Interpreting Chinese Philosophy

Also available from Bloomsbury

Chinese and Indian Ways of Thinking in Early Modern European Philosophy,
by Selusi Ambrogio
Chinese Philosophy of History, by Dawid Rogacz
Cross-Cultural Existentialism, by Leah Kalmanson
Critique, Subversion, and Chinese Philosophy, edited by Hans-Georg
Moeller and Andrew K. Whitehead
Michael Slote Encountering Chinese Philosophy, edited by Yong Huang
Transcendence and Non-Naturalism in Early Chinese Thought,
by Joshua R. Brown and Alexus McLeod

Interpreting Chinese Philosophy
A New Methodology

Jana S. Rošker

BLOOMSBURY ACADEMIC
LONDON • NEW YORK • OXFORD • NEW DELHI • SYDNEY

BLOOMSBURY ACADEMIC
Bloomsbury Publishing Plc
50 Bedford Square, London, WC1B 3DP, UK
1385 Broadway, New York, NY 10018, USA
29 Earlsfort Terrace, Dublin 2, Ireland

BLOOMSBURY, BLOOMSBURY ACADEMIC and the Diana logo are trademarks of
Bloomsbury Publishing Plc

First published in Great Britain 2021
This paperback edition published in 2023

Copyright © Jana S. Rošker, 2021

Jana S. Rošker has asserted her right under the Copyright, Designs and
Patents Act, 1988, to be identified as Author of this work.

For legal purposes the Acknowledgments on p. vi constitute an extension
of this copyright page.

Cover image: Stone wall carvings of ancient chinese philosophy in 'Seven Star Park'
(Qixing Gongyuan). Feargus Cooney / Alamy Stock Photo

All rights reserved. No part of this publication may be reproduced or transmitted
in any form or by any means, electronic or mechanical, including photocopying,
recording, or any information storage or retrieval system, without prior
permission in writing from the publishers.

Bloomsbury Publishing Plc does not have any control over, or responsibility for, any
third-party websites referred to or in this book. All internet addresses given in this
book were correct at the time of going to press. The author and publisher regret any
inconvenience caused if addresses have changed or sites have ceased to exist,
but can accept no responsibility for any such changes.

A catalogue record for this book is available from the British Library.

Library of Congress Cataloging-in-Publication Data
Names: Rošker, Jana, 1960-author.
Title: Interpreting Chinese philosophy: a new methodology / Jana S. Rošker.
Description: London; New York: Bloomsbury Academic, 2021. |
Includes bibliographical references and index. |
Identifiers: LCCN 2020055562 (print) | LCCN 2020055563 (ebook) | ISBN 9781350199866
(hardback) | ISBN 9781350199873 (ebook) | ISBN 9781350199880 (epub)
Subjects: LCSH: Philosophy, Chinese–Methodology.
Classification: LCC B5231 .R668 2021 (print) | LCC B5231 (ebook) | DDC 181/.11–dc23
LC record available at https://lccn.loc.gov/2020055562
LC ebook record available at https://lccn.loc.gov/2020055563

ISBN: HB: 978-1-3501-9986-6
PB: 978-1-3501-9990-3
ePDF: 978-1-3501-9987-3
eBook: 978-1-3501-9988-0

Typeset by Deanta Global Publishing Services, Chennai, India

To find out more about our authors and books visit www.bloomsbury.com
and sign up for our newsletters.

Contents

Acknowledgments		vi
Prologue: Chinese Philosophy—Fact or Fiction?		1
1 Referential Framework		9
	1.1 Problems of Transcultural Research	11
	1.2 A Contrastive Analysis of Two Frameworks	30
	1.3 Specific Features of the Chinese Model	35
2 Basic Paradigms		57
	2.1 A Structural Network of Dynamic Relations	57
	2.2 Vital Potential or Vital Creativeness	64
	2.3 Dialectical Thought and Proper Measure	68
3 Chinese Logic as a Basis of Classical Chinese Theory		73
	3.1 Semantic Nature of Chinese Logic	74
	3.2 Chinese Analogies	83
4 Methods and Approaches		101
	4.1 Analytical and Hermeneutic Procedures	102
	4.2 Problems of Transcultural Comparative Philosophy	121
Epilogue: Relation as the Core of Understanding		137
Notes		141
Glossary		165
Sources and Literature		170
Index		184

Acknowledgments

I gratefully acknowledge the financial support from the Slovenian Research Agency (ARRS) in the framework of the research core funding *Asian Languages and Cultures* (P6-0243) and in the scope of the research project N6-0161 (Complementary scheme) *Humanism in Intercultural Perspective: Europe and China*.

I am sincerely grateful to many of my precious friends and colleagues who have supported, inspired, and encouraged me in the writing of this book. Here are the names of just a few of them: Selusi Ambrogio, Roger Ames, Federico Brusadelli, Robert A. Carleo, David Chai, Paul D'Ambrosio, Carine Defoort, Bart Dessein, Fabian Heubel, Huang Chun-chieh, Yong Huang, Lee Hsien-chung, Lee Ming-huei, Li Chenyang, Eric Nelson, Gregor Paul, Graham Parkes, Karl-Heinz Pohl, Dawid Rogacz, Geir Sigurðsson, John Makeham, Ady Van den Stock, Andrej Ule, Ralph Weber, Brook Ziporyn, and—last but not least—my most treasured friend and colleague, who is also my spouse and lover, Téa Sernelj.

I dedicate this book to one of my dearest and oldest friends (and most reliable partners in crime), Evi Wollner.

Jana S. Rošker

Prologue

Chinese Philosophy—Fact or Fiction?

Chinese philosophy still represents a riddle for most Western intellectuals. First of all, they have not yet succeeded in clarifying the question of whether it can be denoted as philosophy at all. Of course, we could well try to avoid the dilemma which will be described in the paragraphs that follow and simply designate it with the term traditional Chinese thought, but the meaning and the connotations of this word are much too broad, for they also pertain to literary, sociological, medical, spiritual, or even artistic content of Chinese intellectual heritages. Why is the term Chinese philosophy problematic?

Whenever sinologists speak of Chinese philosophy, they are unavoidably confronted with the question of the suitability of this term. In the best case they have to accept the necessity of explaining certain specific features of traditional Chinese thought, its epistemological roots and its methodology to Western-trained philosophers and to the colleagues from other disciplines of humanities. This interdisciplinary issue, however, has been preconditioned by a necessity to clarify and to define certain concepts and categories, which have been rooted in East Asian traditions.

Scholars trained in Western philosophy, on the other hand, have only limited access to the general theory and genuine philosophical aspects of Chinese thought. Hence, for the majority of them, these features of classical Chinese discourses continue to appear obscure, unsystematic and therefore lacking any theoretical reliability. Consequently, we must inspect the basic dilemma or question of whether it is possible at all to declare that certain discourses of traditional Chinese thought are philosophy. This question becomes increasingly significant, for especially in our present, interconnected, and globalized world, efforts to obtain a cross-cultural understanding of reality are more essential than ever. It seems rather clear that any attempts to gain an insight into the modes of such comprehension without considering the philosophical perspective of others seem to be not only arrogant, but also—to put it mildly—quite naïve.

In his article entitled "There Is No Need for *Zhongguo zhexue* to Be Philosophy," Ouyang Min—as many other scholars—argues that philosophy is a Western cultural practice and cannot refer to traditional Chinese thinking except in an analogical or metaphorical sense. Hence, he proposes to replace the term "Chinese philosophy" with the notion "sinosophy" (Ouyang 2012, 199). However, the original meaning of this notion, which represents a compound of the ancient Greek words for "China" and "wisdom" is, in fact, nothing other than the translation of the Western expression "Chinese wisdom" into ancient Greek language. The philosophizing or abstract traditions within Chinese thought, on the other hand, go far beyond the sole notion or the discourses of wisdom; therefore, they cannot be reduced to it.

It is certainly not our intention to reinterpret Chinese tradition in terms of Western concepts, for philosophy as an academic discipline has arisen from the essential human need to philosophize. This need or this feature of human thought and sentiment is something universal, as for instance, the human ability to generate language. Although the ability or the potential to create language and thus linguistic communication is universal, each individual language and the grammatical structures by which it is defined is culturally conditioned. Thus, the expression "Chinese philosophy" does not refer to a geographic dimension of this universal term, but is rather an expression of the cultural conditionality which defines a certain form of philosophizing, or of a certain system of philosophical thought with a typical paradigmatic structure. As Carine Defoort (2001, 394) exposes, we are perfectly accustomed to use "Continental" or "Anglo-Saxon" philosophy, denoting different types or genres within the philosophical tradition; the problem with the term Chinese philosophy, however, goes further.

The simplest and most frequent argument against the notion of "Chinese philosophy" is based on the assumption that philosophy as such designates a system of thought, which arose exclusively within the so-called European tradition. In this context, philosophy is thus defined as a theoretical discipline that is based on the specific and unique premises and methods of the Western humanities. According to this supposition, every system of thought, which arose within the context of any other tradition, is thus necessarily irrational (or at least unscientific). Hence, it cannot be applied within any "truly" academic discipline; because it cannot contain abstract academic theories of any kind, it can by no means be regarded as philosophical. During his visit in China in 2001, Jacques Derrida also stated:

> There is no problem with talking about Chinese thought, Chinese history, Chinese science, and so forth, but obviously, I have a problem with talking about the Chinese "philosophy" of this Chinese thought and culture before the introduction of the European model.... Philosophy in essence is not just thought. It is linked with a sort of specific history, with one type of language, and with an ancient Greek invention. It is an ancient Greek invention, which then underwent "transformation" by Latin translation and German translation and so on. It is something European. There may be various kinds of thought and knowledge of equal integrity beyond Western European culture, but it is not reasonable to call them philosophy. (Derrida, quoted in Jing 2005, 60–1)

According to such statements, we are allowed to say that China has thought, but absolutely not "philosophy" in the strict sense of the word. Hence, various forms of ideology and intellectual discourses of all civilizations in the world are "thought," but Western thought is "philosophy." This means that "Chinese civilization, Indian civilization, and Western civilization all had 'thought,' but only Western thought took the form of 'philosophy,' and is therefore called 'philosophy'" (Zhang 2006, 40).

Two centuries earlier, Hegel explained the issue more in detail: he upheld that "genuine" philosophy originated in ancient Greece. In his view, the thought of the "people from the East" was still permeated with the holistic one substance; hence, they were hitherto unable to acquire individuality and had yet to attain spiritual consciousness and self-awareness. What people generally called "Chinese philosophy" was in his view not yet a philosophy but merely some moral preaching. Hegel even wrote the following about Confucian works: "For their reputation, it would have been better if they had never been translated" (Hegel 1969, 142).[1] Hegel described Confucius as an ancient "master" who had disseminated a collection of thoughts on morality without creating any real philosophy. This naturally implies that his work did not contain any transcendent dimensions. This superficial (mis)understanding of ancient Chinese texts continues to hold sway in Western theory not only with respect to Confucius, but in terms of Confucianism in general, and the whole of traditional Chinese thought.

Derrida, however, did not mean to diminish the value of "Chinese thought" with his abovementioned statement, for he was critical toward Western philosophy, which was, in his eyes, much too logocentric. But ultimately, the important thing is that both, Hegel as well as Derrida, firmly believed that China had no philosophy of its own. However, when dealing with such beliefs, we must be aware of the fact that such questions include not just the acceptability of the concept and the term. They also pertain to a series of further problems, such as the position, the assessments, and also the research methods, and even the legitimacy and competence of doing such research. These disquieting problems confuse Chinese scholars and Western sinologists who investigate Chinese philosophy because, as already mentioned, in present time, philosophical categories, conceptual systems, and knowledge structures are all based on Western norms. Hence, it is quite understandable that the Westerners look at Chinese thought in terms of their own norms and standards; however, explaining and sorting out the Chinese intellectual traditions exclusively (or even predominantly) in line with Western standards might not be the best method to achieve transcultural philosophical understanding. Hence, in methodological terms, the argument according to which philosophy is an exclusively European issue is Eurocentric par excellence. It is also advisable to look upon this issue through the lens of the postcolonial critique of Orientalist approaches to intellectual and cultural heritages.

> Under normal circumstances, saying that China had no philosophy would be the same as saying that the West had no Confucianism, Daoism, or any of the four great inventions, and would be no cause for alarm. The problem is that the paths of modernization and globalization traveled by the world as a whole have all been opened up by the West, and the standards of evaluation have also been set by the West. Against such a background, saying that China had no philosophy is, to a large extent, regarded as an insult, as it suggests that the civilization of ancient China never attained relatively high theoretical or ideational levels despite its splendor and magnificence. Confronted with such a question, we can hardly state with equanimity that this is no more than an academic issue. However, unless we can prove that the question of whether China, in the final analysis, had a philosophy constitutes an issue of ideology and by no means one of academics, we should deal with it with an academic orientation. (Zhang 2006, 40)

This Eurocentric dimension of the argument against the existence of Chinese philosophy becomes very clear in the very beginning, namely when one takes into consideration the etymology of the term "philosophy." As every child knows, philosophy originally meant the love of wisdom. Can anyone seriously maintain that Socrates, Plato or Aristotle loved wisdom more than Laozi, Zhuangzi, or Wang Shouren?

On a somewhat more complex level, the assumption that the word "philosophy" in the European tradition signifies a special kind of love of wisdom also holds good; in this tradition, it means a kind of wisdom that deals with specific questions of metaphysics, ontology, phenomenology, epistemology, and logic. None of these clearly defined disciplines were ever developed in traditional China.[2] Here, we have to consider a more differentiated approach, for in this way it can be seen that this argument actually lacks a rational basis: firstly, because Chinese philosophy is, in fact, not a philosophy in the traditional European sense, but a different philosophical discourse, based on different methodology and with different theoretical concerns and secondly, because traditional Chinese thought also developed certain mutually discriminated forms and branches of philosophical inquiry that greatly differ from those that were generally developed within classical European discourses.

Indeed, one could argue in the same manner that traditional European philosophy is not a complete philosophy, since it did not fully develop any of the most significant philosophical categories and methods which form the core paradigms of traditional Chinese theoretical discourse, such as the method of correlative thought, binary categories or the paradigm of immanent transcendence and the One-world view. We could also state, for instance, that Western philosophy is underdeveloped and lacks important approaches to the coherent comprehension of reality, because it lacks the disciplines *xuanxue*,[3] and *mingxue*,[4] or the philosophical branches *qiongli gewu*,[5] *xinxing*[6] and *liqi*[7] respectively.

If we wished to be really provocative, we could even invert the argument and claim that the opposite was true, that it is European thought which cannot be considered as true philosophy, for if philosophy is the love of wisdom, then philosophy as a scientific discipline with its rigid, almost technocratic delimited categorical and terminological apparats (precisely that discourse which, in Europe and throughout the world, is considered as philosophy in a strict, essential sense) cannot be regarded as philosophy at all. At best, it can be considered as "philosophology," in the sense of teaching, researching and writing *about* the love of wisdom.

In her famous article "Is There Such a Thing as Chinese Philosophy?" Carine Defoort states a position which is not grounded upon an absolute denial, but neither on an absolute affirmation of the question. In this context, it could be said that the tradition of the "Chinese masters" (*zi* 子) is comparable with the wider Western philosophical tradition (and not merely its modern variant) to a degree that "allows us" to denote it as philosophy. After all, these discourses are opening questions of deep human concern while proving the ideas they contain with rational arguments (Defoort 2001, 403). The complexity and richness of both the concept clusters and the ways in which the clusters themselves are supported through persuasion, appeals to authority, standards of arguments, and aesthetic integration provide strong reasons to consider even the earliest Chinese thought as philosophical. To diminish this richness and depth to a weak account of "Western" philosophical conceptions, or even to dismiss them because they are "different" leads to a loss of methods to forefront possible culture-wide assumptions and the loss of access to the conceptual and ideational assets created and developed in the Chinese tradition (Creller 2014, 196). These assets could namely be useful for many different purposes, such as resolving long-lasting philosophical difficulties within the Western tradition, or simply sparkling the imagination, which belongs to most important outfits of any genuine philosophical inquiry.

On the other hand, this position points to the fact that the Chinese themes and forms of reasoning are sometimes "so fundamentally different from those of their Western counterparts that they offer a unique opportunity to question, in a critical and philosophical manner, the currently prevailing notion of 'philosophy' itself" (Defoort 2001, 403).

Recognizing the comprehension, analysis, and transmission of reality based on diversely structured sociopolitical contexts as a categorical and essential postulate offers the prospect of enrichment. Hence, instead of following the rudimentary horizon of Western discursive patterns and problems, we should try to approach the Chinese tradition from the perspective of language and writing, to which it belongs. If we try to follow the inherent laws of its specific concepts, we can gain a completely different, much more autochthonous and much less "exotic" image of this tradition. But how can we bridge the abyss between different cultures, if we no longer possess a generally valid, commonly shared horizon of expressions and imaginations? Certainly not by trying to "think like the Chinese," in the sense of using some different logic. We should, as proposed by Chad Hansen and Heiner Roetz, seek to establish a methodology of transcultural research in accordance with the principles of the so-called "hermeneutic humanism." Humanism is namely the keynote in Chinese philosophy: human beings are in the forefront of Chinese philosophers and human society has occupied their attention throughout the ages.

For centuries, Chinese philosophy has, similar to other philosophies all over the world, been the central driving force for creating ideas and shaping knowledge which forms and develops human understanding, launches human curiosity, and inspires human creativity. Therefore, the previously "absurd" assumption that the "Western" theory of knowledge does not constitute the sole, universally valid epistemological discourse, something which would have been unthinkable for the majority of "Western" theorists less than a century ago, is gradually becoming a generally recognized fact among most present-day cultural exponents and communities. It has become clear to most people that "Western epistemology" represents only one of many different forms of historically transmitted social models for the perception and interpretation of reality. Hence, polylogues between different forms of such intellectual creativity are not only possible, but also a most sensible thing to do (Ames 2015, 109–10). If we consider their value and significance within the framework of contemporary global developments, we can with an easy conscience ask ourselves what role will be played, and what share modern and adequate reinterpretations of classical Chinese philosophy will have in this process.

1

Referential Framework

In his book *The Methodological Problems of the Chinese Philosophy*,[1] Feng Yaoming[2] assumes a certain grade of incommensurability between the methodological systems of the so-called Western and East Asian traditions (Feng 1989, 291–2). He asserts that this phenomenon is connected with the "frameworks of presumptions,"[3] and is based on the non-transferability of concepts[4] from one socio-cultural context into the other. All this leads of course logically to a certain grade of the impossibility of comparisons or incommensurability of different methodological systems or approaches. In my view, such epistemological difficulties cannot be reduced to differences in presumptions (or, in Gadamer's language, to different prejudices), but are rooted in an even more complex and very dynamic network of continuously changing references, which is being applied as a living pattern of describing vibrant realities of human life. In the widest sense, this framework differs from one individual to another, but social groups and cultures of all kinds provide us with certain general coordinate systems with relatively stable structures of meanings, views, values, and imageries which stimulate our perceptions and feelings, and profoundly influence our language, thought, and behavior. Hence, the incommensurability Feng had in mind is rather a result of differences between discrete referential frameworks than merely between "frameworks of presumptions."

Different cultures produce different referential frameworks, which are, on the other hand, linked to different methodologies applied in the process of perceiving, understanding, and interpreting reality. Here, I am specifically referring to frameworks of reference that define theories and other forms of abstractly ordered cognitive constructions within sciences and humanities. A referential framework in this sense can be defined as a relational structure of concepts, categories, terms, and ideas, as well as values, which are applied in the cognitive processing of the objects of comprehension. It also includes paradigms and perspectives that influence and define the comprehension and evaluation of particular semantic elements within this structure, as well as the structure as a whole.

These problems are, however, not limited only to theories or methods, which spring out of different cultural traditions; they are normally also occurring within every research, focused on objects within one single language or tradition. Actually, what we are here confronting is a universal problem, which has been discussed by a broad scope of Western theories (Kuhn, Quin, Lakatos, Feyerabend, etc.) Feng reminds us here of the well-known example of the relation between Newton's and Einstein's theories: because they represent different referential frameworks, the functions and semantic connotations of the same notions applied in them are also different. In his important book on the structure of scientific revolutions, Thomas Kuhn has explained these phenomena in the following way:[5]

> Within the new paradigm, old terms, concepts and experimentals fall into new relationship one with the other. The inevitable result is what we must call, though the term is not quite right, a misunderstanding between the two competing schools. . . . Consider, for example, the man who called Copernicus mad because he proclaimed that the earth moved. They were not either just wrong or quite wrong. Part of what they meant by "earth" was a fixed position. Their earth, at least, could not move. Correspondingly, Copernicus' innovation was not simply to move the earth. Rather, it was a whole new way of regarding the problems of physics and astronomy, one that necessarily changed the meaning of both "earth" and "motion." (Kuhn 1996, 149)

Feng Yaoming tries to explain this difference through the example of two different types of pans that are used for frying food in Easter Asia and in Euro-American region respectively. He writes:

> We all know, that Chinese people normally use pans with round bottom to fry their food, while people in western countries normally prefer pans with even bottom. Same kinds of food can be fried in both types of pans. But the same food, which has been fried in both types of pans, can stay the same in some of its qualities, and become remarkably different in some other qualities. In both kinds of pans we can fry, for example, eggs. This

is a common property of both types. But the functions, possibilities and limitations of both pans used for frying the same eggs can also differ. These differences give also reasons for different consistence, color, form and taste of the eggs, being fried either in the pans with round or in those with even bottom. (Kuhn 1996, 149)[6]

According to Feng, different referential frames can—in exactly the same way—lead to different descriptions and interpretations of the same objective reality. Different possibilities and limitations of the concrete functionality of both types of pans express different features of different referential frames, their specific shortages or advantages.

This defining role of a referential framework does not only pertain to the meaning of particular notions, but also to their mutual relations. Hence, it is a comprehensive tool used to filter perceptions and to create meaning. In this intercultural philosophic debate, it is important to consider that different referential frames can lead to different descriptions and interpretations of the same objective reality. This is also the reason because of which transcultural research can sometimes produce misunderstandings between different cultures instead of eliminating or at least diminishing them. The greater the structural, semantic, and axiological diversities between two languages and cultures, the more likely the appearance of such misunderstandings. In the following, we shall attempt to perform a contrastive analysis of two different culturally conditioned frameworks of reference that are important for the present study. But before taking a closer look at these systems, we shall illuminate some of the external and more general issues that are also significantly influencing the "Western" understanding of Chinese philosophy in our academic world.

1.1 Problems of Transcultural Research

For Western researchers, the confrontation and understanding of the so-called non-Western cultural traditions is always linked to the problem of differences in language, tradition, history, and socialization processes. The interpretation of various aspects and elements of different cultures is namely always linked to the geographic, political, and economic positions of the interpreter as well as the subject of interpretation. A fundamental premise of the present study is that Western epistemology represents only one of many different models of human comprehension. Therefore, it follows the main methodological principles of transcultural research, taking into account the incommensurability of diversely (culturally) conditioned paradigms, or theoretical frameworks deriving from diversely formed discourses of different cultural and linguistic environments. In Western research on Chinese philosophy, the non-reflected use of a scientific analysis, which is a result of specific (Western) historical processes and the related, typical organizational structure of societies, often proves to be a dangerous and misleading mechanism. Concepts and categories can namely not simply be transferred from one sociocultural context into another.

In my view, a suitable methodology for studying Chinese philosophy—which is hitherto still often been interpreted based primarily on premises deriving from the traditional Western social sciences and humanities—is found not only in the recognition of a "different theoretical model," but in the relativization of the value systems and perception structures. Here, it is important to clarify that such a relativization of values does not imply that all values are equally good and reasonable or sensible. In other words, it does not imply that elementary issues, which are not beneficiary for humanity, or even in contradiction with preserving the integration and dignity of human beings, can be pursued and implemented in the name of some "specific culturally conditioned values." This catchphrase should be understood in a different context, namely as an instrument for preventing a one-dimensional understanding of values, or an absolute, general universalization of criteria for evaluating values by one single axiological discourse or one single axiological doctrine.

Since the dominant discourses in Western philosophical theory are based on the concept of truth, the awareness that there are very few objective, universally valid values is of utmost importance for those Western scholars who are concerned with Chinese philosophy. While the value systems that shape modern Western societies are based upon concepts like individualism and free will, in East Asian societies a strong sense of familism and belonging to a community was (and, to a certain extent, still is) prevalent. These concepts and identification patterns represent the foundations of different values systems, which should thus be seen as being relative.

If we want to consider all abovementioned differences, we need to gain insights into the conceptual structures and connections among the concrete historical, economic, political, and philosophical systems that underlie Chinese social reality, shaping and modifying the complex entity usually called Chinese culture. The awareness of these underlying rudiments—which also unavoidably influence the elementary theoretical approaches, methods, and conceptual frameworks—constitute a platform which might allow us a better understanding of Chinese philosophy at its most profound levels.

In this context we should clarify the nature of our approach to reading Chinese philosophy. Since this book is written mainly for Western readers, it automatically deals with its subject through the lens of cultural differences. When reading Chinese philosophy, readers born, educated, and socialized in Western languages and social environments are confronted with different epistemologies, different perspectives, perceptions, and patterns of knowledge acquisition and transmission. To a certain extent, and especially when it comes to ancient and traditional philosophies, this problem also affects today's Chinese readers who live in a globalized world where the standards of conception and understanding have been adopted from Western cultures.

Therefore, our approach to Chinese philosophy is intercultural in the sense of interaction and engagement of several cultures. Interculturality is a specific type of interaction or communication between discourses, where differences in cultures play a role in the formation of meaning. Intercultural interactions therefore involve the process of transferring meanings between cultures (Ongun 2016). However, many contemporary scholars (e.g., Welsch 1999) criticize that the concept starts from a conception of cultures as "islands" or "spheres" and creates a separatist character of cultures. In today's globalized world it is therefore important to understand that cultural factors have become transcultural. The transcultural understanding of cultures offers us a multi-perspective and inclusive approach rather than an exclusive and isolated approach (Ongun 2016). Transcultural philosophy is a long-standing discourse, but with constantly changing and evolving paradigms. For at least half a century it has been an important field of philosophical investigation. It began with Eduardo Valera's construction of its methodological foundations (Valera 1972a; b) and has developed more or less continuously in the following decades (see, for example, Fredericks 1988; Nielsen 1995; Siegel 1999; Heubel 2011, 2014; Lee 2013; Dai 2020 and many others).

> The suffix "trans-" in the term "transcultural" suggests transcending not only one's borders, one's limits, while enriching, updating oneself. It suggests also the possibility to step beyond the very fragmentation and separateness of various cultures and philosophies. (Silius 2020, 275)

Transcultural approaches therefore aim at overcoming the outdated, static, and immobile concept of culture. This does not mean, however, that there is no culture. It is still a real thing, like language, for example. Both are dynamic, historically grown, and constantly changing entities without fixed borders. Therefore, the ontological assumption underlying the concept of culture does not necessarily refer to a metaphysics of an abstract substantial being. In this book, the concept of culture is understood to be based on a metaphysics of relations. In this sense, I continue to use the two terms, that is, both intercultural and transcultural: although it is impossible to draw firm and constant boundaries between them because they form a complex and often overlapping web of meaning, I use the former when referring to concrete interactions between different cultures[7] and their various elements, and the latter when referring to the goal and results of such interactions, that is, to see oneself in the other.

To enable such a reflection in our investigation of the methodological framework of Chinese philosophies and their formal, semantic, and conceptual foundations, we must first take a closer look at some of the external elements that also strongly influence our interpretation and the modes of our understanding. These external elements are linked to the historically developed structures of power relations within epistemology.

1.1.1 Orientalism and Reversed Orientalism

In the context of the present study, it should first be clarified that the terms "East" and "West," which are commonly denoting vast multicultural areas in Asia and within the so-called Euro-American cultural tradition, are somewhat problematic, for they are based on generalized and essentialist views of areas covering multifaceted pallets of different historical, political, and cultural developments.[8] Usually, such characterizations are based upon a superficial view, according to which developmental traits of different cultures are fixed and predetermined; such views completely (and arrogantly) disregard the importance of variations among particular social, ideational, and axiological developments within various cultures, belonging to the two umbrella categories.

Bearing this in mind, I will in this book—for the sake of practicability—nonetheless apply the terms "Western" and "Chinese"; in the framework of the present study, however, they have to be understood as expressions, which do not exclusively refer to a certain geopolitical area (i.e., China vs. Europe, America, Australia, and New Zealand), but are rather based upon the prevailing and distinct *differentia specifica* that profoundly marks the dominant currents in their respective ideational development, namely the demarcation line between immanent and transcendent metaphysics.[9]

Sinology as an academic discipline was constituted within the scope of Orientalism, which laid the foundations and conditions of the colonialist approach to the study of cultures which are not the fruit of the so-called "Western" tradition. This is why the criticism of elements of Orientalism in sinology is simultaneously the criticism of the violent nature of the classical relation between knowledge and authority or knowledge and power.

In his famous book on Orientalism, Edward Said has defined the concept as "a style of thought based upon an ontological and epistemological distinction made between 'the Orient' and (most of the time) 'the Occident'" (Said 1978, 2). For him, Orientalism was also

> the corporate institution for dealing with the Orient—dealing with it by making statements about it, authorizing views of it, describing it, by teaching it, settling it, ruling over it: in short, Orientalism as a Western style for dominating, restructuring, and having authority over the Orient. (Said 1978, 3)

In the Orientalist framework, the ideal of European identity was seen as a superior one in contrast to all non-European cultures and their people (Said 1978, 7). This alleged "superiority," however, has to be viewed in the context of the existing global economic (and consequently also political) and power relations. Hence, Orientalism is a discourse or a framework of reference, which is inherently connected to "Western" institutions of power. Therefore, it is not enough to try and overcome it by simply affirming the "Orient" or the "East" over the "Occident" or the "West." This is because the "Orient" or the "East" can never be a free subject of thought or action, simply because in itself, it is a creation of the West (Hahm 2000, 103). Besides, it is completely clear that affirming one pole of the binary oppositional pair does not imply the overcoming of the dichotomy as such.[10] The sensible thing to do would then be to strive to find a completely independent epistemological position. However, this desire to get "outside," to establish an "objective" bird-eyes view is itself a typically Western ideal at least since Plato (Hahm 2000, 103). Hence, in this postmodern era, many intercultural discourses were based upon a presumption that it is impossible to surpass the boundaries of the semantic and axiological frameworks to which we are bound through our native languages and socio-cultural education. Thus, the postmodern approach of deconstructing various expressions and representations of reality can never be complete. As Chaibong Hahm (2000, 103) points out, deconstruction is different from destruction precisely because it cannot "wipe the slates clean of Western prejudices."

Moreover, we cannot forget that all histories of ideas and all cultural discourses are ethnocentric. In an un-reflected ethnocentric view, one's own people "historically stand for civilization and its achievements, whereas the otherness of the others is a deviation from these standards" (Rüssen 2004, 62–3). In this sense, Eurocentrism as an either formally or informally institutionalized discourse, which represents a psychological foundation and a central approach of Orientalism, is simply a form of ethnocentrism, one among many others. Orientalism functions by applying Eurocentric views and validations of reality. And because Orientalism is a discourse of power, Eurocentrism naturally forms a part of the same power. In a certain sense, they are simply two sides of the same medal. It is precisely this fact which makes Eurocentrism something more influential than most of other ethnocentrisms—the fact that it is an ethnocentrism based upon a "higher" position of economic and political supremacy, which is a result of specific social, ideational, and historical developments.

Some scholars[11] believe that the domination of "multiculturalism" leads to the end of Eurocentrism. Similarly, the global redistribution and restructuring of economic power could, along with the fragmentation of traditional cultures, also lead to an end of Orientalism. However, the solution of these problems is not as simple (and automatic) as it seems at first sight. The very term multiculturalism, to begin with, is misleading, for it does not only refer to cultural fragmentation, but also undermines the underlying traditional forms of production and social networks. Because of this, the end of Eurocentrism might be an illusion, for its internal structure remains a predominant part in the constellation of postmodern, global societies (Rošker 2016, 53). Arif Dirlik, for instance, is convinced that

> the apparent end of Eurocentrism is an illusion. Capitalist culture, as it has taken shape, holds Eurocentrism in the very structure of its narrative, which

may explain why, even as Europe and the United States lose their domination of the capitalist world economy, culturally European and American values are still dominant globally. It is also noteworthy that what makes something like the East Asian Confucian revival plausible is not its offer to alternative values to those of Euro American origin, but its articulation of native culture into a capitalist narrative. (Dirlik 1994, 51–2)

Arif Dirlik points out that in reality we might even not be dealing with the fragmentation of cultures but rather with the fragmentation of space. According to him, such fragmentation offers new possibilities for global capitalism to solve old problems linked to maximizing profits, controlling the market and freeing the production and marketing from the pressures of social interventions (e.g., integrative labor strikes) or political control (state measures). Such a fragmentation of space also implies the shattered social status of the individual, living in a reality which manifests itself in her or his increasingly precarious situation, subjected to directives of flexibility, instability, and other typical symptoms of the alienation of the modern subject. This is why a one-dimensional criticism of Eurocentrism and its interpretation of history and world structure is no longer sufficient.

And what is especially important for our present discussion is also the fact that in a wider sense, that is, in terms of everyday life, Eurocentrism is no longer limited to Europe, but represents a contemporary, global phenomenon.[12]

Similar to the ways in which Eurocentrism hence is posited against other forms of ethnocentrisms, like Islamocentrism or sinocentrism, Orientalism is posited against Occidentalism, which is also a discourse representing the Western, African, and Muslim worlds as the "Others," often in an equally dehumanizing and ideological way as Orientalism. It can also be seen as a form of nationalist essentialism in the non-European or non-Western world, especially in Asia, which is increasingly redrawing the global map of progress. Here again, however, the difference between both discourses is (similar to the relation between Eurocentrism and, for instance, Sinocentrism) in the abovementioned global power relations, which are deeply rooted in historical and axiological conditions laid by the colonial and postcolonial world.

However, Occidentalism cannot be mixed up with a phenomenon denoted as "reversed Orientalism" or "Orientalism in Reverse," which is rooted in conditions established by the "leading historical role"[13] of Orientalism. One of the most significant features of this discourse can be found in the presumption, according to which there exists a fundamental ontological difference between the natures of the "East" and the "West," that is, between the so-called Eastern and Western societies, cultures, and even peoples.

> This ontological difference entails immediately an epistemological one which holds that the sort of conceptual instruments, scientific categories, sociological concepts, political descriptions and ideological distinctions employed to understand and deal with Western societies remain, in principle, irrelevant and inapplicable to Eastern ones. (al-Azm 1980, 10)

In such a view, differences between "Western and Eastern" societies are not so much a result of complex processes in the historical development of humanity, nor "a matter of empirical facts to be acknowledged and dealt with accordingly" (al-Azm 1980, 10). In addition to all that, they are first and foremost products of a certain "Oriental essence," pertaining to the cultural, psychic, or racial nature of the non-Western "Others." Sadiq Jalal al-Azm calls this form of discourse Ontological Orientalism (al-Azm 1980, 10). Orientalism in this sense provided a fertile basis for the establishment and development of Reversed Orientalism, which manifests itself primarily on the epistemological level. It assumes, for instance, that "only Japanese can understand Japan, only Chinese can understand China" (Lary 2006, 9).

Even the very notion of Orientalism was not unproblematic after it was published in the regions belonging to the so-called Orient: Said's book was welcomed by people who understood its main message; however, by many other scholars, Said's views were also sharply criticized. His arguments that "the Orient" had been diminished and distorted by Western specialists were especially irately rejected by numerous Chinese scholars and intellectuals.

Moreover, in this view, no matter how well-versed Western sinologists are in Chinese language and culture, they can simply never understand Chinese culture. Diana Lary provides a good illustration of such an attitude:

> One example is research on Peking Man, who may or may not have been the ancestor of the present-day Chinese. The fossil remains of Peking Man were discovered in the late 1920s by an extraordinary team of scholars that included Chinese (Pei Wenzhong) and foreigners (the Swede J. G. Andersson, the French Pierre Teilhard de Chardin, and the Canadian Davidson Black). A young Chinese archaeologist who discussed the discovery with me in 2005 would only accept the role of Pei; the Western scholars were dismissed as having done next to nothing. In this view he was following a fairly

common convention in Chinese scholarship that Westerners have made little impact on the study of China. There is a similar unwillingness to give any credit for the discovery a little earlier of the Oracle Bones, the first form of Chinese script, to the Canadian missionary James Menzies. (Lary 2006, 9)

John Timothy Wixted provided us with another illustrative example of Reversed Orientalism in the field of epistemology:

> The expectation on the part of many Chinese is that work on China by non-Chinese is no good. If, however, it is clear that the work is good, then the reaction, which on occasion I have witnessed, can be this: I, as a Chinese, am ashamed, am humiliated, that this work was not done by a Chinese. I have heard Chinese say this (and mean it) about the Takigawa Kametaro's edition of the Shih-chi and certain other Japanese scholarship, about Kalgren's work on Chinese phonology, and even about a volume of my own work. This self-inflicted psychological pain tells us something, I believe, about an aspect of Chinese Reverse Orientalism: many Chinese, in a possessive, exclusionist, self-contained way, consider the study of China their bailiwick and theirs alone; and the inward centeredness of this Chinese cultural world prevents such Chinese from taking active pleasure either in the scholarship itself, in the fact that others are doing work that can redound to the benefit of Chinese and non-Chinese Sinologists alike, or in the fact that such work might increase appreciation of the richness of Chinese culture among non-Chinese. (Wixted 1989, 22)

However, we should not pour out the baby together with the bathing water. First, this situation has much improved during the last decade: the Chinese academic world has become increasingly aware of the contributions of Western sinologists and experts in Chinese studies to the spreading and deepening of knowledge on Chinese culture and society in the Euro-American worlds. On the other hand, the majority of Chinese scholars (and policy makers) has obviously recognized that some issues can be better investigated from a certain distance; and furthermore, they would certainly like to maintain a stronger control over the Western academic production on their country. For all these reasons, a huge deluge of books and articles on Western perception and interpretation of China has been (and is still being) translated into Chinese and published by various Chinese publishing houses and journals.

Second, we should—as Diana Lary points out—not take the Sinocentric academic biases described in this chapter too seriously. First of all, even those

Chinese people who hold such views are willing to acknowledge that individual Western scholars can be quite capable. Such people are usually honored with the label "*Zhongguo tong* 中國通," a colloquial and populistic expression that means that a foreigner has gained a profound and genuine insight into Chinese language and culture. On the other hand, Lary also rightly emphasizes that the basic problem of the Reversed Orientalism is linked to much more general and elementary issues regarding representation and appropriation within the historically developed inequalities:

> Can men write about women, can white people write about blacks? These are concerns that are deeply felt, and that can never be easily resolved, since they are based on perceptions of long-running discrimination and misrepresentation. (Lary 2006, 9)

If we truly want to begin placing, observing, and explaining Chinese philosophy in the historical, linguistic, and methodological context to which it belongs, we cannot ignore the specific processes of global interactions which demarcate its present state. Hence, in this endeavor we have to consider the historical role and the impact of power structures and the consequent establishment of privileged and underprivileged or even discriminated social groups and cultures. On the other hand, however, we have to watch out not to slip into a hole of opposite prejudices. We also have to be aware of the fact that in spite of this principal sociocultural inequalities, of which the European past (and present) is certainly a great part, we need to think through a dialectical interplay between aids and wrongdoings, for "Europe does and has made great contributions to humanity, just as crimes have been committed against humanity in the name of Europe" (West 1993, 148). I cannot but strongly agree with Cornel West who emphasizes (West 1993, 148) that in order to surpass and to go beyond Eurocentrism and multiculturalism, we have to begin reflecting upon these issues in a much more complex way, which includes a nuanced historical sense, a subtle social analysis, and, above all, a radical democratic worldview.

1.1.2 The Hybrid Nature of Sinology

The postcolonial view on recent historical developments in the field of Chinese studies still didn't manage to effectively separate itself from essentialist and Orientalist understandings of contemporary Chinese society.

The recent omnipresence of China in all types of media is still not accorded by its place in intellectual and academic production or expertise (Vukovich 2010, 148). Sinology has been—theoretically and methodologically—accused of unreflectingly repeating the wrongdoings and sins of its colonial and Orientalist past. In the neoliberal presence, the vast knowledge and profound understanding that the Chinese language and its humanistic tradition have to offer are not only seen as being redundant, but often (as many other potentially critical discourses) even as dangerous and hence unwanted. In recent years, most universities have replaced sinology by empirical China studies, which are primarily oriented toward modern and contemporary China and more or less ignoring the richness and the latent, subtle, but sublime impact of its past. Most Western governments have drawn exclusively on information "supplied by 'experts' who, more often than not, are woefully lacking in knowledge of the history, languages, literatures, and customs of the countries they speak about" (Wixted 1989, 25).

Sinology, on the other hand, has hitherto still not solved most of the elementary problems connected to its "hybrid nature." This problem is a different one and must be treated separately from the (equally difficult and complex) problem of its Orientalist roots, which means that numerous scholars inside and outside China who refer to Said still believe that sinology is a form of Orientalism (Gu 2013, 43). In his passionate attack against sinology as an academic discipline, Hans Kuijper dismisses sinologists as pseudo-scientists, for in his view, they are lacking any form of sinological theory. He also thinks that sinology is wrongly defined (namely by the object of its inquiry instead of by the optics on this object) and is not a systematic study (Kuijper 2000, 338). He is convinced that sinologists

> do not see the nexus, or *Gestalt* (configuration), of the object of their study (China), the relationships between, or specific combination of, its elements or subsystems, the whole that is different from the sum of its numerous parts. . . . They do not know how China, as an extremely complex *unity*, works; they do not comprehend its wiring, its deep structure and dynamics. Not seeking to "uncover" and understand the orderliness of China *qua* China, they disqualify as scientists. Indeed, the emperor is wearing no clothes. (Kuijper 2000, 338)

However, Kuijper also offers a solution to this problem; he advises the sinologists either to devote their careers to the project of translating the vast number of important works of Chinese culture that have still not been made available to the Western audience, or to collaborate in those fields of Chinese studies, in which they are interested, with (real) scholars of parallel Western disciplines, because the latter do possess a theory and a specific research methodology.

Notwithstanding Kuijper's well-intended advices, it is certainly not necessary to emphasize that not everybody could agree with his assumptions—at least, of course, those sinologists who have gained an international reputation as brilliant theoreticians. Hence, it is not surprising that according to Denis Twitchett, a renowned sinologist and expert for Chinese history,[14] sinology has "far more unity, a more closely integrated set of techniques, and far more of a corporate sense of purpose than has, for example, history" (Kuijper 2000, 109).

It is doubtless true that in its Orientalistic past (the relicts of which often spooked around even in some of the most distinguished Western departments of sinology until the beginning of the present century) sinologists were seen as a kind of experts for everything regarding China.[15] Nowadays, the only common point that all sinologists (should) possess is their mastering of modern and classical Chinese language and the kind of general education regarding Chinese culture that has to be retained by an average Chinese high school graduate. In the course of their studies, Western students of sinology have thus to obtain at least the basic knowledge of Chinese political, sociocultural, and ideational history; they have to be acquainted with the main developmental trends and paradigms in Chinese literature, art, and philosophy. French students of German studies, for instance, must not learn German philosophy or sociology in the course of their study. But in sinology such subjects necessarily have to be a part of the obligatory curriculum, simply due to the fact that European (or Western) students don't learn almost anything about Chinese history, culture, and society during their high school education.

> That is to say, Sinology should provide us with a broad understanding of Chinese culture and society in all its aspects, to give us the sort of instinctive understanding and orientation which we have of our own society simply by being born and educated in it. Moreover, it should give us the ability to see through the eyes of the Chinese literati who wrote our materials, and thus to enable us to discount their prejudices and preoccupations before reinterpreting what they have written in terms of our own. (Twitchett 1964, 111)

This kind of general education is necessary even for those students, whose main interest is "only" the Chinese language and translations and are therefore mainly interested in a linguistic training, for language is always embedded into a particular thought and culture.

However, sinologists who develop a special academic interest in any of the more specialized fields (e.g., Chinese history, sociology, philosophy, art, anthropology, law) have to go through focused academic training in the respective discipline before they can become experts in the corresponding field. This is not an easy task, because it requires professional training in both Chinese and Western academia. Here, we have to consider the fact that academic teachers in individual sinology departments can offer a specialized academic training only in their own field of research. Hence, the sinological curricula in various departments differ from each other to a greater extent than most of the curricula in other disciplines. In the ideal instance (which is often the case), future sinologists can combine their study with another discipline—and most often it is the same field as the one they want to specialize in within sinology.

But in a strictly methodological sense, such an "ideal" combination is not as trouble-free as it seems to be at the first glance especially in those cases in which the field of sinological specialization is being learned solely in one of the general (i.e., non-sinological) departments. As we shall see in later parts of this book, the optics of Western methodological systems do not always apply to the study of Chinese tradition. On the contrary, sometimes it can be quite disturbing. Academic methodology is namely (at least in the fields of social sciences and humanities) always implying a certain kind of viewing and interpreting reality. In Western humanities, these discrete approaches to reality are results of specific (i.e., Western) historical and ideational developments. Such methodologies provide us with a systematic set of categories and concepts; it furnishes us with a set of methods and with a series of referential frameworks. These are necessary and essential elements of any theory. However, while the specific methodologies that were created in particular disciplines can offer us a special tool to work with, it is precisely the very same tool that simultaneously limits our treatment of the selected subject matter, if it pertains to a different language and culture. If we namely internalize this particular view of reality, we might overlook numerous, often significant, elements that can only manifest themselves when observed from a different viewpoint which lies beyond the methodological framework we are using, because it is embedded in different paradigms of perceiving, understanding, and interpreting reality.

As already mentioned, concepts, categories, and methods of inquiry cannot be automatically transferred from one sociocultural or linguistic area into another. This becomes even more visible if the two areas in question are separated by significant differences in linguistic, grammatical, and semantic structures, by large spatial distances and by diverse trajectories of historical and sociocultural developments.

Nowadays, it is a long-known fact that applying terms and classifications deriving from Western social sciences or Western economic-political theory to the histories and present situations in non-Western societies and cultural areas can be seriously misleading. Even today, several Chinese (and even Western) theoreticians who work with Western sociological categories in an uncritical way, still denote all ancient, medieval, and premodern developmental periods of the Chinese societies with the term "feudalism," although the modes and structures of production in Central and Eastern Asia were completely different throughout Chinese and European histories respectively.[16] The non-European modes of production were always seen as a kind of deviation from the norm—thus, for instance, the establishment of the term "Asian mode of production" along with all its utterly negative connotations. The same applies, for example, to the modernization theories and the role of non-European ideational traditions in these processes. Without a detailed and in-depth sinological research, the clarification of such Eurocentric "misunderstandings" in social sciences would not be possible.

The same goes for most of the disciplines and research fields within humanities. In making history, experts of this discipline cannot surpass difficulties related with discursive representations, simply due to the fact that constructing and writing history as such is necessarily a process of representation grounded upon a discourse. Regarding the writing and the evaluation of Chinese history, sinology and the issues it highlights are substantial in helping historians become more conscious of the problematic nature of history and historiography, and hence more critical to the discourse in which they are working and of which they are a part. It is sinological knowledge that allows them to understand how and why understanding is being standardized, "normalized," and Westernized and to see the implications of such knowledge for the construction of history (Mittal 2015, 1). It is namely by no means sufficient to simply re-place this discourse into the framework of postcolonialism, because this field of research and writing still structures the non-Western problems in the very framework of Western axiology and methodology.

This problem is also well known in the field of comparative literature. Many Western sinology trained experts in Chinese literature emphasize the fact that Chinese literature is not well-served by Western generic classifications. The treatments of non-Western literatures through the lens of the criteria established by Western formal, technical, structural, and narrative approaches still remain rooted in Eurocentric assumptions. However, these have to be critically questioned:

Assumptions are a natural and necessary way of extrapolating and applying information, but it ought to be salutary to examine the ways in which

1) Chinese literature is not, and perhaps cannot be, represented by wholly equivalent terminology when treated in non-Chinese languages, and
2) Chinese literature is treated as forming a coherent and national whole, and whether this accurately reflects the scope of sinophone writing (Stenberg 2014, 287).

Josh Stenberg critically questions such a genre universalism by highlighting that it is still reasonable to ask whether French *roman* and the English novel were "the same thing" (Stenberg 2014, 287), or whether the novel as such is a definable unit at all. It is certainly true, however, that they were at least conceived and developed with a knowledge of each other and thus with a certain sense of equivalence, while also having common areas of reference. None of this applies to the Chinese "novel" (i.e., *xiaoshuo* 小説). "This same concern should run through all of the equivalences made between the European generic terms—*poetry, biography, prose*, perhaps especially *drama*" (Stenberg 2014, 288) and independent traditions with their own names and histories. The same holds true for the classification of literary currents, movements, or styles, because literary works always represent different cultural conditioned interpretations of social problems, connected to different intellectual histories, moral philosophies, social criticism, aesthetic formations, and other fields of reasoning which are of relevance to the way humans interpret meaning.

It is certainly not a coincidence that Lu Xun, for instance, has often been named "the Chinese Gorki" by literary criticism. But nevertheless, the reality from which Lu Xun's "madman" is escaping and which he fears to death, the reality which swallows lives and destroys destinies of all his characters, is completely different from the one from which Gorki's heroes are fleeing and in which they have been helplessly thrown. Not only sinological, but also literary comparatists and theoreticians should always be reminded of such facts, because they still tend to excessively press the creative work of "other" cultures artists into the molds of Western methodological classifications. Therefore, the great works of Chinese literature should not be read through the optics of Eurocentric categories of the so-called Worlds literature.

Perhaps the illiteracy regarding differently structured principles for creating literary or artistic products becomes most visible in the example of traditional Chinese poetry. In their work, almost no traditional Western translator has tried to maintain the very strict metric principles typical of classical Chinese poetry. This kind of ignorance has led to certain prejudices, which underlie most of the public perceptions of traditional Chinese lyrics in Western regions. Chief among these is the false assumption that they belong to a highly "modernistic" style of poetry, based on pure association, and written in a free verse style, without any restrictions regarding rhythm, rhymes, or other prosody or versification instructions. This, of course, is again a completely wrong view, because, as every sinologist knows, most of the traditional Chinese poetry was created under the application and consideration of very strict and complex metrical rules.

All these questions point to the fact that comparative views in any of the disciplines are difficult and much more complex than it seems at a first glance. However, sinology is—in its essence—a discipline that stands and comes into action in any serious comparison or communication between any aspect of Chinese and Western cultures. In its nature, it is a bridge, connecting different cultural, historical, and ideational heritages by introducing and interpreting one to another. And in its specific discourse, which is defined by transitions and by fusions of different cultural, ideational. and linguistic spheres, it developed very specific, albeit relatively coherent, disciplinary methods. The common thread or the general basis of all these methods manifests itself in the methodological framework of a vigorous textual and philological criticism, which necessarily underlies any kind of historically conscious research investigating China and its multifarious cultures. Textual criticism is the analysis and the interpretation of texts via their semantical, syntactical, historical, and cultural contexts. Questions about the life of the author, the way the author's use of language fits in with the text's time period, and so on, are also part of textual criticism (Creeler 2014, 201. See also Shun 2009, 458).

This is a reliable and comprehensive method, which, of course, can only be applied after a long-lasting process of acquiring a wide, profound, and detailed sinological education. This is the elementary methodological paradigm for sinology as an academic discipline, a paradigm that enables us to skillfully navigate and find our safe way between the Scylla of essentialism and Charybdis of evolutionism.

1.1.3 Discursive Translations

As an interpretative and analytical discipline, sinology necessarily includes translations—however, not merely direct translations of a wide opus of classical Chinese works, as advised by Hans Kuijper, although this is doubtless also one of the most important tasks for those sinologists who are specialized in Chinese linguistics and trained in the translation theories. What I have in mind is clearly not limited to merely rendering one language into another, but also involves the "translation" or transposition of different discourses. This form of "translation" is often taking place merely on the abstract level of reasoning and must not necessary be written down, let alone published. It is an essential part of every sinological research and involves interpretations of individual textual and speech structures, categories, concepts, and values that differ depending on their sociocultural contexts. In the process of such work, which relies on both analytical and hermeneutic methods, sinologists often encounter a discrepancy between the etymological and the functional understanding of a given expression. In some cases, the same notion may even be understood completely differently, depending on the general social context of the two different societies in which it appears.

To illustrate this point, I shall shortly explain the results of an intercultural socio-linguistic investigation (see Rošker 2012), which I conducted in Taiwan and partly (for the sake of the comparative perspective) in Central Europe in 1995. The study included inspection and comparison of several different dictionaries and encyclopedias, textual analyses as well as contrastive proportional surveys in Central Europe and in Taiwan.[17] The results of the inquiry clearly revealed that the common understanding of the word *autonomy* in the Central European cultural and linguistic context is closely connected to the notion of freedom in the sense of non-interference. The general perception of its official synonym in the Chinese language (*zilü* 自律), on the other hand, proved to be mainly linked to the semantic complex of "self-restriction" in the sense of self-control and self-discipline respectively. These two kinds of comprehension are not only different but also mutually contradictive, although the etymological meaning of both terms (autonomy and *zilü* respectively) is more or less the same, both implying concepts as "self-law" or "self-regulation" and phrases like "to decide one's own law" or "to establish the law (or regulations) by oneself." The research results have shown that this discrepancy derives from different understandings of the notion of law[18] and its respective traditional connotations in both cultures in question. In Europe, the law was established in order to protect individuals (and their property) from the violence and heteronomy of the others; hence, it included both, not only the restrictive, but also the protective function. The latter was closely associated with freedom, because only a safe person could afford to be free. The person with the greatest amount or degree of freedom was, according to such a logic, the person who had the power to establish the law by oneself. In China, on the other hand, law was never (with a tiny exception of the Qin 秦 dynasty rule, which lasted fifteen years) seen as the main means for regulating human relationships and it was mainly associated with restrictions, prohibitions, and punishments. Hence, to establish a law for and by oneself could only imply self-restriction or self-discipline. These connotations are still reflected in the general understanding of the Indo-European notions of word autonomy, and in the Chinese term *zilü* which was—according to most dictionaries—often used as its synonym.

A broader socio-semantic investigation, which was conducted subsequently, has namely clearly shown that the European term *law* and its Chinese synonym *fa* 法 have the same format and functional meaning; yet their mutual difference arises only from their particular cultural connotations. Although such inquiries might seem redundant, because they seemingly focus upon some trivial and unimportant terminological issues, they can have significant discrete consequences. When an average Chinese person speaks about autonomy, the concept she has in mind is something completely different from what an average Austrian person has in mind when mentioning the same term. If they speak with each other about autonomy, they will therefore often speak about two different things. This is only one small example for illustrating the fact that in-depth sinological research and discursive translation is significant not only for classical studies, but also for understanding contemporary China.

As we have seen earlier in this chapter, discursive translations cannot be limited to a linguistic transfer, but must include the interpretation of specific textual/speech structures, categories, concepts, and values existing in diverse sociocultural contexts. In recent years, there has been a growing demand to revive the classic categories and concepts of traditional Chinese sources. This approach, however, involves the transcultural relativization of the contents based on methodologies that correspond to the specific requirements of research in the Chinese ideational tradition, and comparative philosophy or cultural studies in general. The priority in this approach is preserving traditional Chinese philosophical characteristics and maintaining autochthonous and traditional methodological principles. However, this does not mean denying or excluding an intellectual confrontation with Western (and global) philosophical systems. Global (especially European and Indian) philosophy includes numerous elements that cannot be found in the Chinese tradition. The investigation and application of these elements is not only a valuable means for fertilizing new idea systems, but also offers an important comparative tool for better understanding one's own tradition. At the same time, as the modern Chinese theorist Zhang Dainian[19] cautioned, we must avoid the use of incompatible or incommensurable methods that attempt to study Chinese history through the lens of Western concepts and categories: "Different philosophical theories use different concepts and categories. Concepts and categories used in philosophical theories can differ greatly from one nation to another" (Zhang Dainian 2003, 118).[20]

As a final point, we must also take into account the differences between the original Chinese notions and their semantic connotations that originate in the translations of these notions into Indo-European languages. The expression "*ru xue* 儒學," for instance, is commonly translated as "Confucianism" (also in the compounds as "New," "Contemporary" or "Modern Confucianism").[21] Thus, it automatically connotes Confucius (Kong fuzi)[22] and the various historical phases of the Confucian teachings. But *"ru xue"* actually signifies "the teachings of the scholars,"[23] which means that this expression does not a priori exclude any of the major influences on the history of Chinese thought. In fact, what Confucian and Daoist philosophy, as well as Sinicized Buddhism, all share is this idea of traditional Chinese philosophy as the "teachings of the scholars."[24]

1.2 A Contrastive Analysis of Two Frameworks

All these issues are, as we have seen in this chapter, linked to the fact that different theoretical models are embedded into different referential frameworks. When investigating traditional Chinese theoretical texts, we have to take into account that these texts belong to a concrete referential framework. The specific features of this framework are determined by the application of different concepts and categories (as well as different kinds of relations between them), resulting in different referents and, consequently, in dissimilar methodological procedures necessary for their investigation and their ordering and communication. This leads, as already mentioned, to a mutual incommensurability of the systems or frameworks as such. But this does not mean that the "questions and answers in one tradition cannot sustain meaningful statement in the other tradition" (Wong 2017, 1). Still, cross-cultural (or cross-traditional) references to a common subject matter should always be examined against the respective backgrounds of the elementary conceptual apparatuses, justification practices, and methods applied in both traditions in question.[25]

We were all born into a society with established norms, values, laws, rules, institutions as well as modes of thought and expressions. To a certain degree, we are thus all determined by the set of cultural meanings within which we learn to speak, to perceive reality and to express our feelings and opinions (Sprintzen 2009, 40). The philosophical background that shapes and participates in the forming of these factors within the cognizance of Euro-American researchers (and through the Western-dominated globalization process, also in the understanding of most modern and postmodern theoreticians) is still guided by the paradigms and parameters of modern Western philosophy. It is a philosophy, which is rooted in the seventeenth and eighteenth centuries and dominated by a scientific, that is, rational and analytical worldview, but also profoundly influenced by the ideas of enlightenment and European type of humanism. In a way, we are still living in the period which started with Kant (Willaschek 1992, 13–15). In this period, the entire philosophical agenda and the crucial philosophical questions were reformulated in a way, which still allies to us and is still relevant for our life. In many respects, not only in the academic sense, but also for the understanding of the world and our place in this world, the philosophers of European modernity have quite decisively redefined the essential problems of Western philosophy. In spite of many significant inventions and critical shifts that were created in sciences and philosophy during the twentieth century and in the so-called postmodern era, modern Western philosophy is still the crucial reference point for the thinking and feeling of the majority of contemporary people. It is the background that provides us with basic paradigms with which we begin and to which we are accustomed to respond. This background can also be seen as a referential framework, which could be contrasted with different philosophical frameworks of reference from other cultures. For the requirements of the present discussion, we will contrast it with the theoretical referential framework pertaining to Confucian philosophy, which has also profoundly influenced the entire traditional Chinese society.[26] Following Paul Gregor's basic rules of intercultural philosophy, intercultural philosophy (or any form of intercultural understanding) has to proceed from the basic ascertaining and explicit formulation of similarities and from identifying, describing, and explaining differences (Paul 2008, 23). Hence, we will begin by describing some of the crucial features of two frameworks. The first one (referred to as framework A) consists of the basic paradigms representative of modern European enlightenment philosophy, and the second one (framework B) of the paradigms typical of classical Confucian philosophy.

The following description or contrastive analysis of these two referential frameworks is of course based upon rather bold generalizations and, as such, is rather essentialist. Neither of the philosophical systems belonging to any of the two frameworks fulfills all the requirements for a "pure" A or B framework or possesses all the attributes described in them and none of them can be viewed as a precise and accurate summary of the central characteristics of Confucian or modern European thought. The present schematic differentiation is not based upon definite factual parameters, but rather implies theoretic tendencies and chief guidelines of thought that are not necessary parts of all theoretical systems in the respective discourse. Thus, this schematic overview will serve us only as an additional tool for a better understanding of problems and difficulties we encounter in any comparative or intercultural philosophical investigation.

- The basic setting of framework A is static, while framework B functions in a dynamic and changeable way. This basic setting influences the entire theoretical system integrated in the particular framework, but also each individual part composing these systems, as well as the relations between all these parts. The same holds true for the respective fundamental paradigms of the two contrasting frames, for their central thought patterns as well as their epistemological and interpretative methods.
- Hence, the inner logic of argumentation and the central modes of processing the content are, to a great degree, abstractly formalized in framework A whereas in framework B, they are rather functioning in accordance with variable semantic and axiological connotations.
- The formal logic behind framework A is tightly linked to normative analyses of fixed and stable objects of investigation, that is, of precisely defined objects excluded from the variable continuum of time and space, whereas the semantic logic applied by framework B is highly contextual and relational (i.e., focused upon relations rather than upon individual isolated objects), and the objects of inquiry are continuously modified. Hence, one of the central methods applied in this framework is the method of semantically specified analogies.
- Concepts contained in framework A are chiefly based on the notion of absoluteness (or the presumption of the absolute truth), whereas in B they are rather relational, implying a relativity of reality and suggesting its relativistic understanding.
- While categories are often applied in dual oppositions in both of the two frameworks,[27] the basic structures and modes of interaction of these binary oppositions are fundamentally different.
- While in framework A, the mutually oppositional objects are (due to their following of the three classical laws of Western logical thought) mutually exclusive, in framework B they appear in the form of binary categories,[28] which function in correlative, interdependent, and complementary interaction.
- This dissimilarity is also reflected in the respective models of dialectical thought that evolved from the two frameworks in question. The model belonging to framework A can be historically followed back to ancient Greek philosophy and is in its modern forms rooted in dual representation models like Cartesian dualisms, in which oppositional notions (body and

mind, matter and idea, substance and phenomena, subject and object, etc.) negate and exclude each other and are thus strictly and radically separated both formally and logically. Although in Hegel's theory the two oppositional concepts still form a correlative unity, they are seen as static momenta within this entirety; in the ultimate instance, this unity is nothing more than the sum of its parts, which, as momenta, condition but also contradict and hence exclude each other. In such models the two oppositions are often denoted thesis and antithesis. The tension that results from the mutual negation and contradiction of both poles leads to the synthesis (which can be reached through Aufhebung or sublation in Hegel). This third stage is a qualitatively different and "higher" stage of development, in which parts of the previous opposition are preserved and other eliminated. In essence the dialectical thought in framework A is conceptual (i.e., containing fixedly defined contents), while in framework B it is a process, based on categories (the concrete content of which is exchangeable and replaceable, not only in the semantic but also in the axiological sense). In its earliest form this latter model goes back to the oldest Chinese proto-philosophical classic, the Book of Changes (*Yi jing* 易經), where it appears as a model of "continuous change" or "continuity through change" (*tongbian* 通變) (Tian 2002, 126). It functions by applying binary categories and the principle of correlative complementarity. The oppositions it contains are interdependent and do not negate but rather complete each other. They are oppositional dualities, but not dualistic contradictions. Hence, the model of their mutual relationship and interaction cannot be denoted as an abstract form of dualism, but rather as a process of a dynamic duality. Furthermore, each of them represents the very essence of the other and neither of the two can exist without the other. In contrast to the synthesis belonging to framework A, the totality or unity of both oppositions in framework B is to be found in the very process of their interaction as such; hence, it does not lead to a qualitatively new and "higher" stage or form of reality, idea, or even its understanding (which is the tendency of framework B).[29]

- Framework A presupposes a metaphysic of transcendence; in framework B it is not possible to distinguish between noumenon and phenomena. Although both are recognized as specific states of being, the demarcation line between immanence and transcendence is blurred and subjected to a dynamic process of all-embracing change.[30] Instead, there is an omnipresent unity of culture and nature, of human beings and the cosmos and of transcendence and immanence in the Unification of Heaven and Humans (*tianren heyi* 天人合一).

- In its epistemological aspects, framework A proposes a distinction between knowable and the unknowable reality. While the latter is represented, for instance, by the thing in itself, the knowledge of the former can be obtained either through experience or through a-priori mental forms. In framework B the realm of the unknowable is also accepted, but it does not represent an object of investigation or any kind of elaboration. However, there is also in framework B—similarly as in framework A—a distinction between innate knowledge (which mostly pertains to axiological contents) and external knowledge, which is mainly empirical. The main distinction between a-priori (A) and innate (B) knowledge lies, once again, in the static (A) and dynamic (B) nature of their respective forms. Framework B shows that knowledge about both external and internal reality is obtained through the structural compatibility of human mind and external world. Knowledge within the constructs of framework B can never be separated from practice. Meanwhile in framework A reason is the main method for gaining knowledge; framework B allows for it to be additionally obtained through intuition, emotions, and intentions.
- Ethics in framework A is closely related to the notions of freedom and moral responsibility. This framework suggests that to act morally is to act from a principle. Freedom, responsibility, and ethics can mainly be maintained through the regularity and rationality of universal rules. Ethics here is a social reality, a spiritual entity, or a fact of reason—that is, it is something external to human inwardness.[31] In framework B, ethical rules are less normative and much more contextual and situational. This framework views the universe as permeated with meaning and therefore also as encompassing ethical implications reflected in the humanness (*ren xing* 人性) as a central virtue of humaneness (*ren* 仁). In a concrete human life this humaneness must be properly learned and cultivated through social customs and especially through rituality, which rationalizes the instinctual essence of human natural feelings. However, since humans are seen as being in unity with heaven, nature, or the universe (*tian ren*

heyi 天人合一), humaneness is both the basis of ethics and the core of individual morality; hence, its external cultivation simultaneously means the realization of one's own individual and personal self.

- In framework A contents pertaining to the abovementioned fields of philosophical investigation are structured and ordered into mutually distinct disciplines (logic, ontology, metaphysics, and epistemology). There are on the other hand no strictly defined disciplines in framework B, but rather contexts (or discourses) belonging to these fields. In this framework epistemological thought, for instance, is intermingled, blended, and mixed with ideas from many other fields of philosophical inquiry, particularly with ontology, ethics, and phenomenology.

After this short description of the basic differences, let us take a closer look to some of the most important and influential features constituting the framework B, that is, the system on which rest most of the classical Chinese philosophical approaches.

1.3 Specific Features of the Chinese Model

Essential differences most definitely exist between traditional Chinese philosophical discourses and Western ones, especially with respect to certain fundamental aspects that determine our ways of perceiving the world. The most basic of these differences is to be found in the principle of immanent transcendence (transcendence in immanence) or the (non-monistic) One-world view, which, in terms of its basic characteristics, differs completely from the concept of transcendence metaphysics. This feature is also linked to the problem of spiritual (or sacred) elements within Chinese philosophical discourses, because the nature of these a-theist elements differs profoundly from the religious (mostly monotheistic) spirituality as developed in Western cultures. Another important specific feature of traditional Chinese philosophy is the structurally ordered, holistic worldview which is rooted in binary relations between pairs of (often antagonistic) notions, and which we will denote with the term "binary categories." The process of mutual interactions between the polar opposites that form these pairs manifests itself in the principle of complementarity, which constitutes another basic paradigm and appears in typical patterns of traditional Chinese analogies. This principle is tightly connected with another important feature of classical Chinese philosophy, namely its dynamic nature which displays itself in continuous changing of all that exists.

1.3.1 One-World View or Immanent Transcendence?

The famous contemporary Chinese philosopher Li Zehou[32] described the worldview that has prevailed in the Chinese tradition as a "One-world view."[33] According to such understanding, there is only one world, namely the world we live in, the world we experience. In this world, the human mind is also formed in accordance with the features and laws of this dynamic empirical world. There are no transcendental, preexisting forms of knowledge. There is neither a need for, nor a possibility of, transcending into higher, intangible realms, and there is also no necessity for a higher force or a personalized god. In other words, there is no need to establish another, separate world of any kind of "Heavenly Kingdom." Hence, this holistic worldview is completely different from the so-called two-worlds view, which prevailed in the history of Western philosophy and which distinguishes the noumenon from phenomena, heaven from earth, and body from mind. Li explained it as follows:

> The main difference between the Chinese cultural tradition and the Judeo-Christian tradition, roughly speaking, is the difference between a "one-world view" and a "two-worlds view." The Bible, Plato, and Kant believe in two worlds: this world and the world beyond, this world and the world of ideas, phenomenon, and noumenon. But for the Chinese, there is just this world. Since nature, human society, and the gods are living in this same world, then anything in this world, including the gods, the emperors, even Heaven, must all follow and obey the same cosmic order of this world, which is called the "Way of Heaven" (*tian dao* 天道). The "Way of Heaven" is the same as the "Way of Humans" (*ren dao* 人道). This means that these two are interdependent and interrelated, and human beings can exercise power to such an extent in this world that they can have a significant impact on the cosmos. (Li 1999a, 179)

The specifically Chinese paradigm of the unity of men and nature (*tianren heyi* 天人合一) is, of course, possible only in the framework of such holistic worldview. This is the only realm that enables the complementary functioning of reason and emotion, of objective cognition and subjective judgement, of abstract analysis and emotional imagination. Li sees this as still latently inherent in the cultural-psychological constitution of modern Chinese people.

The one-world paradigm has not only epistemological and cognitive, but also ethical implications. In his *Response to Michael Sandel and Other Matters*, Li Zehou wrote: "I believe that the focus on the integration of emotion and reason rather than mere reason is the philosophical basis for the major divergence between Chinese ethics and Western ethics" (Li Zehou 2016a, 1069). For these reasons, the Chinese tradition contrasts with those that derive their ethical and social codes from some transcendent supernatural beings. In this one-world people's search for existential meaning is confined to the human realm. Hence, it does not value sacrifice, self-abnegation, or the feeling of failure because of the impossibility of reaching a more desirable realm or state (D'Ambrosio, Carleo and Lambert 2016, 720). This is also the reason the one-world realm can produce the culture of pleasure,[34] defined by the pragmatic (and not practical or even less speculative) reason, which is not separated from emotions (or intentions) and does not seek to disconnect human beings from the network of the relationships (*guanxi* 關係) to which they belong. "In a contemporary context this means that Confucianism, especially in terms of the attention it pays to the 'emotio-rational structure,' can function as a corrective to curb certain shortcomings of modern thought associated with liberalism, formal justice, abstract reason, and notions of the atomic individual" (D'Ambrosio, Carleo and Lambert 2016, 720). Precisely because of its one-world orientation, the Confucian tradition upholds the values of human life, concrete experience, and emotion, and discovers pleasure and meaning in the worldly life. Several other crucial approaches and concepts of Li Zehou's philosophy (as for instance historical ontology or emotion as substance) are also necessarily grounded in this One-world view, for in such a view there is no separation between the phenomenal world and the world of substance, nor a clear and fixed distinction between the human and the transcendent world.

From the perspective of the One-world view, Li Zehou has also redefined the notions of ontology and noumenon in Chinese philosophy. He pointed out that precisely because this worldview was not dualistic, traditional Chinese theoretical discourse did not need to raise philosophical questions of being or define various realms of phenomena and noumenon. He states:

> We translate noumenon as *benti* 本體, a word coined from *ben* 本 (root, origin) and *ti* 體 (stem, body). *Bentilun* 本體論 literally means a discussion, theory, study, or views of *benti*, and this compound was adopted to translate ontology in Chinese.[35] So instead of a study of being, *bentilun* is a study of *ben* (root, origin) and *ti* (stem, body) of things. (Li and Cauvel 2006, 40)

In this context, we have to understand that in the One-world view, the existence of everything is necessarily connected with the existence of human beings and that therefore being as such (or any being) cannot be separated from the existence of human beings.

Several contemporary Chinese theoreticians have undertaken this idea of a unified, single world, which is typical for classical Chinese philosophy, constructing their philosophical systems on similar, or even the same grounds. Yang Guorong, for instance, also presupposes that this view entails important ethical implications. He emphasizes that in such a Chinese philosophical "one world" the abovementioned unity of beings also predicates the unity of facts and values:

> Since there is only this world and no other, it could not and does not, in the last analysis, exist in a state of separation or duplication. The relationship between fact and value is conditioned by this fundamental fact. At first sight the real world seems to be characterized by diversity only and not by oneness, but beings in a world of diversity do not exist in separate, discrete conditions. . . . Moreover, although there is more than one dimension in every being and each dimension is different, every being manages to hold these dimensions together within itself. Furthermore, beings that are in a state of diversity are at the same time always involved with a number of actual or potential values. Therefore, when we make the claim that the real and concrete world is characterized by the unity of fact and value as well as by the unity of a variety of features on the level of fact, this unity is rooted in the fact that there is only this one world. (Yang 2008, 272)

Li Zehou maintains that the Chinese "One-world view" is a complicated feedback system in which the relation between Heaven and humankind (or nature and human beings) is but a single element or "moment" of it. On such grounds, it becomes clear why there is almost no conception of "pure truth" or "pure reason" in Chinese philosophy. Li emphasizes that because of such a worldview the Chinese ideational tradition looks down on pure speculative reasoning. It rather emphasizes the value of "pragmatic rationality."[36]

> For the Chinese, "transcendental" or a-priori cannot be the last word. The Chinese mind would ask why something is "transcendental," or where the a-priori comes from. Because of this "one-world view," it would also be difficult to accept the idea of something "absolutely independent of all experience." This is also the reason that Chinese find it difficult to accept the formalism in Kant's ethics. On the contrary, filled with a sense of history, the Chinese mind always searches for some historical interpretation. Thus, the "transcendental" and the a priori must also have their roots in this world, in the movement of history. (Li 1999a, 180)

In such an understanding, the thinking subject cannot be separated from the acting subject, and human consciousness similarly cannot be separated from their physical or material (bodily) existence. Thus, in Chinese philosophy, knowledge cannot be separated from power (action), scholarship cannot be separated from ideology (dominating power), and epistemology is inseparable from ethics and religion.

On the other hand, many other modern and contemporary scholars (who were not less influential than Li Zehou) saw this inseparability of noumenon and phenomena in a different way. This idea was developed most distinctively by Mou Zongsan, who belonged to the most important representatives of the second generation of Modern Confucianism.[37] He held the basic paradigm of the classical Chinese philosophy to be that of immanent transcendence. Li Zehou strongly opposed this idea, because he believed it to be incompatible with his notion of the One-world view. However, before we proceed to the main arguments of this debate (i.e., One-world-view vs. immanent transcendence), let us take a brief look upon the reasons because of which the Modern Confucian philosophers (especially and most distinctively Mou Zongsan) have established this idea.

Modern Confucians are focused on ontological questions because for them ontology can be seen as a key to the modernization of traditional Chinese philosophy. In their view, classical Confucianism saw Heaven (*tian* 天) as the ultimate noumenon. It was the elementary entity, creating and modifying all that exists. For them, Heaven possessed ontological duality, for it was simultaneously transcendental and immanent. Hence, it endowed human beings with innate qualities of humanness (*ren xing* 人性) that were essentially determined by the fundamental Confucian virtue of humaneness (*ren* 仁). This was a development of Mencius's understanding of the human Self, a view that was typical of the Neo-Confucian discourses in which Mencius was defined as the only "proper" follower of Confucius. However, in their explanations of classical schemes, the Modern Confucian philosophers went a step further. Hence, in their discourses human innate qualities or humanness (*ren xing*) became that potential that not only formed the moral or spiritual Self, but also transcended the individual's empirical and physiological characteristics. Therefore, every individual could be, by acting in accordance with humaneness (*ren*), united with Heaven (*tian ren heyi* 天人合一) and thus realize the genuine sense and value of existence.

These elementary features of the Modern Confucian concept of Heaven (*tian*) can also help us understand their view of the difference between external (*waizai chaoyuexing*)[38] and internal (or immanent) transcendence (*neizai chaoyuexing*),[39] with the latter being one of the specific features of Confucianism and Chinese philosophy in general.

In interpreting traditional Confucian thought (especially the idea of Heavenly Dao or the Dao of Nature), the contemporary New Confucians[40] often made use of the concepts of "transcendence" or "immanence." They pointed out that the Confucian Dao of Nature, which is "transcendent and immanent," is diametrically opposed to the basic model of Western religions, which are "transcendent and external" (Lee 2001, 118).[41]

Immanent notions, which are essential to defining Chinese philosophy, are, of course, also necessary products of the holistic worldview. This also explains why notions that are seen as transcendent in prevailing Western philosophical discourses and that are generally perceived as transcending one and proceeding into another (usually higher) sphere are also immanent in most traditional Chinese philosophical works. Most theoreticians attribute to such notions of immanent transcendence the concepts of Heaven (*tian*) and the Way (*dao* 道). Mou Zongsan has explained this double ontological nature of these classical notions as follows:

> The Way of Heaven, as something "high above," connotes transcendence. When the Way of Heaven is installed in the individual and resides within them in the form of human nature, it is then immanent. (Mou 1990, 26)[42]

David Hall and Roger Ames have criticized such an understanding, observing that while Mou accentuates the inseparability of Heaven and humankind and proposes an immanent classification of the idea in question, at the same time he claims that it is transcendent "to the extent that it connotes independence," a definition that, in their view, "seems inappropriate" (Hall and Ames 1987, 205). Rather, they see the concept of transcendence as it has been coined and defined in Western culture as follows:

> A principle A is transcendent in respect to that B which it serves as principle if the meaning or import of B cannot be fully analyzed and explained without recourse to A, but the reverse is not true. (Hall and Ames 1987, 13)

Their concern is that the usage of such notions might lead to still further misunderstandings in the already difficult interchange between Chinese and Western ideational traditions. They also take Mou to task for his distinctions concerning the connection of transcendence with the Decree of Heaven (*Tian ming* 天命): "To have a sense of the Decree of Heaven, one must first have a sense of transcendence, which is possible only if one accepts the existence of such transcendence" (Mou 1990, 21).[43]

Hall and Ames (1987, 205) believe that in such passages Mou is clearly trying to attribute a "strict transcendence" to early Chinese philosophy. For them, such an attitude seems to be problematic. For Lee Ming-huei,[44] however, their criticism is the result of a "misunderstanding":

> When Modern Confucians apply the concept of "immanent transcendence," they are adhering to the basic premise that "immanence" and "transcendence" are not in logical contradiction. This means that they never apply the concept of "transcendence" in the strict sense understood by Hall and Ames. Their critique is thus clearly based on a misunderstanding. (Lee 2002, 226–7)[45]

Lee Ming-huei's main argument is that notions, especially those that are abstract, have a range of semantic connotations. Here, the term "transcendence" is no exception, as it has had several connotations through the history of Western philosophy. The notion of "immanent transcendence" denotes a *certain type* of transcendence; it certainly does not cover the entire spectrum of the possible semantic connotations of this concept, particularly not those connected to "independence" or to the "separation between creator and creation." Hence, for Modern Confucians, immanent notions do not constitute absolute principles, as in the theological idea of Divinity or the ancient Greek idea of substance (Rošker 2016, 131–7).

To a certain extent, Li Zehou's critique of Mou Zongsan's[46] definition of immanent transcendence is similar to that of Hall and Ames. In his argumentation, Li proceeds from the Modern Confucian classification of the Confucian philosophical tradition, and strongly opposes their idea of "three periods of Confucianism." Because the Modern Confucians have completely neglected the entire second period, marked by Dong Zhongshu's[47] reform and his integration of cosmological and legalist elements into the framework of original Confucianism, they have reduced its development to the philosophy of moral metaphysics as elaborated by the Song Neo-Confucianism. Li maintains that such interpretations can only lead to developments of the narrow scope of Confucianism's religious aspects, whereas the Confucian teachings in their entirety could offer a much more complex foundation for the modernization of the Chinese ideational tradition (Li 1999b, 2–5). Li claims that this problem became even more severe because Mou tried to elaborate upon it within the Kantian framework. Thus, on the one hand, Mou describes his theory of immanent transcendence as a theory that is based upon Confucian tradition and that therefore necessarily negates the existence of an external god. In this sense, Mou has tried to establish moral imperative on the foundation of a unity of human and heavenly heart-mind or on the unity of human and spiritual nature.[48] In this sense, he aimed to establish the noumenon based on inherent human morality. However, on the other hand, he also assumed the Western "two-world view," which separates the divine and the worldly, the realm of ideas and the realm of physical reality, and that of noumenon from that of phenomena. Hence, in Mou's view, the human heart-mind and human nature (or humanness) were "transcendent." However, Li emphasizes that in this Western framework "transcendence" necessarily means a realm that surpasses experience and in which the transcendent (god) determines and rules over human beings, who are confined to the realm of experience. Humans, on the other hand, cannot influence God, who is independent and absolute and who represents the ultimate origin of any existence. According to the "two-world view" all that exists in the concrete reality is limited to the sphere of appearances, for substance or essence only pertain to transcendent existence. Li rather sees it that such a paradigm cannot be combined with the traditional Chinese paradigm of the unity of Heaven and humans (*tian ren heyi*), nor with the view that holds substance and function to be inseparable (*tiyong bu er*).[49] In other words, the Western notion of transcendence can by no means fit into the Chinese One-world view. Consequently it is completely wrong to lay stress, on the one hand, upon the traditional Chinese notions of the unity of Heaven and people, and, on the other, to explain concepts that are originally confined to the sphere of sensuality and emotions, like, for instance "humaneness (*ren*)" or "inborn knowledge (*liangzhi* 良知)" as something immanently "transcendent" or "transcendental" respectively. In addition, Li stresses that, precisely because of the "One-world view," the social and ideational development in ancient China could have led to the aforementioned culture of pleasure, because in this framework, human beings have no tense relation[50] toward external deities, or no fear of god. In this context, Li additionally explains:

> Zheng Jiadong discovered that Mou Zongsan has actually proceeded from the supposition of a mutual division of Heaven and human beings, which means that there cannot be any equation of humans and Heaven (in this way, he acknowledged the existence of some sort of external transcendent entity). Only afterwards did he gradually establish the union of human beings and Heaven by emphasizing that the "immanent transcendence," i.e. the human moral self, was actually grounded in the Way of Heaven. People were thus endowed with an "immanent transcendence," which means that god was already in their heart-minds. Why should they then have any "fear" of a transcendent, externally existing god? (Li 1999b, 9)[51]

Since according to Li Zehou, all these contradictions are rooted in the Song period's Neo-Confucianism, Li Zehou believes that Modern Confucianism has not succeeded in creating any genuinely new philosophical approaches or theoretical innovations (Li 1999b, 8) that could serve as a foundation for future philosophical discoveries or new philosophical systems. "Thus, it is solely a modern 'reflection' or a 'distant echo' of the School of the structural principle (*li xue* 理學) from the Song and Ming Dynasties, unable to construct a new period of philosophic investigation" (Li 1999b, 10).[52]

Because of all these reasons, Li claims that Chinese philosophy is thoroughly immanent. Hence, it becomes clear that his "one-world" is exclusively the world of here and now, the concrete world in which we live. Some of contemporary Chinese theoreticians, however, are critical toward such a view. Chen Lai,[53] for instance, agrees with Li Zehou in the conviction that, in contrast to the Western discourses, traditional Chinese ethics was never rooted in a belief in a Supreme Being. However, in contrast to Li, Chen sees the crucial difference between Chinese metaphysics and those of monotheistic religions in the nature of the relationship between the two worlds and not in the lack of a transcendent realm (Carleo and D'Ambrosio 2015). Chen Lai (1996) upholds that, although in Chinese tradition there is a distinction between the concrete and the metaphysical world, this distinction does not equal a separation. This is important to Chen because he believes that Li's assertion that Chinese thought is "one-world" impedes the existence of traditional Chinese metaphysics. Nevertheless, for both thinkers "the West sees a gap between this world and a transcendent, divine world of greater truth or reality whereas China remains focused on divinity occurring within this world" (1996). In this context, however, Chen Lai exposes the importance of Li Zehou's division between the "narrow" and "broad" senses of metaphysics.

> The narrow sense of metaphysics is quintessentially Western and refers to that of the analytical and rational tradition of thought developed from Ancient Greece. This kind of thinking did not become dominant in the Chinese tradition. However, a broad sense of metaphysics as the pursuit of values and the meaning of human life is central to traditional Chinese thought. It also holds great relevance today. (Carleo and D'Ambrosio 2015, 14)

On the other hand, immanent transcendence doubtless refers to the realm of the human inwardness, of the heart-mind, which is rooted and actualized in human consciousness:[54] in Confucian discourses, Heaven (or nature, *tian*) is perceived as a great, infinite organism, of which all of us are parts. In this sense, a human being is separated, but simultaneously also united with it. Hence, in this framework, individuals do not strive to be more than what they are. In so doing, the individual would namely be acting against their own humanness (*ren xing* 人性) and hence against the Way of Heaven (*Tian dao* 天道). Liu Shu-hsien[55] described this in the following way:

> But to teach a complete humanism does not mean that man has to cut all his ties with the transcendent. On the contrary, once he realizes the creative source within himself, he can then participate in the creative process of the universe and forget the sorrows, which pertain only to his small self. A man who has no other concerns than those of the small self is not a fully developed man. Such a man is caught by a sense of anxiety and never feels free. Only if a man broadens his view and realizes that he is a part of the creative process in the universe will his sense of anxiety be completely overcome. He will then gladly accept his destiny without feeling any regret in his heart. What he achieves is not a kind of personal immortality, but a method to live according to the Way and to merge into the transforming and

nourishing process of Heaven and Earth, which will never cease even if the present form of the universe no longer exists. (Liu 1972, 48)

Although the individual human heart-mind is thus restricted by the physical limitations of the body, there is doubtless a deep connection between human consciousness and the infiniteness of the universe, which operates as the Way of Heaven, as we can read in numerous sections of the classics, for instance: "The duke inquired: 'May I ask what it is that the nobleman values in the Way of Heaven?' Confucius answered: 'He values its endlessness'" (*Li ji* s.d., Ai Gong wen, 12).[56]

In my opinion, the most important point regarding the question of immanence and transcendence in Chinese philosophy is that even when denoting this paradigm as a One-world-view, this holistic model still cannot be understood as a monistic worldview, as has been presupposed by some Chinese scholars (see for instance Chongbai Moluo's interpretation in Li Zehou 2016a, 293).[57] As we will see later, in the section dealing with binary categories, this holism was ordered and structured in a binary or dual (but not dualistic) manner. Before that, however, we have to clarify the question of spiritual or religious elements inherent in Chinese philosophy.

1.3.2 The Question of Spirituality and the Unemployed God

When assuming that the Chinese "one-world" was actually a world of "immanent transcendence" (or "transcendence in immanence"), we have to ask ourselves what is then the nature of its sacredness and spirituality. In other words, what is the nature of the relation between religion and philosophy in China?

According to Xu Fuguan's[58] analyses, all cultures find their earliest source in religion and originate in the worship of God or gods. The specific feature of Chinese culture was that it soon descended, in a series of gradual transitions, from heaven to the world of men, and the real life and behavior of human beings. During the Zhou Dynasty (1459–249 BCE), the preoccupation with earthly matters had started: the spirit of self-consciousness was beginning to work and they had developed a clear will and purpose (see Bresciani 2001, 338). They were thus moving progressively from the realm of religion to the realm of ethics. Hence, from this very early stage, the Chinese have been liberated from metaphysical concerns. In contrast to the ancient Greeks, who at the same critical stage in their history moved from religion to metaphysics, they moved from religion to innate ethics.

In China, the Eastern Zhou Dynasty (770–256 BCE) was a period of conflicting local cultures. According to Modern Confucian interpretations, this innate moral ethics, denoted as the "Moral Self" (*daode benxin, daode ziwo*),[59] appeared in China during this period as an ideal core of individual perception and possible identification. For them, its emergence was conditioned by the fact that all of the "feudal" states in the Zhou Dynasty were rooted in diverse traditions that had formed different religious ideas. Just as ancient Greek culture is generally considered the "cradle of European culture," so too the period of the Zhou Dynasty is seen as the "cradle of (Han)-Chinese culture" by official Chinese historiography.[60]

In this framework, the Zhou society resulted from the merging of two different types of culture: an agrarian system typical of the defeated Shang (or Yin) Dynasty (1600–1066 BCE), and the hunting and gathering culture of the nomadic conquerors, that is, the ancestors of the Zhou Dynasty.[61] This theory is supported by the *Shi ji (Historical Notes)*, according to which in spite of the fact that the mythological founding ancestor of the Zhou Dynasty, Hou Ji, was credited with greatly improving Xia (2100–1600 BCE) agriculture, his son Buzhu abandoned agriculture entirely, living a nomadic life in the manner of their Rong and Di "barbarian" neighbors (see *Shi ji* s.d., Zhou benji: 3).[62] Among the consequences of this encounter was the mixing of agrarian and nomadic religions. Xu Fuguan showed that the Zhou society could, in many ways, be seen as a continuation of the Shang culture (Xu Fuguan 1987, 649).

One of the elements appropriated by the Zhou from the Shang Dynasty was the cult of ancestors (Xu Fuguan 1987, 649). Given that the religious ideas of the Shang Dynasty centered on fertility worship, while its economic system was based upon the cooperation and division of labor within family clans, the cult of ancestors as a ritualized worship which united both aspects, gradually became the common thread which can be traced throughout Chinese history.

In Western sinology, the cult of ancestors is still commonly thought to be a religion, for it is rooted in a faith in the afterlife and the propitiation and search for protection from the ancestral spirits by the living members of the family clan. But since Confucius was an agnostic,[63] his emphasis on the importance of the ancestor cult cannot be confused with a religious ritual, but must be understood as a moral one. This aspect was underscored by

Xu Fuguan, in the context of his research into the ideologies of the pre-Qin period.

> With respect to the worship of spirits and deities, while Confucius could not rationally prove that they existed, he could neither prove that they did not exist. Thus, he transformed this ritual into a form of respectful ancestor worship, in which the living could manifest the virtues of respect, humanity and love. This form of worship, which began with Confucius and was further developed after him, is in no way a religious activity, for what it implies is a purification and elevation of the self-centered perception of individuals. (Xu 1995, 614)[64]

This cult provided the basis for the first Han-Chinese ethical codex, as well as the religious ideas of this cultural community. Its basic belief is that the human body contains two souls: the first is animalistic and dies soon after the death of the body, while the second, the so-called soul of human personality can move about freely and continue to exist as long as there are living people who remember and feed it. The family clan that respected its deceased ancestors guaranteed itself their protection and assistance. The new ideologies thus merged the cult of Heaven with the family system, such that the ruler became the "Son of Heaven" (*Tian zi* 天子), thereby legitimizing the quest for absolute power, while also accommodating the original nomadic Zhou culture.

While in the Shang/Yin period, the people's faith in God or the highest ruler (*Shang di*) did not imply any ethical elements, in the period of the Zhou Dynasty this belief was related to morality. In historical terms, the linking of Heaven with virtue not only resolved the problem of justifying and legitimizing the political power of the early Zhou, but also accelerated the development of the original Chinese religion by raising it from a natural to a moral religion. In its role as the highest anthropomorphic deity, Tian was not only the creator of humanity, but also its highest judge, who meted out praise and punishment as recompense for moral or immoral behavior. However, according to Yang Zebo (2007, 2), due to the inefficiency, corruption, and nepotism of the ruling class, this moral-religious consciousness gradually declined, reaching its low ebb at the end of the eighth century BCE, during the transition from the Western to the Eastern Zhou Dynasty. As confirmed by several passages in the *Book of Songs* (*Shi jing* 詩經), by this time the deity was the object of much anger (*tian yuan*) and doubt (*yi tian*).[65]

As Xu Fuguan has shown, the authority of the Heavenly Mandate (*tian ming*) was already much weakened by the time of the ruler You[66] of the Zhou Dynasty. The traditional religious concepts which were rooted in the early Zhou Dynasty had almost completely disintegrated. This period marks an extraordinarily important historical and cultural shift, in which Chinese society entered what Karl Jaspers has called "the axial period."[67] In fact, as opposed to most other civilizations, China did not develop a theology, but separated itself from it (Yang Zebo 2007, 3).[68]

As Chen Lai (1996, 4) points out, instead of people recognizing their own limitations and turning toward some transcendent, infinite entity or monotheistic religion, they recognized the limitations of deities and oriented themselves toward the real world and the ordering of society and interpersonal relations. Thus, instead of a "breakthrough to transcendence," in China there was a "breakthrough to humanity" (Xu Fuguan 1987, 659). While other civilizations were moving toward "more developed" religions during this same period, China turned toward a pragmatic search for an ideal social order.[69]

By not taking these specific historical circumstances into account, Western scholars have always assumed that the main Chinese religion in the late Zhou period (primarily Confucius) was a primitive form of religious faith. Hegel, for example, in his description of this religion (Hegel 1996, 320), concluded that the concept *tian* only referred to the concrete social reality, and that ancient Chinese thinkers (with Confucius at the fore) had thus been unable to gain an insight into the idea of transcendence.

As already mentioned, the Modern Confucians developed their views on the original Confucian teachings and the ethics they implied based on immanent transcendence. The creative transformation of religion into morality thus also served as the foundation of the new Modern Confucian concept of subjectivity. The second-generation thinkers followed the basic supposition that in the aforesaid historical process of social transformation in China, the idea of Heaven (*tian*) was transformed from an anthropomorphic higher force into something which determined the inner reality of every human being (Fang and Li 1995, III/608). As Fang Dongmei[70] puts it:

> At first, this culture was formed on the basis of a religious spirit, but it was then transformed into a culture with a highly developed ethics. This ethics was appropriated and properly ordered by Confucius. (Fang 2004, 99)[71]

Xu Fuguan conjectured that original Confucianism attempted to establish a basis for moral decisions in the idea of a subjective righteousness which was intended to serve as a fundamental criterion and thus replace the former fear of spirits. Xu argues that this transformation represents a higher level of spiritual development than that found in monotheistic religions, which are based upon the idea of an (external) God. In his view, in China this transformation led to a humanism based on a high level of "self-awareness" (*zijuexing* 自覺性):

> All human cultures begin with religion. China was no exception in this sense. But all cultures also form a kind of clear and reasonable idea which influences the development of human behavior; that is, they must develop a certain level of human self-awareness. Primitive religions are, instead, mostly defined by a simple belief in miraculous supernatural forces, which derive from a sense of dread at the destruction that can be caused by heaven. Such religions are not based on any kind of self-awareness. Highly developed religions differ according to the societies and historical periods in which they arose. If we observe the preserved bronze vessels from the Yin period, it is clear that Chinese culture was already highly developed at that time, and that it had a long history behind it. However, if we examine the inscriptions on bones and turtle shells from that same period, we find that spiritual life was still rather primitive, and that their religion belonged to primitive forms of religious faith. People still believed their lives were completely dependent upon various deities, the most important of which were the spirits of ancestors and the highest ruler, Shang di. In the Zhou period, a spirit of self-awareness was incorporated into traditional religious life. In this sense, a culture previously rooted in material achievements was raised to the sphere of ideas. And this contributed to founding the humanistic spirit of Chinese morality. (Xu Fuguan 2005, 15–16)[72]

Like most other second-generation thinkers, Xu Fuguan was convinced that this transformation from a "primitive" natural religion into a system of pragmatic ethics was the Zhou Dynasty's greatest contribution to the development of Chinese culture. Xu points out that while during the Zhou period the people still worshipped and offered sacrifices to various deities from previous natural religions, this no longer occurred within the context of official state religions that could have fulfilled the function of preserving or justifying political power. In the Zhou period, this function had gradually been supplanted by the idea of the "Heavenly Mandate" or "The Decree of Heaven" (*tian ming*). The values criteria of this new idea were defined by the reasonableness or unreasonableness of human performances (Xu Fuguan 2005, 24). The most important innovation here was that the idea of the Heavenly Mandate was no longer an ideology intended to protect a real ruler and his real interests. Instead, the ruler always had to be chosen among those who could prove themselves most worthy of this position through their reasonable, responsible, and righteous actions. The concept of the Heavenly Mandate was thus no longer something remote, incomprehensible, and miraculous, as with the previous ideology of spirits and deities, but a concept which was both sacred and yet completely human and comprehensible. It could therefore guarantee a reasonable structure of society and politics, and enable individuals to attain a fair degree of independence (Xu Fuguan 2005, 24).

Xu Fuguan has explored this process of the formation of morality and the internalizing of the spirit of humanity in great detail. He believed that Confucius was the figure who most influenced this transformation of primitive belief (Xu 1995, 613). Of course, even before Confucius there were various germs of moral ideas in China, which served both as generally accepted behavioral criteria and as a legitimization of affiliation to a given social class. But the gradual process of the "humanization of heaven" and the discovery of its humanistic dimension (*tiande renwenhua*)[73] did not begin before the Spring and Autumn period (770–476 BCE). By that time, the ideas of reverence (*jing*)[74] and rituality (*li*) had become fairly important as central manifestations of the socialization of morality. Previously, moral ideas had merely represented sets of axiological meanings which served as criteria for the good and reasonable in the ordering of society and interpersonal relations. Moral ideas were thus something external; in Confucianism they instead acquired a new dimension and became part of a completely different discourse:[75]

> Before Confucius . . . moral and ethical ideas manifested themselves merely in the form of external knowledge and behavior. They were woven into relations in the objective world and were not understood as something that could be consciously applied to open up the inner world of humanism. Only through Confucius' creative reform was this humanism of the objective world transformed into a world of inner humanism. Individuals were thereby endowed with the possibility of striving for self-improvement (completion) and a spirit of Chinese morality was formed. (Xu 1995, 614)[76]

Xu Fuguan explains that the philosophical reforms enacted by Confucius manifested themselves in two significant ways:

1. in the reform of the worship of traditional spirits and deities, which was transformed into symbolic ancestor worship by Confucius and
2. in the internalizing of traditional religious concepts, such as Heaven/Nature (*tian*), the Heavenly Mandate (*tian ming*) and the Way of Heaven/Nature (*tian dao*); these concepts were also transformed from abstract external ideas into symbols denoting various forms or states of an inner moral substance.

Confucius distinguished between two levels of transmitting and interpreting his philosophy, as synthesized in his famous phrase: "My studies lie on the physical level, and my penetration rises to a metaphysical one" (*xia xue er shang da*).[77] The former approach was exemplified in the moral teachings for the uneducated and mostly agrarian population, where in order to express his concept of immanent transcendence Confucius relied on traditional notions that were already familiar to his listeners in order to denote specific aspects of the inner substance. In applying this dual approach, he used real human experience in order to elaborate a philosophical discourse on the concept of a morality which transcends the one-dimensional nature of human existence.

> Confucius expressed concepts such as Heaven/Nature, the Heavenly Mandate or the Way of Nature with the most direct and simple language; but he was actually talking about a morality which supersedes experience. (Xu Fuguan 2005, 81)[78]

In order to spread his teachings, these moral-philosophical concepts assumed the function of appropriate symbols that people could apply in their lives through moral conduct and rituality. The Heavenly Mandate could thus become a part of everyday life, while thanks to their familiarity with this traditional idea the common people could become aware of their unity with its moral dimension, and its relevance for them in terms of moral responsibility.[79]

The fulfillment of these internalized moral-humanistic values thus gained the dimension of perfecting one's personality.[80] By linking the innate personal attributes of individuals with the Heavenly Mandate (*tian ming*), Confucius created a new moral content with a deeper significance that superseded the traditional idea of "righteousness" (*yi* 義). This concept, with which all

Confucian discourses were permeated and which constitutes their conceptual core, was expressed by the idea of humanity or mutuality (*ren*), as representing a state of complete individual and social consciousness.[81]

Thus, in Xu Fuguan's reading, Confucianism is not a religion, but a discourse that represents both a practical moral teaching and an abstract philosophy of immanent transcendence. While Confucius' works have generally been understood and interpreted in the former sense, it was primarily the Neo-Confucian philosophers of the Song and Ming Dynasties who would develop its philosophical aspects. We might well ask therefore, and notwithstanding his detailed and painstaking philological research into original Confucianism, whether Xu Fuguan has not projected the discoveries and results of later Confucian philosophies and interpretations onto the original teachings.[82]

However, if we take modern Chinese scholarship as a whole, the reinterpretation of this teaching as embodying something sacred is clearly evident. Although it has been described as a religion without God, that is, as an atheistic religion (similar to Buddhism) the correctness of this interpretation remains open to debate.

While using a very different approach from Xu, Heiner Roetz (2008, 370) has also contextualized original Confucianism within the transition from a religiously determined to a purely pragmatic ethics. He points out that in original Confucianism, "Heaven" (*tian*) never appears in the function of external provisions or regulations, since it "never speaks."[83] Another reason for his skepticism as to the religious dimension of original Confucianism is that a non-religious reading of these ancient texts can, if based on a proper interpretation and adaptation, allow for a unitary conceptualization of modernization which is not limited to instrumental rationality, but which also does not negate social progress, understood as a necessary consequence of enlightenment.

Precisely because Chinese philosophy never implied the need for attaining transcendence or some "Kingdom of God," it could focus its discourses on the refinement of the subject in the world in which it was embedded, within the actuality of here and now. In short, the *Summum bonum* can only be realized in the here and now. The need for a transcendent God condemns this realization to failure in advance (Liu 2003, 485). Furthermore, the Moral Self which manifests itself through its innate moral substance (*xingti* 性體) unites in itself all three essential postulates of practical reason, that is, free will, the immortality of the soul, and the existence of God.

Morality, even of a kind which is grounded on the autonomy of a higher (infinite) heart-mind, that is, on a basis which far surpasses the simple pragmatism of interpersonal life, does not require any higher force beyond this a priori reflexive awareness. In this way, the European God became unemployed. If we stipulate (as Kant did) the creation of the unique and unrepeatable world in which we live on a static and immutable line of time and space, then this world which has been "created" by God cannot be changed or improved, in contrast to a human being who—as a subject—possesses the possibility and urgent need for moral development.

1.3.3 Binary Categories and the Ever-Changing World

As we shall see in the paragraphs that follow, the questions of immanent transcendence and the atheist spirituality of a Moral Self who is rooted in and conditioned by their physical, phenomenal existence cannot be separated from the methodology of binary categories.

It is well known that the traditional Chinese world view was a holistic one.[84] Hence, traditional Chinese thinkers did not strictly (i.e., formally or categorically) distinguish between the spheres of matter and idea, nor between any other dualistic connotations resulting from this basic dichotomy.[85] Far less known or recognized is the fact that this holism was by no means indiscriminate; the traditional Chinese holistic world was not a sort of homogenous unity in which everything was connected to everything else, without demarcations or distinctions. On the contrary, the traditional Chinese world view was logically ordered based on relatively strict binary oppositional patterns. On a mental-reflective level, these patterns formed a series of specific Chinese analogies[86] which provided the bases for the prevailing method of logical thought (Cui and Zhang 2005, 14). Some of these pairs are very well known, as for instance *yin* 陰 and *yang* 陽 (sunny and shady), which is—even outside China—the most renowned and perhaps most general binary category. However, there are many others, which are not so famous outside the Chinese cultural circle, like for instance *tiyong* 體用 (essence and function), *mingshi* 名實 (name and actuality), *liqi* 理氣 (dynamic structure and vital creativity), and *benmo* 本末 (roots and crown).

Binary categories can be seen as one of the fundamental characteristics of traditional Chinese philosophy. They represent a kind of duality that seeks to attain the most real (possible) state of actuality through relativity, expressed in the relation between two oppositional notions:

> Distinctions are seen in binary terms, and primarily between pairs of opposites (with even figure and color reduced to square/round and white/black); having drawn them, and recognized some recurring or persisting pattern (for example large, round, hard, heavy, and white) we detach a stone from other things as we cut out a piece of cloth or chop off a piece of meat. Things are not seen as isolated each with its own essential and accidental properties; on the contrary, distinguishing characteristics are seen as mostly relative. (Graham 1989, 286)

Of course, binary patterns as such are by no means a specific feature of Chinese philosophy, since in their contrastive, divisional, and distinguishing effects they form a basic condition of human thought as such. What distinguishes the Chinese binary categories from traditional Western dualisms is the principle of complementarity, which represents the basic method of their functioning.

What we have here is a structural pattern of binary oppositions, which, however, is fundamentally different from the model of Cartesian dualism. The latter is based on the tree fundamental laws of traditional logic, that is,

1. law of identity $(p = p)$
2. law of contradiction $\sim(p \cdot \sim p)$
3. law of the excluded middle $(p \vee \sim p)$.

Since these laws (which are, in fact, merely different forms of one and the same principle) involve static and universally valid postulates, this model of dualism forms a basis for a dialectic posited upon the relation between the mutually exclusive and polar opposites of thesis and antithesis, determined by a contradictive opposition. This contradiction creates a tension in which the reciprocal negation of thesis and antithesis creates a synthesis. The complementary model, which was prevalent in the Chinese tradition of thought, is instead based upon a non-contradictory opposition between two poles which do not exclude but complement each other, and which are interdependent. Such binary patterns do not produce any separate syntheses that can preserve "positive" elements of the previous state, while simultaneously eliminating the "negative" ones. Zhuangzi described the relation between the two binary poles of a complementary model as follows:

> Therefore I'm saying: why don't we preserve truth and abolish falseness? Why don't we preserve order and abolish chaos? If we think in this way, we do not understand the structure of nature, nor the state of being in which everything exists. This would mean preserving earth and abolishing heaven, preserving *yin* and abolishing *yang*. It's quite clear that this wouldn't work. (*Zhuangzi* s.d., Qiu shui: 5)[87]

Such valuations of binary relations differ a great deal from those logo-centric dualisms developed in the Hellenistic and Judeo-Christian traditions that were grounded upon mutual contradiction of both anti-poles, tending to preserve one of the poles while eliminating the other. The most important specific features of complementary relations, which distinguish them from the binary Cartesian type of dualisms, are therefore the non-contradictive nature of both antipodes, their interdependence, their axiological equality, as well as their mutual supplementation. The latter characteristic is also the reason for the fact that neither antipode can obtain an absolutely primary position: their existence is conditioned by their mutual interaction which surpasses the limitations of spatial and temporal conceptualizations. Zhu Xi 朱熹 (1130–1200), the central representative of the Neo-Confucian renovation, described this in the following way:

> When we speak about *yin* and *yang*, saying that function is *yin*, while substance is *yang*, we (have to know) that movement and stillness are without end, and *yin* and *yang* are without a beginning. Here, we cannot distinguish between before and afterwards. If we speak about it from the point of origination, then there is always stillness before movement, there is always substance before function, silence before perception and *yin* before *yang*. But before every silence, there is also perception and before stillness there is movement. What should be taken as prior and what as posterior? We cannot simply say that today's movement is taken to be the beginning and neglect to mention the stillness that was there yesterday. This is like breathing: if we express it by exhale–inhale, it sounds right. We cannot describe it as inhale–exhale. But in fact, there is an inhalation before every exhalation and before every inhalation there is inhalation there is exhalation. (Zhu Xi 1996, 11)[88]

Here, we could clearly sense the dynamic nature of reality, in which binary categories are embedded. Because the antipodes or oppositional notions as perceived in the Cartesian dualisms are, as mentioned, based on and conditioned by the three basic laws of formal logic, they are formally and essentially always identifiable with themselves, notwithstanding the modifications of time and space. In contrast to such a model, the demarcation line dividing the two oppositional notions in the binary categories pattern is continuously changing and therefore blurred. Hence, they cannot be perceived (or written down) in a formal way. They do not produce any kind of separate and definable synthesis as a qualitative new stage of evolvement; if we would seek for a synthesis in patterns of binary categories, we could at best find it in the very process of interaction between the two mutually complementary and corresponding oppositional antipodes.

It is precisely this dynamic nature of relational interactions which—among others—causes a lot of problems for most Western scholars who are not trained in Chinese philosophy. As an example we could mention the important Chinese concept of the "middle way" (*zhong yong* 中庸), which has often been translated into Western languages as "the doctrine of the mean." When seen from a viewpoint of traditional formal logic, it can be understood as a very conservative method of always choosing the middle in a way of achieving stative (and thus often necessarily insensible) compromises between two oppositional alternatives. In fact, the "middle way" is different. We have to look upon it from the viewpoint of a dynamic perception of the ever-changing reality. In such a view, it is not a formal, statically unchangeable "middle," but a state of equilibrium, which is different in every single moment.

It is interesting and revealing to analyze the Chinese models of dealing with dual (binary) categories, because the structure of opposition (or, in a less determined sense, of relation) between two or more different ideas, beliefs, notions, presumptions, images, or concepts always decisively influences the developmental mode of any theory. Although we cannot see this when looking to them through the lens of formal and static frameworks, the mode of development as such is crucial for the Chinese theoretical models, because, as already implied, they are rooted in an explicitly dynamic, resilient, and flexible framework. Therefore, the concepts and ideas that were shaped in the Chinese ideational tradition occur within this framework in a highly contextual and situational manner, continuously fluctuating and modifying the structural pattern of thought into which they are embedded. Such a system allows (and even necessitates) dynamic changes and the continuous evolution of the all-inclusive structure of any theory.

2

Basic Paradigms

2.1 A Structural Network of Dynamic Relations

As we shall see in this chapter, traditional Chinese philosophy had developed a theoretical standard based on the concept of structure, or the assumption of a structurally ordered world. This idea of a structural, relational order[1] is reflected in most classical Chinese philosophical works and disciplines. Hence, the structural cosmic order constitutes a basic paradigm of the classical Chinese philosophy as such.[2]

The structural understanding of the cosmos, and all that exists within it and forms a vital part of it, is a specific feature of the classical Chinese holistic worldview. The interconnection between everything that exists forms a system which is based upon a structural order. This basic structure, however, is not merely a static formal system which prefigures and conditions the composition of the universe, but also represents an organic and vital formation. As a dynamic organism that pervades everything that exists, it is therefore systemically compatible not only with all the inanimate objects contained within it, in accordance with the rational, structural patterns of the universe, but also with the organic constitution of living beings that form its vital natural parts.

However, the structure of existence which manifests itself in this paradigm is also conditioned by another important aspect, given that its system, which is based upon an ontological duality of immanent transcendence or the One-world-view (including, as it does, both the ideal principles as well as the concrete particulars of existence), is also infinite and therefore open. This is precisely why the traditional Chinese worldview is not, in essence, deterministic, for everything that exists forms a part of a structure that exceeds the conditions of its concrete actuality. Human will is thus a factor which can—though, of course, only within the narrow limits of an individual existence—also act against the structural norms of the cosmic order, even if most traditional philosophers discourage such a course of action.

The theory of structure as it was developed in the Chinese intellectual tradition was rooted in the concept *li* 理, which denoted both a fundamental framework (and network) and the basic nature of all that exists. It provided an insight into reality which can be described within the scope of the conceptual design of the term *li* and which, at the same time, represents its fundamental presupposition. The common acceptance of this structural theory thus enabled human beings to establish certain prognoses and instructions for concrete (either individual or political) modes of action and behavior. We can conclude, therefore, that at the core of the theory of *li* there is a structural model of reality which implies its ontological, epistemological and, last but not least, axiological aspects.[3]

Structure and structural networks play significant roles in all spectrums of Chinese philosophy. If we, for instance, proceed from the basic properties of classical Chinese epistemology, we will see that, according to this discourse, the fundamental precondition of human perception and comprehension of the external world was the structural compatibility of that same external world and the human mind. Specific Chinese models for theories of knowledge were thus premised upon a structurally ordered external reality; since natural (or cosmic) order is organic, it naturally follows the "flow" of structural patterns and operates in accordance with structural principles or patterns that regulate every existence. In this worldview, the human mind is also structured in accordance with this all-embracing but open organic system. The axioms of our recognition and thought are therefore not coincidental or arbitrary, but follow this rationally designed structure. The compatibility or correspondence of both the cosmic and mental structures is the basic precondition that enables human beings to perceive and recognize external reality. As we shall see, this paradigm of structural epistemology can already be found in the earliest Chinese theories of knowledge. In the Chinese tradition, this structural (or networking) worldview was closely linked to a structurally conditioned understanding of the universe. The mutual compatibility between cosmic and cognitive structures enables our perception and comprehension of reality; this is an essentially quite simple principle, which becomes very clear when we consider the original meaning of the Chinese character *li* and its later semantic connotations. Subsequent developments of the Chinese intellectual tradition must likewise be understood as being rooted in the basic meaning of the concept *li* which implies a structural order.

2.1.1 The Concept *li*: Structuralism and Its Chinese Ancestors

This meaning is already apparent in the original The term *li* is among the central concepts of Chinese philosophy, and while interpreting it to mean structure may appear highly unusual, there are some very good reasons for doing so. The etymology of the character *li*, which is composed of the phonetic element *li* 里, and the radical *yu* 玉, that designates jade (originally, it denoted the lines or colored stripes in jade). Wolfgang Bauer points out that when this character was used figuratively in classical Chinese, it also denoted structure (for example, in the crystal net that represents the immaterial principle of ordered matter) and was already used in this sense in the Confucian commentary on the *Book of Changes* (Bauer 2000, 256–7).

A. C. Graham, a modern pioneer in the study of ancient Chinese logic, is one of the very few sinologists who considered the concept *li* as the expression of both a structural pattern and a structure:

> *Li* is the patterned arrangement of parts in a structured whole, of things in an ordered cosmos, of thought in rational discourse, and in *Names and Objects*,[4] of words in a completed sentence. Its emergence in the Sung Dynasty (AD 960–1279) as one of the central concepts of Neo-Confucianism was the culmination of a long development. In pre-Han philosophy it attracts attention especially in the *Interpreting Lao-tzu* of Han Fe tzu,[5] who uses it to mean the specific configuration of properties ("square or round, long or short, coarse or fine, hard or soft") in each kind of thing. (Graham 1978, 191–2)

The philosopher cited by Graham, Han Feizi,[6] was one of the founders of the legalist school and described the concept *li* as follows: "We call *li* that which is long or short, square or round, hard or soft, heavy or light, white or black" (*Han Feizi* s.d., Jie Lao: 29).[7]

The Norwegian sinologist and specialist in Chinese logic Christoph Harbsmeier uses this quotation to support his conjecture that the concept *li* designated the attributes of objects (Harbsmeier 1989, 238). However, he specifies that in this context the term *li* can only refer to those characteristics that can be perceived by our senses. His doubts about the correctness of this translation are evident in the following comment: "By way of experiment, I shall hazard the translation 'attribute' for *li*, which is an extension of the meaning 'visible pattern,' as is well attested to in early literature" (Harbsmeier 1989, 238).

In fact, in the earliest sources, *li* was understood as a visible structure, such as we find in the lines in jade. As Xunzi[8] (ca. 310–235), one of the two main successors to Confucius, declares in his main work, *Rectifying names* (*Zheng ming* 正名): "Form, color and structure can be discerned with the eyes" (*Xunzi* s.d., Zhengming: 9).[9]

This structure can apply to any physical thing. In the *Book of Rites* (*Li ji* 禮記), for example, it appears as a notion that denotes a structure of veins and sinews in the flesh of animals: "The beef we are using must be fresh. We cut it so as to cleave its structure" (*Li ji* s.d., Nei ze: 53).[10]

The term *li* was also used in this sense by Zhuangzi,[11] in reference to the art of butchering, for when cutting beef the master butcher should always: "follow its natural structure" (*Zhuangzi* s.d., Yangsheng zhu: 2).[12]

The concept *li* was already mentioned in the oldest commentaries on the *Book of Changes*, where it denotes the basic structure of heaven and earth. While neither Confucius nor Laozi use the character *li* in their works, it appears frequently in the writings of their immediate successors.

As with the majority of classical Chinese words, the notion *li* can appear in either verbal or substantive form. As a noun, it signifies "pattern" or "structure," and seems to indicate the sum of all the attributes perceivable by the senses (length, color, consistency, weight, form). If we wish to "cultivate" any given object, we must follow its intrinsic structure. Hence, when the character *li* appears with a verbal function, it signifies the process of ordering certain things and phenomena in accordance with its intrinsic structure. In its original verbal form it meant the cultivation of raw jade in accordance with the lines that determine its structure, as for instance in the following example: "Thus, the king ordered the jeweler to cultivate the raw stone (in accordance with its structure) in order to obtain the gem" (*Han Feizi* s.d., He shi: 1).[13]

In the framework of Confucian rituality, the term *Li* with a verbal function already appears in the classical *Book of Rites* (*Li ji*), where it is applied in the sense of regulation: "At the age of thirty, he already had his own home and began to engage in the affairs of men (i.e., to conduct himself in accordance with the prescribed activities of men)" (*Li ji* s.d., Nei ze: 80).[14]

In one of the oldest Chinese encyclopedias, the *Explanation of Texts and Interpretation of Characters* (說文解字),[15] we find the following definition of *li*'s verbal function: *Li* (means) to order (cultivate) jade (*Shuowen jiezi* s.d., 28).[16] It is of paramount importance that this ordering (or cultivation) occurs in accordance with the structure, expressed by the substantive function of the term *li*. Translating its verbal form with the term "to structure" is thus appropriate. However, in the Indo-European languages, this verb has the connotation of establishing a structure in something which is unstructured, while *li* in its verbal function instead expresses the ordering (or "squaring") of an object in accordance with a preexisting system which is intrinsic to it:[17]

> After the structure of a certain thing has been defined, it can be cultivated (squared). If we want to square it in a proper (square or round) form, we have to follow its model. These models are part of every existing thing. The sages can always follow them and this is why they succeed in everything they do. The structures can be divided into square, round, long, short, soft and hard. This is why, once their structure has been defined, all things can follow the Way. (*Han Feizi* s.d., Jie Lao: 29)[18]

The term underwent numerous semantic variations. The original sense of cosmic structure was first enriched with social connotations; then with the structure of language and meaning and, finally, of mind and consciousness: "All things have their different patterns (*Li*), but *Dao* treats them all in the same way; therefore, it is nameless" (*Zhuangzi* s.d., Ze yang, 10).[19]

From the Song Dynasty (960–1279) onward, all these specific kinds of structural patterns were unified in a single, general, and basic rational structure characterized by its fundamental compatibility with an unlimited diversity of structural patterns. The basic structure of the universe is defined by its fundamental pattern which can be established in countless particular forms: "Thus, the structure of Nature in its totality is contained in every particular thing" (Zhou Dunyi s.d., I, Taiji tu shuo: 9).[20]

This unification of particular, specific structural patterns into one single, general and basic structure, only became possible through a progressive semantic abstraction of the term *li*, which has, as we have seen, originally denoted the physical (i.e., visible) structure of lines in a jade. This process lasted several centuries and must be viewed within the context of the more general changes in Chinese culture and society. In practical terms, it was defined by the political and economic development of traditional China, while ideologically it was the result of factors as varied as the formalization of Confucianism as state doctrine, the new approaches formulated by Neo-Confucian theorists, and specific elements of Buddhist philosophy.

We can reduce this process of abstraction somewhat schematically to three phases (Rošker 2012a): the phase of ontologization (*li* as the cosmic structure or as the structure of nature and society), the phase of structural semantics (*li* as the structure of language and meaning), and the phase of epistemologization (*li* as the mutually compatible structure of external word and mind).

Because this notion represents one of the central concepts of Chinese philosophy, we can assume that the philosophy which derives from it is structuralist in essence. This assumption concurs with certain specific features of Chinese culture, in which the concept of the individual was never attributed the function of the highest axiological criterion, but only acquired value within the framework of a correlative relation with society.[21]

2.1.2 *Lunli*: Relationalism and the Role Ethics

The structure we have introduced in the previous section is a structure of relations, which—inter alia—also manifests itself in networks of human relationships. Hence, it is by no means coincidental that even the modern Chinese term for ethics, *lunli* 倫理, literary means "the structure (or patterns) of human relations." Traditional Confucian ethics, which prevailed as the dominant ethical discourse throughout the Chinese history, was namely likewise based on structural networks of relations. This ethical model, which is rooted in kinship relations, was rooted in the "five cardinal relations" (*wu lun* 五倫) and is called "role ethics"[22] in modern sinology (see, for instance, Cua 1971, Ames 2011 and 2016, etc.). This concept was fully developed by Henry Rosemont and Roger T. Ames (Ames 2011, Rosemont and Ames 2009, 2016). They coined this new term because Confucian relational ethics does not fit well in any of the existing Western categories of ethical models. In contrast to the Western image of the individual, entering into particular social relations as an independent, isolated self, the Confucian role-constituted person does not play a particular set of roles, but lives them. Hence, in this framework, a person is the roles that they live, because they cannot be abstracted from their relations with other fellow humans. This understanding has been placed into Ames' concept of process ontology, in which there are no substances that bear property or essence; every existence is dynamic and relational (Elstein 2015, 242). In such an understanding it is completely natural that the community exists before the individual, for the latter is constituted through social relations and cannot exist without them.

> Confucian role ethics begins from a relationally constituted conception of person, takes family roles and relations as the entry point for developing moral competence, invokes moral imagination and the growth in relations that it can inspire as the substance of human morality, and entails a human-centered, a-theistic religiousness that stands in sharp contrast to the Abrahamic religions. (Ames 2016, 141)

In China, the historical roots of such relational social networks were formed through patterns of the so-called relationalism (*guanxi zhuyi* 關係主義). According to Li Zehou, Neolithic humans living in the land occupied by modern-day China were rather advanced and based their societies on small-scale agricultural production, in which communities were mainly constructed through kinship relationships. Such an economic and cultural background has gradually led to the formation of the "relational selves,"[23] or, in Li's own words, to "relationalism" as a form of social interaction pattern which can be identified neither with individualism nor with collectivism. This notion mainly refers to the social significance of relationships between people, which in Chinese culture were shaped by the historical importance of family clan systems. In this socio-historical paradigm, relation—not only as a set of ordered pairs, but also as a basic element of a wider systematic network—has an instrumental function. The corresponding collective social consciousness manifested itself in the condition of the relational individual, who was necessarily and existentially an organic part of a social group. Such consciousness was reflected in the manner in which any given individuals came to view themselves as a part of their group and in which patterns of commonality among individuals brought legible unity to interhuman relations.

The distinction between the emphasis on relationalism and individualism respectively is hence a fundamental dissimilarity between the two types of ethics, which in turn correspondingly prevailed in the Chinese and in the Euro-American cultural milieus.

2.2 Vital Potential or Vital Creativeness

The concept of *qi* 氣 is among the most important, but at the same time the most difficult and complex notions in Chinese philosophy. It implies the basis of all life and the foundation of every living organism. One must rely on *qi* in order to live and to grow strong. Sickness decreases *qi*, and death depletes it. Hence, *qi* was seen as something immensely precious, as the fundamental precondition of life. In ancient Chinese philosophy, *qi* is thus a limitless source of all creation forming an omnipresent cosmic creative flow. Since the ancient Chinese worldview was holistic, and based upon an inseparable unification of heaven (or nature) and men (天人合一), this creative flow is visible in both cosmic and human breath. In this sense, *qi* is a basic vital rhythm connecting everything that exists in the great symphony of life. Therefore, it could be described as vitality, a vital potential, or vital creativeness. However, since it applies to a variety of different connotations, it is very difficult to define or translate. Hence, similar to the notion of *dao*, many sinologists don't translate it at all and apply the original Chinese term instead.

In most traditional sources, the notion implied an organic state, linked to breath. Since the exchange of gases and oxygen underlies any form of life as we know it, *qi* is of fundamental and vital significance for any organic existence. This organic state is internalized in the human body, but simultaneously it connects all existing beings in the universe that are endowed with life. Such a notion of *qi* can be found, for instance, in *Guanzi*,[24] in which we come across the notion of a quintessential *qi* (*jing qi* 精氣), which is responsible for life: things live because they have *qi*[25]—as soon as they lose it, they die.[26]

2.2.1 The Concept *Qi* as the Origin of the Living World

Since the very early Chinese philosophic discourses, it belonged to the most basic categories for the understanding of reality. It is already mentioned in the *Guoyu* 國語 (*State Records*), a work that goes back to ca 500 BCE In this book, the notion *qi* apparently referred to an earthquake. According to this categorization, earthquakes were results of an imbalance of the *tu qi* 土氣 (the earthly *qi*). When the *yang qi* 陽氣 (the dynamic, active *qi*) was suppressed and could not get out, the situation resulted in the explosion of the *tuqi*, that is, the *qi* of the earth (see

Guoyu s.d. Zhou yu I: 6).[27] An earthquake, however, was only one of the many different ways of explaining natural events in terms of the dynamic of *qi*. The notion can already be found in the oracle inscriptions of the early Zhou Dynasty (1066–771 BCE), symbolizing the cloudy vapors in the air (Cheng 2003a, 215). It contained the idea of air and was therefore mostly connected with the process of breathing. Hence, it is probably not coincidental that already in the sources from the sixth century BCE, the term *qi* is seen as the cause of natural events, and not only as a means to describe them (Cheng 2003a, 215). In this context, one can already distinguish various versions of the theory of *qi*, including a theory of its close connection to the interactions of the five powers (*wu xing* 五行) that create life and the universe. In its recent form, it is mostly applied in the compound *kongqi* 空氣, which means air (in empty space). Hence, it is something that is physically real, but at the same time invisible.

It thus manifests itself as the vital force that underlays any form of life, as the principle of vital creativity, as the cause of any change and transformation, which in Chinese philosophy thoroughly has been seen as the fundamental precondition of life. In the process of breathing, one can see the evidence of life. Breathing in air and breathing it out results in the circulation of blood in the body, and so *qi* implies the meaning of internal life force. This life force is by no means limited to the automatic bodily functions; on the contrary, it also produces consciousness and awareness, and thus comprises the very foundation for every form of knowledge and wisdom. Because it is the power of continuous change, it elevates and becomes a cosmic (and even cosmological) power of creation (Geaney 2002, 9).

Eventually, the concept of qi acquires the meaning of both energy or force and vitality, and thus becomes "vital energy" or "vital force," but it has not lost its naturalistic or even materialistic reference of meaning. In fact, what we have observed about the visible natural qi can be extended to the invisible internal qi of an organism. It is even extended to the atmosphere—which is invisible but can be experienced.

In the human body, however, *qi*'s activity does not remain limited to the function of breathing. It underlies every function of all organs, of blood and seminal fluids. It is also closely connected with the very bases of traditional Chinese medicine, for it also underlies the invisible electric neural currents that represent the foundation for healing various diseases with acupuncture, acupressure, or with the help of psychosomatic exercises.

Although in ancient sources, the concept of *qi* has thus almost exclusively been associated with the meaning of some kind of vital power or vital energy, it appeared often as "matter" in the earliest French and English translations. This erroneous understanding is connected to some general problems of intercultural understandings, which have already been treated in the previous chapters.

What is important for our present study of the notion of *qi*, however, is the cosmological (or ontological) paradigm, expressed through the mutually complementary interactions between the principles of *Li* and *Qi*, whereby the former was understood as structure (or structural patterns) and the latter as (vital) creativeness. Hence, even though this cosmological system was binary ordered, it is important to know that traditional Chinese thinkers never strictly distinguished between the spheres of matter and idea, or any other dualistic connotations resulting from this basic dichotomy.[28] In the system of classical Chinese cosmology, the world was not composed of matter and idea, or of material and ideational elements. It was created through correlative interactions between the dynamic, all-encompassing structural patterns *li* that were mutually compatible with and endowed with life through the vital potential *qi* (Rošker 2012b, 280).

While in ancient and early medieval China, the notion of *qi* has mostly been applied in the sense of an independent concept, things changed in later medieval and premodern China. In the scope of the Neo-Confucian philosophies of the Song (960–1279) and Ming (1368–1644) Dynasties, it was seen as a part of the bipolar (or binary) category of structure (*li*) and creativeness (*qi*), which represented the basic cosmological pair that underlays every form of existence.[29]

2.2.2 The Binary Relation of *Qi* and *Li*

When the first sinologists (who were mostly Christian missionaries) initially came to China in the seventeenth century, the prevailing ideology they encountered was based on the Neo-Confucian philosophy. Hence, for them, it was perfectly natural to interpret its bipolar conception of the world, consisting of something called *qi* and organized in accordance with something else called *li*, in terms of, respectively, matter and idea. However, in our view, the concept *li* cannot be understood as idea or principle in the "Western" sense, but rather as structure or a structural pattern, which can, of course, also pertain to the sphere of abstractions or ideas. Similarly, and based on a more profound understanding of Neo-Confucian philosophy, it is evident that the concept *qi* can hardly be understood as matter in the "Western" sense. In fact, the Neo-Confucian philosophers defined it as something that is not necessarily substantial, for air or even vacuum (the great void *tai xu* 太虛) are composed of it. Thus, it represents a concept that could be more appropriately defined as creativity, or a potential that functions in a creative way. Hence, Zhang Zai[30] (1020–77), a pioneer of the Neo-Confucian thought, described it in the following way: "In the great void, qi condenses and dissolves again. This can be compared to ice dissolving in water" (Zhang Zai 1989, 389).[31]

According to most traditional Chinese interpretations, in its condensed form *qi* pertains to the sphere of matter, whereby it belongs to the sphere of abstract entities in its finest, most dispersed state.[32] However, the majority of traditional European and American sinologists have (as we have noted above) translated this concept as matter. To illustrate this point, we can cite the translation of the above quoted passage by the renowned French sinologist from the beginning of the nineteenth century, Le Gall (1858–1916), in which the notion *qi* is clearly understood as atom(s): "Le condensation et les dispersions *des atomes*[33] dans la T'ai-hiu peuvent se comparer a la fonte de la glace dans l'eau" (Le Gall 2006, 49).

This translation of the concept *qi* is problematic, for it derives from a profoundly intrinsic sense of the criteria, based upon the model of Cartesian dualism. Although Zhang Zai's comparison with water explicitly states that *qi* is a continuous state, and not an aggregate of atoms, the analogy with matter was so deeply rooted in Le Gall's perception that he automatically saw the notion *qi* as an entity, which contains or is composed of atoms. Hence, for centuries, Le Gall and other sinologists who followed his reading have misled scholars regarding the question of whether traditional Chinese philosophy applied the concept of atomicity (Graham 1989, 61).

As we have seen in the previous section, the concept *li* indicates the notion of structure, a structural pattern, and the structural order of things. Taken as a whole, *li* represents a cosmic pattern, defining lines of movement or the dynamicity of men and nature. These structural lines are seen as relations that define both the sphere of ideas and that of phenomena. At the same time, they make possible the mutual adjustment of binary oppositions with complementary functions, as well as their orderly fusion within cosmic unity. Agnus Graham described it in the following way:

> The concept *li* is not obeyed or violated like a law; instead, one either goes with or against the grain of it, as in chopping wood. Le Gall translated it as *forme*, thus remolding the whole neo-Confucian cosmology after the analogy of Aristotelian form and matter (atoms). J. Percy Bruce instead translated this term as "law," thereby incorporating into neo-Confucian terminology itself the wrong answer to the question "Are there laws of nature in China?" (Graham 1989, 61)

It is hence completely clear that in these Neo-Confucian discourses, *Li* and *Qi* are complementary concepts, which can be explained as a structure (or structural pattern) and a creative formative potential (creativity). Both are of immanent nature and can therefore be realized in the spheres of both ideas and phenomena. Euro-American philosophy offers no precise equivalents for these two terms. If we want to comprehend the modes of their existence and their functions, we must first free ourselves from reasoning in terms of Cartesian dualisms and try thinking based on the model of analogy, which arose from and was prevalent in the immanent metaphysic of traditional Chinese thought.

2.3 Dialectical Thought and Proper Measure

In previous sections, we have already explained the main differences between the Hegelian dialectic of contradictions and the principle of complementarity, which is typical for the Chinese mode of ordering the world and the reasoning. A most important element of this principle is its inherent tendency toward a well-balanced equilibrium, a harmonious, but dynamic and ever-changeable unity of two opposite fields. The theoretical foundations of this model can be found in the *Book of Changes*, but in the Confucian classic *The Principle of Equilibrium*[34] it mostly refers to human relationships.

The structure of opposition (or, in a less determined sense, of relation) between two or more different ideas, beliefs, notions, presumptions, images, or concepts always decisively influences the developmental mode of any theory. The mode of development as such is particularly crucial for traditional Chinese philosophy, which is rooted in an explicitly dynamic, resilient, and flexible framework. Various concepts and ideas occur within this framework in a highly contextual and situational manner, continuously fluctuating and modifying the structural pattern of thought into which they are embedded. Such systems allow (and even necessitate) dynamic changes and the continuous evolvement of the all-inclusive structure of the theory. Hence, the understanding of such a theoretical system is conditioned by the understanding of the specific dialectical model in which it is rooted. An insight into the latter can offer us, on the other hand, a key to the perception of the former.

First, we must consider that dual oppositions are an important foundation of dialectical thought. Precisely because it allows dynamic alternations and because it offers possibilities of multifaceted insights into the complex nature of reality, dialectics facilitates and advances the development of philosophic reasoning. Hence, it is by no means surprising that, as a method of discussing and examining opposing ideas in order to reach a new level of reasoning, dialectics is present in both traditional Euro-American as well as in traditional Chinese thought. As we have seen in this chapter, the concrete method of dialectical thought differs in both discourses: while in the modern European form, which crystallized with Hegel, the two oppositional notions negate each other, they appear in the traditional Chinese model as binary categories, which are mutually complementary and correlative. As already mentioned, the conception of this model goes way back to the earliest proto-philosophical works of ancient China, namely as far as to the *Book of Changes* (*Yi jing* 易經). The Chinese model is first introduced in this ancient classic through the concept *tongbian* 通變 (*Zhou Yi* s.d., Xi Ci I: 5.1), which can in this context be translated as "continuity through change" (Tian 2002, 126). Quite a few rather clear explanations of this dynamic philosophical paradigm can also be found in Laozi's *Book of the Way and the Virtue* (*Daode jing* 道德經).[35]

Thus, in this model the binary oppositions that continuously interact through permanent dynamic change are co-relative, mutually complementary, and interdependent. However, in these complementary structures, there is always a dominant and prevailing element that triggers the complementary interchange in a certain direction and along a certain trend.

Some scholars have criticized this predomination, arguing that it actually devaluates or practically destroys the theoretical complementarity: "Eventually, it is the subjugation of the senses to reason, the natural to the sociocultural, the individual to the community, rather than the harmonious coexistence of the two" (Wang 1996, 104). However, even the predominant position of one of the two elements within the mutually oppositional structure is not absolute and eternal, but changeable and modifiable as all the concepts and categories of the Chinese referential framework. They cannot be judged as isolated moments in a certain frozen and fixed formula, taken out of time and space. On the other hand, this predominant element conditions the genuine development of the model and its dialectical progress.

Here, we have to consider the ideational development which has taken place in the Chinese intellectual history. In its original form, the complementary dialectical model (as has been, for instance, described in the *Yi jing* or *Laozi*) was namely limited to dynamic interchanges of both antipodes. The emergence of the primary or decisive element can be traced back to the Song Dynasty Neo-Confucianism, or, more precisely, to Zhu Xi's interpretation of the aforementioned relation between the structural (*li*) and the creative (*qi*) potentials.

Besides, the predominant element, which is in each particular model of complementary dialectics connected to the permanent variable of human life, is never a necessary, but nonetheless a sufficient, condition of its own oppositional antipode. This also means that although this predominant element conditions the other one, it does not determine it. This is a small, but significant difference in comparison with typical Western dialectical theories, which are grounded not only on empirical and logical, but also on ontological domination of one particular antipode.

It is also important to note that in such dialectical models the predominant element is always the one that contributes most—in a given situation and a particular context—to sustainable nature, to the preservation and evolution of life. Besides, in this pattern of dialectic development, synthesis is not necessarily an automatic product of mechanistic laws of reason or logic, but rather a result of human deeds and the actively chosen decisions and practice of human beings. Ultimately, the development of human societies and cultures is to a large degree defined by such decisions and the actions resulting from them. But what is the criterion for good and reasonable decisions? In Chinese tradition, the best possible way to select is always to choose in accordance with the so-called proper measure (*du* 度); Li Zehou describes its potential in the following way:

> This is what I often defined as the "Chinese dialectics." It is not P v 'P, but rather P ≠ P±. If you do something exaggeratedly well, it is the same as doing it lousily. This is the State of Equilibrium or the Mean. (Li 2015, 38)[36]

This model suggests that by virtue of our specifically human sensibility and rationality we can solve our dilemmas and make our decisions in accordance with a sense of balance among various elements. Choosing in congruence with reason and emotion will allow us to preserve the balance between all aspects embedded into the innumerable structures of the multifarious complementary relations comprising our individual and social lives.

According to such views, (proper) measure is the ever-changeable, flexible, undeterminable criteria of human (but also animal) adaptability, which enables living beings to exist and develop. "*Du*" is necessarily changeable, dynamic, and different in every moment because the conditions of human life are also continuously changing.

Most of the traditional Chinese theories are determined by their tendency toward the mean, which is designated with the abovementioned classic Confucian term, "*zhong yong* 中庸." Choosing the mean hence entails developing a sense of the proper measure (*du*): "Since ancient times, Chinese thought has always stressed the 'Mean' and 'harmony,' which are nothing other than the objectification of '*du*'" (Li 2002, 3).[37] But "*du*," which is not a transcendent external force, a concrete object, or a pure abstraction, but a human creation and product, is also closely linked to human life and human activities. The "State of Equilibrium or the Mean (*zhong yong*)" is thus of paramount importance, for it makes us aware of our limitations, while also encouraging us to see and explore the unlimited space within this limited framework (Li Zehou 1985, 298).[38]

3

Chinese Logic as a Basis of Classical Chinese Theory

Before dealing with traditional or classical "Chinese logic" in more detail, we have to clarify some basic questions, related to the very nature of this thought.[1]

Is logic a universal discipline, which means there is only one kind of logic? Or is it culturally conditioned, with many different logical systems? These questions are similar to the ones that have been raised in the introduction to this book and the answers depend on how we define logical reasoning. If we follow the narrow definition, which identifies or equates logic with the logical concepts, categories, and methods that were developed in what we can call the Aristotelian or Stoic tradition, we could conclude that in traditional and premodern China there was no logic.[2] But if logic is instead understood as a rational form of reasoning focused on valid argumentation and its principles, many different approaches are possible. Furthermore, like human language, logical propositions imply both universal and culturally conditioned elements.

> We think in relationships, patterns and sequences in which we connect idea to idea, experience to experience. I would stress here that all such connections are made in our thinking and not in or by the objects experienced, or the symbols we use to sign ideas. It is this aspect of thought that is the essence of recognition. To recognize either objects or ideas is to relate them to mental contexts, determining thereby in our thinking the similarity and dissimilarity of one idea or experience with/from another. It is this relating which is the origin and purpose of all logics. The patterns and orders may be quite different, but "patterning" itself is common to the human mind. (Benesch 1997, 4)

While the ability to express the perceived reality by means of linguistic terms and structures is one of the most basic and distinctive features of humanity, this common feature has evolved in countless different ways in different cultures, with each distinct language emphasizing different patterns of reasoning.

3.1 Semantic Nature of Chinese Logic

In China, logical reasoning was closely connected to language, especially with respect to semantic issues and was determined by its tight relation to ethics (e.g., *Mozi* s.d., Jing xia, 155). However, this does not mean that in classical texts which are not immediately identifiable with metaphysical and ethical discourses there were not also forms of logical and methodological thought. Although Chinese philosophy developed in connection with ethical ideas and metaphysical concepts, there was a close relationship between moral and metaphysical thought, on the one hand, and logical reasoning, on the other.[3]

Classical Chinese logical thought never neither elaborated any explicitly systematic and comprehensive formulation of the laws of reason nor produced a coherent system of symbolism for abstract reasoning. Prior to the eighteenth and early nineteenth centuries, Chinese thinkers had rarely encountered a systematic and well-formulated logical work. But as Cheng Chung-Ying (1965, 196) points out, this does not mean that classical Chinese thought lacked logical depth or consistency.

3.1.1 Historical Background

The origins of Chinese logic can be traced back to the earliest known works, such as the *Book of Changes* (*Yi jing*), which dates from the seventh century BCE, while its main development occurred during the so-called golden Age of Chinese philosophy, in the Warring States (*Zhan guo*) period (475–221 BCE). This period gave rise to the "Hundred Schools of Thought," which includes the most influential philosophical discourses, that is, Confucianism, Mohism, Daoism, and legalism. This was a time of extraordinary intellectual development, which was conditioned by the political chaos and constant armed conflict among the warring states. This period ended with the first unification of China and the rise of the totalitarian Qin Dynasty (221–206 BCE). Traditional or classical Chinese logic generally refers to the logical thought that was developed during this era (Chmelewski 1965, 88). These discourses were developed without external influences. However, Chinese logicians were part of a small subculture, whereas in India and Europe, logicians belonged to the mainstream of intellectual development (Harbsmeier 1988, 7).

In ancient China, logical themes appear in various philosophical works, such as the *Book of Changes*, the oldest known Chinese philosophical text, and later, in a number of works by Confucius and his successors (Wang 2009, 1).

In this period, questions such as the relation between concepts or names (*ming* 名) and realities or objects (*shi* 實), the criteria of identity (*tong* 同) and difference (*yi* 異), or the standards of right/true (*shi* 是) and wrong/false (*fei* 非) formed the objects of inquiry across the entire philosophical spectrum, regardless of ideological orientation (Kurtz 2011, 3). The Chinese interest in logical problems grew out of the methodology of debates or disputations.[4] The earliest evidence of this interest is found among the so-called dialecticians or debaters (*bianzhe* 辯者), whose discourses dealt primarily with theories of names (*mingxue* 名學), which led to their becoming known as the "School of Names" (*Ming jia* 名家). The leading figures in this heterogeneous current were Hui Shi[5] (ca. 370–310 BCE), who formulated ten paradoxes on the infinity of time and space, and Gongsun Long[6] (ca. 320–250 BCE), who was famous for the logical defense of his *White horse paradox*, which claimed that "white horses were not horses" (*Bai ma fei ma*).[7] These discourses made important contributions to logic, together with the works of the "later Mohists" (*Houqi Mojia*),[8] who elaborated theories of argumentation (*bianxue* 辯學). They represented a current of the school of Mo Di,[9] whose teachings were collected in the *Mozi*[10] which includes a series of brief definitions and explanations outlining procedures for determining the validity of conflicting assertions, a theory of description, and an inventory of "acceptable" (*ke* 可) links between consecutive statements.

In some fundamental aspects, the *bianxue* discourse resembled the Indian Buddhist logic Hetuvidya (in Chinese: *Yinming xue* 因明學), which is a specific way of disputing general theses. In *Yinming* debates, the thesis had to be challenged by the parties, and the disputants were only allowed to use premises that were acceptable to the opponents, whether they themselves believed in them or not, and the minor premise had to be supported by examples, both positive and negative. However, at the beginning of the *bianxue* development, there was most likely no direct contact between the two schools, since *Yinming* logic was not introduced to China until the seventh century, when its crucial parts were brought to the Middle Kingdom from India by the Buddhist monk Xuan Zang (玄奘).

The Confucians also made important contributions to logical thought in ancient China. For example, already in the *Analects*, which was compiled by Confucius' disciples, we come across a passage dealing with the so-called Theory of Proper Names (*Zheng ming lun* 正名論.), which elaborates on the proper relation between names or concepts and (social) reality.

One of Confucius' most famous followers, the philosopher Xunzi (ca. 310–235 BCE), appropriated the late Mohist logical findings in order to defend the Confucian ideals of state and society. His legalist disciple, Han Feizi (ca. 280–233 BCE), who formulated the totalitarian ideology which brought the golden age of Chinese philosophical and logical reasoning to a close after the unification by the Qin, in 221 BCE, instead relied on "names and disputation" (*ming bian* 名辯).

3.1.2 Concepts And Methods

The classical Chinese logicians did not use a unique term that corresponds to the English concept of "true" (Graham 1970, 39). According to Hansen (1985, 515), they neither focused on a distinct notion of semantic truth.[11] A name or complex of names applied to an object either fit (*dang*) or erred (*guo*), while the validity of certain judgments was expressed by the term "assertible" (*ke*). The terms "so" (*ran* 然) and "not so" (*bu ran* 不然) were also frequently used to indicate that a predicate for something was true. While Chinese logicians did not use any distinct and explicit concept of truth-functional contradiction, they often applied paradoxes (e.g., "going to Yue today and arriving there yesterday,"[12] *Zhuangzi* s.d., Qiwu lun: 4) to expose the relativist nature of reality and thus reveal unorthodox redefinitions of important terms in order to influence people's behavior and their values (De Reu 2006, 282). However, reconstructing the reasoning behind the paradoxes contained in classical works is still problematic and based mainly on indirect evidence.

The relation between names (concepts) and actualities (*ming, shi*) was one of the key notions developed by classical Chinese logicians, especially those belonging to the School of Names. Most of these philosophers were seeking a proper (or most rational) standardization (*chang* 常) of this relation, which was seen as a basic precondition for the unification of language and the establishment of legal norms.

The later Mohist logicians were, instead, more interested in investigating the concept of kind (*lei* 類).[13] They argued that classifying names were supposed to apply to kinds and not only attempted to determine rules for the correct use of classifying names, but also the principles governing the distinction between any two classifying names.

Together with the concepts of evidence (*gu* 故)[14] and structural principles (*li* 理), kinds (*lei*) form one of the three basic components of any thought pattern.

Propositions and logical constants also constitute important themes in classical Chinese logic. While propositions (*ci* 辭) are used to elucidate ideas or meanings (*yi* 意), logical constants[15] were applied to indicate different types of propositions in the language (Liu and Yang 2010, 110).

One of the most important issues in later Mohist thought concerned the concept of "hard-white" (*jianbai* 堅白). This was a technical term for the relation between two things or two features of a thing that are inseparable and "mutually pervasive," in the sense that they completely coincide throughout the same spatial extension (Fraser 2012, 329). The paradigm for this notion is the hardness and whiteness of a completely white stone.

Along with many other logical discourses, the debate on the relationship between hardness and whiteness was gradually suspended in later periods. In the Han dynasty, Confucianism became the main ideological pillar of the new state formation. Thereafter, ethics gradually moved to the forefront of the new ideologies, and pure logical or theoretical thinking was increasingly seen as superfluous and irrelevant. In his work *Bao Puzi*[16] (The Master Who Preserves Simplicity) Ge Hong[17] (283–343) from the Wei-Jin period even wrote: "The debate on 'Hardness and Whiteness' is completely useless. . . . In fact, it is an evil discourse" (Ge Hong s.d. Wai pian, Chong yan, 2)[18].

The Mohists have also developed a concept of dimensionlessness (*wu hou* 無厚), although it was seldom applied. According to the Mohists, something which is "dimensionless" does not "fill" anything (*Mozi* s.d., Jing shuo shang: 66). The dimensionless tip of a solid object (*duan* 端) was used to clearly distinguish different bases or "starting points" for using a term. Thus, a "starting point" or "tip" (*duan*) is the basis for a distinct way of using a general term (Fraser 2013, 17).[19]

Because it was based on inferential patterns of kind, Chinese logic was essentially analogical and was based upon semantic parameters and an epistemology centered on exposing distinctions (Cui and Zhang 2005, 27). Reasoning and argumentation were not formed by means of syllogisms or premises-conclusion arguments. Instead, ancient Chinese logicians were concerned with how certain processes differentiating or predicating terms normatively required making additional analogous distinctions or predications. Inferences were commonly understood as the act of predicating the particular terms of something, as a consequence of having identified that thing as similar to a model for the kind (*lei*) of thing denoted by that term. Inference is thus an act, or a sequence of acts, based on the recognition of structural patterns. The concept of structure (*li*) is crucial for such analogical inferences, given that similar cognitive methods follow a cognitive process in which a known segment of reality forms a model that can be used in order to recognize another unknown part of that same reality, thereby linking them through a network of identical properties. In this network, analogy depends on the order of parts in the source and target. The ordering not only regards objects, but also connections among both objects and relations.

As we will see in the next section, the Chinese model of analogical inferences differs in many respects from the Greek or Indian models.[20] Formal logic seeks to distinguish between general forms of cognitive processes, and the object of investigation. Instead, Chinese logicians were less interested in defining general abstract formulas of propositions and analogies, than in creating semantic (rather than formal) structures, which they then tried to define by means of descriptive explanations and practical examples. However, the later Mohist School and the School of Names were much more analytical in their approaches than either Confucianism or Daoism, in the sense that they tended to proto-theorize their philosophical arguments with an analytical language.

This focus on contents rather than form in ancient Chinese logic led to the classification of analogisms into four main types, which the later Mohists named "*pi*," "*mo*," "*yuan*" and "*tui*." As we shall see later (in the chapter on Chinese analogies), all these types were based upon descriptive methods. According to Fung Yiu-Ming (2012, 341), their expressions relied on the "material mode of speech."

In ancient China, this attention to contents led to fundamental peculiarities in the development of inferences. The structural systematization which defines the general (i.e., traditional European) model of analogical inferences dictates a proposition by which certain relations necessarily imply other relations, regardless of the concrete domain or context (Holyoak 2008, 150). Instead, the Chinese analogical method also distinguishes within this general model between different types of inferences with respect to the semantic and axiological elements of the relations they include. Thus, in the Chinese model, the validity or non-validity of analogical inferences also depends on the valuation of both preceding propositions. As already mentioned, we will deal with this type of analogical inferences a bit later. First, let us take a closer look upon the relation between language and thought in classical Chinese logic.

3.1.3 Logic and Language

Most scholars agree that all these peculiarities were influenced by the specific structure of the classical Chinese language. Classical Chinese characters evolved in accordance with the ancient Chinese thought structure. This inevitably affected the development of Chinese logic, which was thus profoundly influenced by specific Chinese forms and representations (Shen Youding 1980, 90). Most authors also agree that due to its specific structure, classical Chinese contributed greatly to the development and amplification of a system of logical reasoning, which was far less formalized as, for instance, the ones developed in ancient Greece. Because classical Chinese expressed meaning by differences in the word order and sentence structure, rather than by morphological changes, the generation and development of informal reasoning would be greatly influenced by these characteristics. Wang Kexi (2005, 30ff) has shown how the Chinese method of comprehension is a result of distinguishing meanings independently from the grammatical form. In order to grasp the meaning and the semantic construction of a Chinese sentence, it is necessary to analyze it within its context. This rather flexible understanding of Chinese determined the mode of informal thought. Chinese is a language without changes of location, case, and form. Semantic differences are not expressed by morphological forms, but depend on word order and sentential structures. Classical Chinese sentences cannot always be analyzed by the grammatical rules of the Indo-European languages, for they are based upon a different epistemological system (2005, 32). Another important feature of classical Chinese is the lack of copula, since it developed other types of sentences to express judgments. A detailed examination of texts from the Warring States period (2005, 30ff) shows that very few sentences have a structure that uses linking verbs and predicates.

In general, the interdependent and interconnected relation between language and logic is still a controversial, rather than a settled issue. Some scholars believe that the Chinese language has little impact on deep linguistic structures as elaborated by Chomsky (1968, 8) and hence it may have little impact on patterns of logical reasoning. However, Zhang Dongsun's (1886–1973) interpretations were tightly linked to this cognitive-linguistic, interconnectedness.[21] In his comparison between Indo-European languages and Chinese, he pointed out that the latter (especially ancient Chinese) made no clear distinction between subject and predicate, while in morphological terms it did not add suffixes to express time, gender, or number (Zhang Dongsun 1964, 360). Furthermore, in Chinese, the subject is not distinguished and, thus, the predicate is not indicated either. The Chinese language also does not generally use sentential subjects, as opposed to Indo-European languages, which omit sentential subjects only in exceptional cases. Thus, the Chinese quite often omits the subject entirely, which implies that, for the Chinese speaker, the subject is not necessary (Zhang Dongsun 1964, 363). Another difference is that Chinese lacks the equivalent of the expression "it" or the form "it is," which expresses the existence of something, but not its attributes. And yet this distinction is a basic precondition for forming the concept of substance. However, the most important difference Zhang identified was the lack of the expression "to be" in Chinese, which means that it is difficult to form the subject-predicate propositions of "standard" (i.e., Western) logic.

A. C. Graham (1989, 323) also stressed that the verb "to be" was the origin of many metaphysical problems throughout the history of Western philosophy, for beyond its function as a copula, it implies an unchanging identity and existence.

Due to the absence of the linguistic (and thus also cognitive) category "subject" and the absence of the expression "to be" in both ancient and modern Chinese, traditional Chinese philosophy never established or developed the explicit, formally distinguished concept or discipline of ontology.[22] Because the ancient Chinese worldview was based on an implicit, dynamic, and changeable structure of being, the classical Chinese philosophy never fully developed formal logic based upon fixed (static) theorems, or even the basic laws of traditional European logic, which meant that the law of identity was alien to Chinese thought. Zhang Dongsun concluded that Aristotelian logic, based upon the law of identity, developed the structure of dichotomies based upon contradictions of the type "A and not-A." Such relations were mutually exclusive (Zhang Dongsun 1964, 364). But Chinese thought did not function in this way. Although it also applied dichotomies, their mutual relation was structured in a different way: in the thinking modes that have prevailed in China, dual oppositions[23] were seen as mutually defining and interdependent, guided by the underlying principle of complementarity or correlativity.[24]

The classification of the type "A and B" makes it possible for something to be neither A nor B. Such non-exclusionary distinctions were quite common in Chinese logic.[25] Logical definitions in the Aristotelian sense are statements of identity, in which the symbol of identity connects the definiendum and the definiens. Jiang Xingyan (2002, 75) shows that, following ancient Chinese logic, the meaning of a word can be understood or clarified by looking at its opposite.[26] For this reason, definitions found in Western logic do not exist in Chinese logic. For example, a "wife" is a "woman who has a husband," and a "husband" is a "man, who has a wife." This is not a strict definition in the received Aristotelian sense of the term, requiring genus and specific difference. The Chinese logic was relational and therefore based on relational propositions, just as Western logic was based on the proposition of the subject-object structure. The correlation between dual, but complementary oppositions (e.g., above-below, before-behind) thus represents a specific approach of ancient Chinese logic. The representatives of the Mohist school and the School of Names expressed judgments by means of comparisons, causes, enumerations, and explanations. Due to the absence of judgments structured by linking verbs and predicates in a strict sense, ancient Chinese scholars could not fully comprehend the concepts of generality and particularity. As opposed to Aristotelian logic, in which a concept is the predicate of its positive "umbrella-concept," and the latter is the subject of the former, the ancient Chinese logicians preferred to explore "resemblance" (analogies) and the characteristics of the concept of "kind" (*lei*). However, the ancient Chinese concept of "kind" was not limited to the division of the extension of concepts, but also included the resemblance between two events or actions. This also explains why in ancient China, logical analysis in the Aristotelian sense was underdeveloped and why analogism became the dominant type of classical Chinese logic.

The last few decades have seen a resurgence of interest in these issues on the part of contemporary Western and Chinese theorists. Chad Hansen (1983) offers a provocative and innovative theory regarding the nature of classical Chinese. He argues that the classical semantics of Chinese nouns resembles mass nouns. Thus, Chinese logicians tended to organize the objects of the external reality in a so-called "stuff-whole" model, based on the relations of the parts to the whole.

Hansen's hypothesis is still controversial and has been challenged by many scholars. For example, Christoph Harbsmeier (1989) argues that there is a clear grammatical distinction between count nouns and generic or mass nouns in classical Chinese, and demonstrates this view based on the semantics of counting. Bo Mou (Mou 1999, 45) basically concurs with Hansen's mereological approach, but argues that the implicit ontology revealed and reflected by the semantics and syntax of Chinese nouns is a nominalist ontology of collection-of-individuals, rather than a mass-stuff model of reality. Chris Fraser (2007, 420) instead acknowledges that most classical Chinese nouns indeed function as mass nouns (though with certain essential distinctions), but then goes on to say that this does not necessarily mean that one is obliged to accept Hansen's hypothesis. Based on an exhaustive analysis of pre-Qin logical sources he argues that their authors did not appeal to part-whole relations in order to explain the use of general terms. Still other scholars, such as Cheng Chung-ying (1987), David Hall and Roger Ames (1987), criticize Hansen's model through the lens of classical Chinese relational structured worldview, that is, by exposing that in this worldview, particular, concrete things interact within continuous, dynamic patterns, and the universe behaves as an organic entirety with the parts reflecting the structure of the whole. This ontological feature of combining universality and particularity, abstractness and concreteness, activity and its result was also reflected in the structure of the classical Chinese language (see Rošker 2012a). Many Chinese researchers apply the term "field" (*chang*) to define these relations between "parts" and "wholes" (Luo and Zheng 1994, 1–3).

Despite the many diverse interpretations of the relation between language and thought in the classical Chinese logic, most scholars agree that the pre-Qin logic emphasized the (social) regulative function of language rather than its descriptive use.

There can be little doubt that understanding ancient Chinese practices and theories of reasoning has a broad cross-cultural value. There has always been considerable debate concerning the proper approach to classical Chinese logic. This debate corresponds to different phases in the reception of Western logic in the Chinese scholarly community. However, any survey of the views involved indicates just how rich and fascinating this discourse is, and how variegated the interpretative spectrum (Liu, Seligman and van Benthem 2011, 2). The reconstruction of classical Chinese logic offers a paradigmatic case of the epistemic shifts that continue to shape interpretations of China's intellectual history. It thus remains one of the most important areas of research in contemporary Sinology.

3.2 Chinese Analogies

The present chapter aims to expose some aspects of the specific features of classical Chinese analogisms, which form a very important thought pattern prevailing in the entire Chinese intellectual tradition.[27]

Firstly, I would like to reveal that this type of analogism did not focus exclusively on forms without considering their content, that is, that it was linguistically and semantically determined. Secondly, it also aims to show that the classical Chinese analogies are based upon structural relations between the objects in question, which constitute the similarity of two types (or kinds) of things that share certain attributes. This chapter additionally sheds light upon the question of how and why the structure underlying these relations represents a semantic and axiological referential framework that functions as the methodological foundation of the tight connection between logic and ethics in ancient China.

Analogism as the dominant type of classical Chinese logic was developed during the pre-Qin era (776–221 BCE), by which time the earliest Chinese philosophers of that period were already investigating, developing, and applying it to a wide and variegated range of ideologies. This model is a form of cognition, belonging to so-called relational reasoning (Knowlton and Holyoak 2009, 1005), which is based on the distinctively human capacity to see analogies between disparate situations and which requires the ability to mentally represent and modify the relations among concepts. *Chinese analogisms*, which have the property of general analogical inference, are grounded in the similarity of two kinds of things that have certain attributes in common. Upon confirming this likeness, it can then be deduced that these two kinds of things must also be similar with respect to the rest of their attributes:

> If we have two objects (A and B) with a series of common properties (e.g. P1, P2 ... Pn) and if object A has the property q, then we can analogically infer that object B also has the property q. (Cui and Zhang 2005, 26)

The Chinese type of analogical inference is not only an inference drawn between one particular/specific and another; it is also a type of inference in which the premises do not logically or deductively entail the conclusion. The connection between the premise and the conclusion pertains to the sphere of probability; hence, this type of inference belongs to the category of probability inferences.

As already mentioned, such models of analogical inferences differ in numerous features from the Greek or Indian models.[28] While formal logic differentiates between universal formulas of thinking progressions on the one, and the objects of examination on the other hand, classical Chinese scholars were rather interested in generating structures of meaning than in defining generally valid forms. They aimed to delineate these forms by descriptions, clarifications and by concrete samples.[29] Nonetheless, the Chinese method of analogical logic met the basic requirements of scientific demonstration, that is, it clarified the origin of a certain knowledge and the logical inevitability of its sources, and it provided the supporting demonstration (Cui and Zhang 2005, 29).

One of the most important aspects of classical Chinese analogism is that it did not focus exclusively on forms without considering their content; this is a useful method for justifying one's own ideas, while refuting the arguments of others. At the same time, it also provided a basis for an awareness of ethical, political, and social issues. We should also stress that this kind of analogism, as an inference based upon similarities between the known and the unknown, was not only a model that could be applied to existing experience, but also had certain epistemological effects.

This type of analogical reasoning was closely connected to language, especially with respect to semantic issues, and was, as mentioned, determined by its close connection to ethics. It is well known that the prevailing streams of Chinese philosophy developed in almost inextricable tandem with ethical ideas and metaphysical concepts. It is less widely known, however, that there was also a close relationship between moral and metaphysical thought on the one hand, and logical (and analogical) reasoning on the other.

The relation between names (concepts) and actualities (*ming* 名, *shi* 實) was one of the key notions developed by classical Chinese logicians, also manifesting itself in their attempts to establish theoretical grounds for analogies (e.g., *Mozi* s.d., Jingxia: 155). In the pre-Qin period, most of these philosophers were seeking a proper (or the most sensible) standardization (*chang* 常) of this relation, which was seen as a basic precondition for the unification of language and the establishment of legal norms. Such issues were especially important for the representatives of the School of Names. The later Mohist logicians were, however, more interested in investigating the underlying concept of kind (*lei* 類), which could connect (or separate) various concepts.

Because it was founded on kind-based inferences, Chinese analogism was essentially rooted in semantic theory and an epistemology centered on drawing distinctions (Cui and Zhang 2005, 27). Reasoning and argumentation were not elaborated upon by syllogisms or arguments leading from premises to conclusions. Instead, classical Chinese scholars were rather concerned with how certain procedures for differentiating terms normatively required additional analogous distinctions or predications. Inferences were generally understood as the act of predicating the particular terms of something as an implication of discovering that particular things belong to the same kind (*lei* 類) of thing denoted by the term in question (Fraser 2013b). Such references are therefore an act, or a series of acts, grounded upon structural patterns. In this chapter, I shall argue that the idea of structure (structural pattern, structural principle or congruence), *li* 理, is essential for such analogical inferences, given that similar patterns of reasoning follow a thought process by which a known aspect or segment of reality shapes a model that can be applied in order to recognize another unknown aspect or segment of that same reality, thus connecting both segments through a structure of identical or related properties. In this framework, analogy depends on the mapping or alignment of elements in the source and target, which not only regards objects, but also relations between particular objects and relations between relations. Hence, this mode of analogical reasoning was determined by the structure of such relations and the fabric of this structure was tightly connected to language and meaning.[30]

In order to clarify the abovementioned suppositions, we will first more closely examine the general establishment and development of the classical Chinese analogism. In this context, we shall mainly investigate ancient Confucian and Mohist philosophy, for the members of these two schools have dealt with analogisms in a most comprehensive way.

3.2.1 Early Developments

The incipient forms of such analogisms can already be found in the Confucian commentaries on the *Book of Changes* (*Zhou Yi* 周易), as well as in the *Analects* (*Lunyu* 論語) of Confucius. Many important elaborations of these elements are contained in the *Mohist Canon* (*Mozi* 墨子) and in the principal works of Mencius (*Mengzi* 孟子) and *Xunzi* (荀子). The theory of analogies was further developed by Lü Buwei 呂不韋 in his *Commentary on Confucius' Annals of Spring and Autumn* (*Lü shi Chunqiu* 呂氏春秋). All these works contain clear indications that the application and investigation of analogies was quite common among Chinese scholars and can be traced back to at least the sixth century BCE.

Confucius (551–479 BCE) is supposedly the author, or, better, the main inspiration of the *Analects* (*Lunyu*), which can doubtless be regarded as the main source of the earliest Confucian teachings. Yet, in this source, Confucius never systematically epitomized or explained the abovementioned analogical model, although it appears obvious from many of his quotations that he considered its application an important part of ethical and political learning. The following quotation from the *Analects*, in which he is described by his disciple Xue Er 學而, clearly shows that Confucius was well acquainted with the type of reasoning that is rooted in acquiring knowledge through analogies and that he often applied this reasoning in his methods of inference from known to unknown elements: "I gave him a hint and he knew its proper sequence" (*Lunyu* s.d., Xue er: 15).[31]

This was an example of inferring from the known to the unknown. A similar transfer of information was rooted in the assumption according to which elements with similar properties could be treated with the same criteria. The *Analects* also indicates that Confucius often trained his disciples in this kind of reasoning.

> I do not open up the truth to those who are not eager to obtain knowledge;
> I will not help out anyone who is not anxious to find an explanation by

himself. When I have presented one corner (of a subject) to anyone, and he cannot from it learn the other three, I do not repeat my lesson. (*Lunyu* s.d., Shu er: 8)³²

Making inferences regarding the other three corners based on the one that is given is a kind of analogism. The four corners of the subject are namely supported by similarities; seeking the other three corners when one is provided is thus a process of analogy (Cui and Wen 2001, 51). One of the reasons we can assume that this kind of analogical method makes use of the aforementioned relational reasoning lies, as we shall see later, in the fact that it is based on the structural relations between the objects in question, whereby these relations can interconnect two types of things that are similar on account of their common attributes. If such a relation cannot be established, the two kinds must remain separated and cannot be applied in analogical inferences.

Even the central Confucian virtue of humaneness (*ren* 仁) was, according to the *Analects*, established as an analogical model of a person who infers the nature of his fellow human beings based upon his own nature:

> The man of perfect virtue, wishing to be established himself, seeks also to establish others; wishing to be successful himself, he also seeks others to succeed. To be able to take one's own feelings as a guide may be called the art of humanity. (*Lunyu* s.d., Yong ye: 30)³³

In this quotation, which can be understood as a Confucian version of the Christian "Golden rule," we find the term *pi* 譬, which in later texts is used to signify "analogy," in the sense of a cognitive process or transfer of information from one individual to another. In ancient texts, this character means "figuration." Contemporary scholars often translate it as "to match" (Cui and Wen 2001, 56). Hence, *pi* can be interpreted as explaining a truth by using appropriate matching or corresponding examples.

Mencius inherited and developed this ideology by analyzing the thought and methods within the theory of "taking one's own feelings as a guide" and developed a foundation of logical thought clearly distinctive from that of Confucius. His treatises reveal the analogue thought based upon the supposition, according to which human beings are of the same kind.³⁴ Mencius said, "Shun³⁵ is human, I am also human" (*Mengzi* s.d., Li lou xia, 56).³⁶ Hence, for him it was clear that "Saints and ordinary people are of the same kind" (*Mengzi* s.d., Li lou xia, 56, Gongsun Chou shang 2).³⁷ As we shall see in the next section, the concept of kind (*lei*) was already an important part of analogies for Mencius.

3.2.2 The Concept of Kind (*Lei*)

For Confucius, this concept remained a latent supposition that he considered, but never explicitly defined.[38] The logical definition was later provided by his follower Mencius.

The two examples, provided in the previous section, give us the essence of the Mencian ideology regarding "humankind." In order to explain the notion in more detail, he defined the concept of kind as follows:

> All things belonging to the same kind are similar to one another; why should we doubt this when it comes to human beings, as if they were the only exception to this? The sage and I belong to the same kind. (*Mengzi* s.d., Gaozi shang: 7)[39]

Gu Longzi, Mengzi's counterpart in this debate, also agreed with him, pointing out that "dogs and horses do not belong to the same kind as people" (*Mengzi* s.d., Gaozi shang: 7).[40]

Since I am of the same kind as other people, we must have "something in common." In this instance, the concepts are those of "self" and "other," and the inference consists in the possibility of establishing a cognitive process that links the first concept with the second. According to Mencius, the similarity of their heart-minds (*xin* 心) is the basic similarity that defines human beings (*Mengzi* s.d., Gaozi shang: 7).[41] Hence, since their minds are structured in the same way (*Mengzi* s.d., Gaozi shang: 7),[42] they can communicate directly and be kind with one another.

Xunzi appropriated these findings in order to defend the Confucian ideals of state and society. His analogies were already founded on an even stricter classification of objects into different kinds:

> All things have their origins in kinds . . . fire can be amplified by adding firewood, soil can get moist by watering. Trees and grasses are flourishing, and birds and animals swarm into the flourishing forests. Everything belongs to its own kind. (*Xunzi* s.d., Quan xue: 7)[43]

He explained the concept by providing an example: "Sprouts, trees, branches, and leaves necessarily belong to the kind of plants with roots" (*Xunzi* s.d.,

Fu guo: 14).⁴⁴ For him, kinds were necessary tools for ordering both human thought and human society: "With the help of kinds, we can handle the diversity, and with the help of unity, we can manage the multiplicity" (*Xunzi* s.d., Wang zhi: 18).⁴⁵

The concept of kind was also profoundly investigated and elaborated by the later Mohists.⁴⁶ In their attempts to establish a detailed definition of the notion of kind (*lei*), their arguments deal primarily with the "difficulties connected to the theoretical definition of analogies" (*Mozi* s.d., X, Jing xia: 102).⁴⁷ Their achievements are of utmost value for the further development of the methods of analogical inference (Graham 1978, 12). Their canonical work *Mozi* 墨子 includes several chapters that, both directly and indirectly, seek to resolve central questions connected to the methods of such inferences. In this context, the Mohists were especially concerned with their concrete application and logical classification. Departing from the results of earlier investigations, they systematically elaborated and developed these methods into a coherent, integral theory of analogies.

They argued that classifying names was supposed to apply to kinds. However, it was not only attempted to determine rules for their correct use, but also to define the principles governing the distinctions between any two classifying names. This approach was based upon the following assumptions that also represented—inter alia—the basic principles of analogical thought:

1) Each kind is determined by some crucial properties, being common to all the objects of that kind.
2) All objects belonging to the same kind are similar or the same. They called this "the sameness/similarity of kind" (*leitong* 類同), which can refer to relations between objects and kinds, respectively. The sameness (or similarity) of two kinds is that which clearly distinguished them from other kinds and from objects that do not belong to them.⁴⁸
3) Analogous to this view of sameness or similarity (*tong* 同), the later Mohists also explored distinctions and differences (*yi* 異), focusing on "distinctions or differences in kinds (*leiyi* 類異)." The demarcation line between distinction and difference (and, analogously, between sameness and similarity) was established later in the later Mohist commentaries from the fourth century, in the differentiation between similarity (*tong*) and distinction (*yi*) on the one hand, and sameness (*zhi tong* 至同) and difference (*zhi yi* 至異) on the other (*Mo bian zhu xu* s.d., 2).⁴⁹

According to Chris Fraser (2013, 6), the Mohists specify three categories of general criteria for distinguishing kinds:[50]

a) "shape and visual appearance" (*xing mao* 形貌),
b) "residence and migration" (*ju yun* 居運),
c) "amount and number" (*liang shu* 量數).

Also, some things are so different they cannot intelligibly be compared at all, and so they probably have no respects in which they could be considered "of a kind" (2013, 6). Wood and night, for instance, belong to different kinds. Hence, we cannot measure them by a common criterion, asking "Which is longer, a piece of wood or a night?" (*Mozi* s.d., X, Jing xia: 7).[51] The Mohist called the analogical inference "extending kinds" (*tuilei* 推類), which means "extending" our judgment of what counts as "of the same kind" to include new cases: "In practice, 'extending kinds' amounts to taking the judgment that things are 'of a kind' (*lei*) in one or more respects as a basis for treating them as 'of a kind' in another" (Fraser 2013, 5).

3.2.3 Names (*ming*), Meanings[52] and Axiological Evaluations of Kinds

As we have seen, Chinese logic differs from Western formal logic, which seeks to discriminate between general forms of cognitive processes and the object of investigation. Chinese logic differs in this respect, for its creators were not so much interested in defining general abstract formulas of propositions and analogies. Instead, they created semantic (not formal) structures, trying to define them with practical examples and descriptive explanations.

As we have also seen, the Mohist approach to the methodological suppositions of analogical inference was determined by their desire to arrive at a detailed definition of the notion of kind. Hence, they were the first philosophers to engage in extensive debate on the notion of kind (*lei* 類) in relation to naming (*ming* 名), both of kind and the objects belonging to it. They defined names as entities, which they divided into

- unrestricted,
- classifying (belonging to particular kinds),
- individual (*Mozi* s.d., X, Jing shang: 79).[53]

The explanation of this passage reads:

> Naming some "thing" as such is unrestricted, since any actuality necessarily requires this name. Naming something "horse," however, is a classification, because for actualities of this type we are compelled to employ this appellation. Naming someone "Zang" is individual, because this name remains limited to this particular reality. (*Mozi* s.d., X, Jingshuo shang: 79)[54]

For the Confucian Xunzi, it was moreover of great importance to apply "proper" names; thus, he exposed that this propriety was an essential precondition of correct inferences:

> Only if we continuously apply the proper nomenclature will our analogies match the reality and we will be able to avoid mistakes in distinguishing particular things. Only on this basis will our inferences not be in contradiction. (*Xunzi* s.d., Zheng ming: 11)[55]

But the Mohists also defined the notion of kind with respect to the concepts of similarity or sameness (*tong*) and difference (*yi*). They started this analysis with a definition of the similarity (or sameness), which they understood as appearing in four categories:

- identity,
- units,
- being together,
- being of a kind (*Mozi* s.d., X, Jing shang: 87).[56]

This is explained in the following way:

> If there are two names but only one object, this is the similarity of "identity." Not being outside the total is similarity "as units." Both occupying the same space is the similarity of "being together." Being similar in some respect is similarity in being "of a kind." (*Mozi* s.d., X, Jing shuo shang: 87)[57]

Difference was perceived in an analogous way:

- two,
- not units,
- not together,
- not of a kind (*Mozi* s.d., X, Jing shang: 88).[58]

An explanation of this concept follows:

> Different: If there are two (objects), they are necessarily different, being "two." (Objects that are) not connected or attached are "not units." (Objects that are) not in the same place are "not together." (Objects that are) not the same in some respect are "not of a kind." (*Mozi* s.d., Jing shuo shang: 88)[59]

Things of the same kind can appear in analogies as the carrier or object of the information transfer. Analogical inferences follow a structure that connects all elements within a particular kind. It is hardly accidental, therefore, that in such discourses structure functions as one of the basic elements that make analogies possible. The Mohists established three conditions that determined the formulation of the so-called phrase, which served as the basic tool for analogical, inferential, and cognitive processes. These phrases (ci 辭) were defined as elements that express meaning: "Names denote realities, and phrases express meaning" (*Mozi* s.d., XI, Xiao qu, 1).[60]

Subsequently, an even more detailed definition of this term was given by Xunzi: "A phrase is a way to express a coherent idea by combining different names, which denote different realties" (*Xunzi* s.d., Zheng ming: 11).[61]

The Mohists proceeded from the presumption that analogical inferences (lit. transferring the kinds) are difficult because of their sizes:[62]

> If we speak about animals with four legs, then oxen and horses are included. But, ultimately, (all) things differ in something; therefore, this is a question of the sizes (of kinds). (*Mozi* s.d., X, Jing shuo xia: 102)[63]

The relation between the size of kind, and sameness/difference was therefore fundamental, and would be formulated in greater detail by the representative of the School of Names Hui Shi (ca. 370–310 BCE).[64] In fact, differentiating among kinds with respect to their extension[65] implied the (im)possibility of analogical inferences based upon transferring information from these kinds. For example, in the quote provided in the previous paragraph, the kind of animal with four legs is a sort of generic umbrella kind that "covers" many more limited kinds of animals with different names. The Mohists thus cautioned that when inferring we must be aware of the extent of a particular kind, for the broader it is, the less the objects belonging to it will possess common attributes and criteria. Analogical inferences should therefore apply criteria that are appropriate for the dimensions of a particular kind.

However, objects should not be shifted from larger into smaller kinds arbitrarily, as this could lead to false conclusions:

> We cannot claim that oxen and horses are different because the former have teeth, while the latter have tails. They both have teeth and tails. But neither can we claim that an ox is different from a horse because it has horns, while a horse does not. If we take the fact that oxen have horns, while horses do not as an example in order to clarify the differences between them, it is a kind of nonsense, just like the example that an ox has teeth and a horse has a tail. (*Mozi* s.d., X, Jing shuo xia: 167)[66]

The Mohists thus asserted that the criterion for distinguishing the sameness (similarity) or difference (*tong* or *yi*) between individual objects should be how general the possession or non-possession of a given attribute was (Cui and Zhang 2005, 34). It was wrong to distinguish an ox from a horse because it has teeth, whereas a horse has a tail. Teeth are not a unique, specific characteristic of oxen, just as tails are not a unique feature of horses. But distinguishing them because oxen have horns, while horses do not, is likewise wrong, for horns are not a *differentia specifica* of oxen, but also a characteristic of sheep and goats. Only a unique feature can serve as a criterion for distinguishing objects within a certain kind.

> If things have some common unique similarities, they are of the same type; if not, they belong to different types. So, if we want to judge whether certain things belong to the same type or not, we can only take unique differences or similarities (which manifest themselves in their general attributes) as a standard. Otherwise, the average differences or similarities (in their general attributes) cannot help us in judging whether these things belong to the same type or not. Hence, similarities in the evidences of analogism are relationships between things with the same unique attributes. (Cui and Zhang 2005, 34)

In such contexts, content was clearly more important than form and this priority has led to the classification of analogisms into four main types, which the Mohists named *pi, mo, yuan,* and *tui*[67] (Cui and Zhang 2005, 40). While the *pi* type was based on explanation by example, the *mo* type referred to deduction from a parallel series of words, phrases, or sentences (*ci*). The *yuan* type was instead based upon potentially similar views and the *tui* type on agreements with certain views through the negation of contrary views. All these types were apparently based upon descriptive methods.

In pre-Qin China, the focus upon the contents rather than forms led to basic characteristics defining this kind of inferences. The basic typography that determines the specifically Western model of analogical inferences suggests a proposition where some relations necessarily determine the existence of other relations, regardless of the particular context in which they appear (Holyoak 2008, 150).[68] Besides, the basic scheme of specific Chinese analogies also makes additional differentiations within this basic model: different types of inferences are distinguished according to the axiological assessment of the relations they contain. Hence, analogical inferences are also evaluated according to the ethical meaning of both propositions.

> Black horses are horses. If we ride a black horse, we ride a horse. Female slaves are human beings. If we love a female slave, we love a human being. (*Mozi* s.d., XI, Xiao qu, 4)[69]

If we replace "female slave" with "thief," we obtain a formally and structurally equivalent inference worded as follows: "Thieves are human beings. If we love a thief, we love a human being" (*Mozi* s.d., XI, Xiao qu, 5).[70]

Although both examples are structurally equivalent on the formal level, and their premises are doubtless true, for the later Mohists the first inference was correct, whereas the second was not, for the former accorded with common sense, while the latter did not.[71] In their view: "Thieves are human beings, but to love a thief does not mean to love a human being" (*Mozi* s.d., XI, Xiao qu, 5).[72]

They explained this conclusion as follows:

> How can this be explained? If we do not like thieves, this does not mean we do not like human beings. And if we desire that there be no thieves, this does not mean we desire there be no human beings. This is the same everywhere in the world. And if this is true, then it is likewise true that to love thieves does not mean to love human beings. (*Mozi* s.d., XI, Xiao qu, 5)[73]

In this case, the Mohist interpretation does not hold up to closer formal verification, for thieves (as female slaves) are a subspecies of human beings. One equivalence is thus correct—the argument affirming that the thieves and human beings belong to the same kind—but the vice versa is not, however, correct necessarily, for even if all thieves are people, clearly not all people are thieves. Thus, the Mohist statement is certainly true in the negative form, for if I do not love thieves, this does not mean that I don't love people. On the other hand, it is by no means true in the affirmative form, that because I love thieves I should also love people.

This argumentation is clearly about ethical issues. It is about value systems and about axiological evaluation, which for the late Mohists was a very basic one, since it "is the same everywhere in the world" (*Mozi* s.d., XI, Xiao qu: 5).[74] It is clear that this evaluation puts different criteria to judge objects that belong to certain kinds. Although thieves are people, they are not viewed (merely) as a subspecies of people (such as, for example, female slaves), but as a different kind (of people), one that belongs to a completely different ethical context and that cannot be measured by the same criteria as other subspecies of people (for instance slaves). In this frame of different axiological valuations of specific elements in the premises of both of the above inferences, it is evident that to love female slaves still means to love human beings, while to love thieves does not necessarily mean to love human beings.

Such elements of semantic and axiological connotations are even more evident in the following example of Mohist argumentation: "A dog is the same as a cur, but to kill a dog is not the same as to kill a cur" (*Mozi* s.d., X, Jing xia: 155).[75] Here, the problem at issue is that both dog and cur are names that can refer either to the same—or to a different—actuality. Although they can refer to the same specific animal, the difference between the two notions (i.e., dog and cur) is to be found in their respective ethical evaluation which is rooted in their different semantic connotations: while a dog has positive connotations, a cur implies something negative.

In the Chinese tradition, the various kinds of inferences were thus always further defined by semantic and axiological connotations. These models of inference, grounded upon semantically determined analogies, were extremely important in classical Chinese logic, as is clearly evidenced by many influential works of the pre-Qin era.

The underlying semantic structure was provided by the structural principle or the principle of structure patterns, that is, by the dynamic structure of li, which has been more in detail treated in Chapter 2.1.1 ("The concept Li—Structuralism and its Chinese ancestors").

3.2.4 Linking Objects and Values

Hence, ancient Chinese philosophers did not focus solely upon the human ability to grasp analogies, but also upon the capacity to combine them into structures of a higher order. They also stressed that in order to make our relational capacity operational, an elaborate symbolic system, such as human language, was necessary.

> According to Mencius, the similarity of minds is the basic similarity which defines human beings. Since their minds are structured in the same way, they can directly communicate and be "kindred" with one another. His treatises reveal a form of analogical thought based upon the theory that human beings are of the same kind. Obviously, these analogies were developed on the basis of Confucian teaching, which required people *"to be guided by their own feelings"* when dealing with one another. (Cui and Zhang 2005, 30)

Thus, objects that belonged to the same kind, and could thus be treated with the same criteria, were clearly connected through some form of coherent constitution. As noted already in the *Book of Rites*, these objects had to be mutually connected through the same structure:

> The structural pattern of every existing thing interacts on the basis of its kind. (*Li ji* s.d., Li qi, 30)[76]

This conception of the world, which enabled ancient Chinese philosophers to create analogies based on structural connections, was already expressed in the earliest sources:

> The *Book of Changes* (易經) argued that universality included the logic of the world; it applied the Eight Trigrams as symbols, expressing structural connections to the laws of Nature. These symbols were also applied as criteria for the classification and epitomizing of all worldly situations. The reason for this "epitomizing" of all universal laws by the scheme of the Eight Trigrams is found in the method of "comprehending by analogy," which was applied by interpreting these symbols. This method was one of gradual (step by step) deduction, based upon analogies. (Cui and Zhang 2005, 40)

Each of the basic binary symbols was rooted in a structure that was integral and all-embracing and could therefore be expanded to include a limitless number of things that belonged to the same kind as this singular, concrete symbol. Based on this premise, communication between human beings is only possible because the human brains are structured in the same way (Cui and Zhang 2005, 30).[77]

Distinctions within the all-embracing cosmic order, which follows the Way (*dao*), are also made in accordance with structural patterns (*li*). Such understanding of the relation between the two notions[78] appears already in the earliest sources, for instance in *Guanzi* (circa seventh century BCE):

> Dividing different relationships and their proper distinguishing is called structure (*li*). To follow these structural patterns without losing them is called the Way (*dao*). (*Guanzi* s.d., Jun chen I: 8)[79]

This order was structured in accordance with kinds, and hence proper kinds could not generate contradiction within it. This basic structural scheme was seen as something eternal. In this context, Xunzi wrote:[80] "The kinds do not generate contradictions, and so, no matter the duration, the structural patterns (*li*) are the same" (*Xunzi* s.d., Fei xiang: 7).[81]

In this context, the concept *li* denotes a structure (or a structural network) underlying particular kinds, which is comparable to the aforementioned referential frameworks underlying or determining discourses, paradigms, theories or other cognitive systems (Feng 1989, 291–2). The same words or notions (and even same phrases) can imply a completely different meaning, when appearing in different referential frameworks (or networks).

For the Mohists, phrases were fundamental elements of well-regulated communication, based upon principles of semantic logic. Phrases could thus provide the bases for analogies and were also viewed as sentences or propositions (Cui and Zhang 2005, 23). The Mohists stressed that the existence, composition, and application of phrases could not be arbitrary, otherwise people would not be able to communicate clearly and understand one another. The three necessary conditions that determined phrases, as well as analogies, were reasons, structures, and kinds:

> Before starting an argument, three elements are necessary: phrases originate from reasons, they are guided by structures (or structural patterns, principles) and are transferred through kinds. Forming phrases without a clear knowledge of their reasons leads to chaos. (*Mozi* s.d., XI. Daqu: 25)[82]

The passage stating that phrases were "guided by structures (or structural patterns)" can be explained in this context as a presumption according to which phrases had to be applied within a well-regulated semantic structure of language and meaning (reasoning). The "transfer of phrases through kinds," that is, the cognitive processes that are based upon analogies, follow a structure that determines the intrinsic constitution of language and thought. Structure (*li* 理) thus signifies well-ordered (i.e., proper and reasonable) relations between reasons (*gu* 故) and kinds (*lei* 類) (Cui and Zhang 2005, 38).

3.2.5 Ethical Implications

Bearing these elements in mind, let us now re-examine the question of axiological criteria determining the similarity or difference of kinds. Let us first more closely examine the Mohist example regarding the difference between killing a dog or a cur. Even though the two are synonymous (*chong tong* 重同) and refer to the same being with different connotations, a specificity of Chinese logic emerges in understanding the structure of relations that form models of analogical inferences. This framework is based upon an important assumption by which a sentential structure is not merely a formal, static structure with immutable functions, but also implies dynamic variations in meanings that can influence the correctness or inaccuracy of a given inference.

Li as the semantic structure (or a referential network) underlying the evaluative criteria of objects belonging to particular kinds obviously brings rise to ethical implications. A dog (*quan* 犬) and a cur (*gou* 狗) can both refer to the same object in the same kind, that is, the kind of four-legged hairy animals that eat meat and bark, whereby the cur is by no means a subset of the dog, although their sameness[83] is expressed in the manner that is often used to denote relations between a kind and a subkind.[84] Although they can refer to the same specific animal, the difference between the two terms lies in their semantic connotations, which are linked to their ethical evaluation: as already mentioned previously, a dog implies something positive, while cur has negative connotations. These evaluations manifest themselves especially clearly in our actions toward the objects to which they belong. Hence, they are usually implied in transitive verbs referring to a dog or to a cur as their object. Therefore, they belong to the same kind regarding their physical attributes, but to different kinds in respect to our actions (or attitudes) directed toward them, for the latter are necessarily embedded in a proper (generally accepted)[85] ethical structure or the ethically determined referential framework in which our life is embedded in turn. In this framework, it is completely clear that to kill a dog is not the same as to kill a cur. Analogously, thieves and humans belong to the same kind referring their particular physical characteristics; the difference between them becomes clear only in our attitude toward them. At least the late Mohist logicians believed that loving thieves contradicted the premises implied in the referential framework of the all-embracing and generally valid ethical structure. This is the reason why, for them, loving thieves was something completely different than loving people. In this presumption, the late Mohists went even a step further; in order to demonstrate the "reasonableness" of the capital punishment they were advocating, they concluded that, "killing a thief was not the same as killing a human being" (*Mozi* s.d., XI, Xiaoqu: 5).[86] The Confucian Xunzi, who was, of course, one of their worst enemies, attacked them for this statement, replying that with such phrases they apply names in a confusing way, creating chaos in the naming of objects (*Xunzi* s.d., Zheng ming:10).[87] Such critiques are certainly grounded in common sense, even though they do not diminish the value of this type of logic, for in traditional formal logic there is no shortage of examples that run afoul of common sense.[88]

It follows that semantic logic, which is imbued with ethics and ideology, is just another way of perceiving, ordering, and transmitting reality. Although the abovementioned Mohist examples can by no means be accepted as arguments for capital punishment, a similar, reverse statement (with which the Confucians—including Xunzi—would doubtless agree), might be a more illustrative (and persuasive) example for this type of logical reasoning: "Huo's parents are people, but when serving his parents, Huo is not serving people" (*Mozi* s.d., XI, Xiaoqu: 5).[89] Our parents are, of course, not just (any) "people." Although Huo's parents are a subset of the umbrella kind people, they are not merely a subset of people regarding Huo (and his actions), since for him, they belong to a completely different and very special kind of people, namely to the ones that are closest to him. The question about how the relations between a kind and its subsets change is namely a human decision and not one of some automatic formal laws[90] on which we have no real influence. The crucial element in judging and evaluating kinds and their mutual relations, as well as the relations between them and us, is our attitude toward them, which is rooted in our very understanding of the world. In this sense, we are the ones governing reality and not vice versa. The decisive factor here is the human heart-mind, which functions in accordance with a structural network that is—like the universe itself—imbued with rational, as well as ethical premises.

4

Methods and Approaches

Because of the growing attentiveness regarding the specific features of the Chinese philosophical tradition, the debate on the philosophical dimensions of Chinese texts and their role in the context of Chinese thought has been developed increasingly successfully under the aegis of rediscovering and applying specific traditional Chinese methodological approaches, concepts, and categories. Based on the awareness of the importance of such revival of classical Chinese philosophical methodologies, such approaches aim to elaborate a renewed but coherent methodological system based upon a modernized and upgraded traditional methods and partly on their combination or synthesis with certain approaches derived from the Euro-American discourses.

Proceeding from a short discussion on the two most widely applied methods, namely the analytical and the hermeneutical one, we shall try to evaluate their integration into the referential frameworks typical of Chinese philosophy. The concluding section will deal with a method, which is also widely used and thus very important, namely the comparative approach. Here, we shall debate the nature and the value of the specific insights it can offer us, but also critically reflect on its inherent dangers and misconceptions to which it can lead.

As regards the current situation, scholars researching Chinese philosophy still mostly apply modern and contemporary versions of the analytical and hermeneutical methods belonging to the Euro-American methodological tradition. However, as we will see later in this chapter, both approaches were also developed in the course of the Chinese intellectual tradition, although they differ in several aspects from the "Western" ones.

In this last chapter, I will expose some problems linked to a superficial application of both abovementioned approaches. On this basis, I will propose an innovative mode of hermeneutics, which is based on the fusion of aesthetic realms (*jingjie*),¹ aiming to replace (or at least radically modify) the controversial usages of Western hermeneutical methods, rooted in the concept of the fusion of horizons. Given that modern methods, which proceed from analytical and hermeneutic approaches respectively, are mostly applied in their Westernized (modernized) form, which is, in itself, necessarily a product of the European intellectual history and the corresponding socialization processes, we have to take into account that we are dealing with discourses that do not belong to any of the Western traditions. This means that even if we preserve the Western analytical or hermeneutical methods in investigating traditional Chinese theoretical texts, we have to consider that these texts belong to a different referential framework. The specific features of this framework are determined by the application of different concepts and categories and resulting in different methodological procedures.

As mentioned, the chapter will conclude with a debate on the advantages and shortcomings of comparative perspectives, which also belong to the most widely used—albeit sometimes dangerous—methods in investigating and explaining Chinese philosophy and placing them into a broader transcultural context.

4.1 Analytical and Hermeneutic Procedures

In the Chinese linguistic environment, many books and articles, dealing with problems of applying the Western scientific methods while researching objects, connected with specific elements of Chinese tradition, were published in recent years. The debate on the inherent semantic dimensions of classical Chinese texts and their role in the context of traditional Chinese thought is in modern studies more and more successfully turning in the direction of the rediscovery and use of specific traditional Chinese methodological approaches and traditional categories. There are still many controversial opinions regarding the questions of the proper method of comprehension and interpretation of classical Chinese texts.

As already mentioned, I will here—due to space limitations—only present two main approaches and shortly introduce the research methods they are advocating. The first approach is analytical; scholars, advocating this method, mainly belong to the field of analytic philosophy or logic (including the research in traditional Chinese logic). The second one is recommending traditional and modernized hermeneutic methods. Representatives of this stream mainly belong to the current of Modern Confucianism, but they also include some other contemporary philosophers who are concerned with the revival of traditional Chinese methodological procedures.

The demarcation line between the two approaches is extremely blurred, for very often they are being combined. However, the first systematic approaches to a modern categorization and ordering of traditional Chinese philosophy were proceeding from the analytical standpoint, so we will first take a short look at the development of the analytic method in Chinese philosophy.

4.1.1 The Uncertain Paths of Chinese Analytical Philosophy

The germs of the analytical tradition were formed already by the Mohist and Nomenalist schools of thought in the pre-Qin era. Later on, the analytical methods of investigating Chinese texts were further developed partly by the Donglin academy,[2] by Gu Xiancheng[3] (1550–1612), Gao Panlong[4] (1562–1626), and Wang Fuzhi[5] (1619–92). In the premodern era, that is, before the confrontation with the "Western-style" analyses, the "Chinese type" of analyses was further elaborated on by several traditions of text criticism (*kaozheng* 考證) that were flourishing in China between 1600 and 1850, with its two most prominent representatives Gu Yanwu[6] (1613–82) and Huang Zongxi[7] (1610–95), but also in the framework of the new methodologies developed by Dai Zhen[8] (1724–77).

Later on, after the first encounters with Western thought, numerous Chinese scholars have already upgraded or modified Western analytical methodology with various intriguing approaches, derived from classical Chinese thought (Liu 1996, 16). Here, we have to mention at least some of these interesting theoretical innovations. One of the pioneers of such approaches was doubtless Feng Youlan.[9] Together with Hu Shi, he belonged to the first Western-trained scholars who attempted to order and systematize traditional Chinese philosophy with the help of logical analysis. First of all, he divided Chinese philosophy into the "Period of the masters"[10] and the "Period of the Classics."[11] He also subdivided all central philosophical schools into several different streams: the legalist school, for instance, consisted of proponents of power, of tactics and of law. In a similar way, the School of Names was categorized into the group of unifying identity and difference (*he tongyi* 合同異), which was represented by Hui Shi, and by the group of separating hardness and whiteness (*li jianbai* 離堅白), represented by Gongsun Long. He was the first interpreter who categorized the Neo-Confucian school into the school of the structural principle (*li xue*) and the school of the heart-mind (*xin xue* 心學). The notion of heaven (*tian*) was also classified into five categories. Besides, Feng also tried to compare some of the crucial notions from Euro-American and Chinese philosophy. He proposed that the Neo-Confucian binary category of *Li* and *Qi* was similar to the ancient Greek concepts of form and matter. According to him, Gongsun Long's "*zhi* 指" is comparable to the notion of universals (Zhao 2007, 2). Although nowadays it is clear that we have to be very careful when applying the Western logical methods and categories to the field of Chinese philosophy, and very aware of the dangers that can be brought about by such practices, we cannot but admire Feng Youlan for his contribution to the modernization of Chinese philosophy.

Many of his followers have further elaborated on different modifications of the existing analytical methods in order to create a suitable analytical tool for investigating Chinese philosophy. Here, we should mention Jin Yuelin's[12] elaboration of the Chinese concept of *Dao* in the sense of mattered form (or formalized matter) as a fundamental entity within a modern system of modal logic. Jin organized this system in terms of possibility, rather than actuality, and suggested unnamable and unknowable matter, which he called "the given" (*suoyu* 所與), as "pure potentiality and pure activity that, in realizing diverse possibilities, determines knowable and namable objects and underlies the substantiality of those objects" (Bunnin 2003, 347). As opposed to his role model Russell, however, Jin viewed analysis merely as a method, and not as the essence of philosophy. For him, the analytic method represented the most efficient tool for the construction of new philosophical systems. Therefore, Jin can be considered a follower of Russell's school only in methodological terms, and should not be regarded as a "pure" analytical philosopher.

In this context, the philosopher Zhang Dainian and his elder brother Zhang Shenfu[13] should also be mentioned. Zhang Shenfu translated Wittgenstein's *Logical Philosophical Treatise* and proposed a combination of Russell's philosophical analysis, dialectical materialism, and traditional Chinese philosophy. Hence, in his work, he combined analytical, Marxist. and ancient Chinese thought. Zhang Dainian, on the other hand, has proposed a "creative synthesis"[14] of analytical philosophy, dialectical materialism, and classical Chinese traditions of thought. Apparently, this combination decidedly contributed to a reasonable continuation of traditional Chinese philosophy:

> The continuation of the Chinese tradition was already apparent in the philosophical works of Jin Yuelin and Feng Youlan. With Zhang Dainian, this continuity finally became a conscious, self-aware methodology. It can be said that Zhang Dainian, as opposed to Jin or Feng, was not only vigilantly preserving the special characteristics of traditional Chinese thought but, more importantly, was also preserving and continuing traditional methodological principles. . . . In terms of its range, Zhang Dainian's continuation of the Chinese philosophical tradition goes far beyond Jin Yuelin's and even Feng Youlan's. His work represents a genuine synthesis of the continuations of traditional philosophy. (Hu Weixi 2002, 230)[15]

A further aspect of the influence of philosophical analysis can be seen in Chinese responses to Kantian philosophy, especially in the works of Zhang Dongsun, Mou Zongsan, and Li Zehou (Bunnin 2003, 349).

Zhang's analysis was based upon a revision of Kant's philosophy, in which he followed his own system of so-called panstructuralist cosmology, which was to a certain extent also influenced by the chan-Buddhist philosophy upon which his own worldview was based. His cultural epistemology was founded upon a pluralistic theory of knowledge (*duoyuan renshilun* 多元認識論), and proceeded from the premise that knowledge was culturally determined and therefore essentially of a cultural nature, an aspect of his philosophy which still remains quite topical, especially in the field of transcultural research. His cultural-philosophical studies are based upon detailed comparative analyses of Chinese and European thought, with a special attention to the influence of linguistic structures upon various philosophical systems, and the connection between culturally determined differences and systems of logical reasoning in different traditions of thought.

Mou Zongsan analyzed and ordered Chinese philosophy in accordance with his "two tiered ontology" (*youzhi cunyoulun, wuzhi cunyoulun* 有執存有論, 無執存有論) in order to establish a new theoretical framework of incorporating modernization, science, and democracy via the inner dialectical development of Confucianism. In his most important work, *Intellectual intuition and Chinese philosophy*,[16] he analyzed the specific Chinese understanding of the structure of existence. In doing so, he drew certain parallels with Heidegger's ontology and pointed out inconsistencies in Kant's theories. Mou was convinced (see 1975, 37) that along this line of thought he could build a valid moral metaphysics, which Kant did not succeed in building.

Li Zehou's philosophy has helped modify and transform the antiquated patterns of Chinese intellectual discourses. His innovative, imaginative, and unique approach to a wide range of basic theoretical problems, grounded in solid arguments and analyses, has created new styles of intellectual investigation into the post-Mao period, and presented a new challenge to the tedious and monotonous theories delivered by the official Party ideologists. Through his analyses, Li placed the central framework of Kant's philosophy upon a social and materialist foundation by simultaneously recovering the original Marxist definition of human beings as "homo faber," that is, as living beings developed through practice and able to apply tools in a systemic, continuous way. Humans are thus, in Li's view, recreating both their environment and their inwardness into something he called "humanized nature." His analyses could be described as the ordering of a vast material, offering possibilities for a coherent synthesis between Western and traditional Chinese thought. It was driven in order to elaborate a system of ideas and values capable of resolving the social and political problems of the modern way of life. In most of his works, he attempted to reconcile "Western" (especially Kantian and Marxist) theories with "traditional Chinese" (particularly Confucian, but to a certain extent also Daoist) ideas, concepts, and values, in order to create a theoretical model of modernization that would not be confused or equated with "Westernization."

Lao Sze-kwang,[17] a Hong Kong-Taiwanese scholar who did not belong to any of the prominent contemporary streams of thought but is nevertheless widely regarded as an important modern Chinese theoretician, has established a new criterion for the analysis of classical Chinese texts, namely the so-called "fundamental source (*jiyaun* 基源)" approach. He defines it as a method, which is based on the unified criteria for analysis and interpretation of various philosophical problems:

> The so-called method for investigating fundamental sources of problems proceeds from the logical meaning and is complemented by the method of historical evidence in order to unify all particular philosophical activities under one clearly defined criterion. If we want to revise a philosophical theory, we first have to understand that all philosophical theories, no matter whether they were established by individuals or by particular philosophical

schools, have to search for an answer to certain questions or for a solution to a certain problem. As soon as we find this problem or this question, we can obtain an insight into the general context of this theory. And, on the other hand, all the contents of this theory are, in fact, founded on this problem or this question. (Lao 1980, 16)[18]

In this context, contemporary Taiwanese scholar Duh Bao-Ruei[19] exposed in his book on the methodology of Chinese philosophy (2013, 12) that in regard to Chinese philosophy, this kind of problem-awareness (or research questions) is much more closely linked to certain philosophical schools than to the works of individual philosophers. He also proposes a new classification of Chinese philosophy. Instead of blindly following Western disciplines of logic, epistemology, metaphysics, ontology, phenomenology, etc., the research in traditional Chinese philosophy should mainly be oriented upon investigations in the theory of skills[20] and/or the philosophy of aesthetic realms (*jingjie zhexue* 境界哲學) (2013, 11). Another contemporary Taiwanese philosopher, Lee Hsien-chung,[21] an expert in Chinese logic, aims to develop and upgrade his newly coined concept of "thought units" (*sixiang danwei* 思想單位). However, the aforementioned analytical philosopher Feng Yaoming (Fung Yiu-ming) has probably made the hitherto most important contribution to the development of the analytical method in the research in Chinese philosophy with his numerous articles and books.

Many other scholars in the Chinese-speaking area are presently still continuously elaborating on the further development of analytical method and its adaptation for an in-depth research in Chinese philosophy. They are far too many to be mentioned in this short study. For now, it can only be said that if we take into consideration the abovementioned specific methodological features, which represent the methodological basis for classical Chinese philosophy, the analytical methods can—in an adapted form and besides other approaches—doubtless prove themselves as appropriate tools for investigating, interpreting, and evaluating Chinese theoretical writings.

4.1.2 Lacking Contextuality: The Problem of *Dao*, *You*, and *Wu*

However, this holds true to a certain extent only. Following Wang Bo's[22] investigation (1991), I will try to illustrate the limitations of this method by virtue of three different examples that are dealing with an interpretation of the relation between the three crucial concepts from Laozi's[23] *Dao de jing* 道德經, namely *you* 有 (presence), *wu* 無 (absence), and *dao* 道. In addition, we shall see that the application of the same analytical method (or, more concretely, the analytical method implying logical inferences) can lead different scholars not only to different but even to mutual contradicting results.

First example: Hu Shi[24] believes that *dao* is identical to *wu* (absence) (as cited in Wang Bo 1991, 40). Hu illustrates his point by quoting Laozi's following statement:

> The *dao* produced One; One produced Two; Two produced Three; Three produced All things. (*Laozi* s.d., 42)[25]

Then, he reminds us that, in another context, Laozi also writes that

> All things under heaven sprang from *you* (presence), but *you* (presence) sprang from *wu* (absence). (*Laozi* s.d., 40)[26]

Hu Shi thus concludes that both, *dao* and *wu*, are equally the origins of all existing things, and that they are thus equal (as cited in Wang Bo 1991, 41).

Second example: Yan Linfeng,[27] on the contrary, is convinced that Dao is identical with *You* (presence), and he grounded this opinion upon the following analysis: in the beginning, he quotes the same section from the 42nd Chapter of Laozi's *Dao de jing* (as cited in Wang Bo 1991, 41):

> The *dao* produced One; One produced Two; Two produced Three; Three produced All things. (*Laozi* s.d., 42)[28]

He explains this quotation as implying that *dao* is the "mother of all things."[29] After that, he quotes the first part of the sentence that was previously quoted by Hu Shi:

> All things under heaven sprang from *you* (presence). (*Laozi* s.d., 40)[30]

In addition, he also quotes another statement from the first chapter of the *Dao de jing*:

> *You* (presence) is the mother of all things. (*Laozi* s.d., 1)[31]

Hence, he concludes that both *you* (presence) and *dao* are the "mother of all things" and are therefore identical (as cited in Wang Bo 1991, 41).[32]

Third example: Zhang Dainian[33] believes that *dao* is both *you* (presence) and *wu* (absence). To demonstrate his view, he quotes a section of the first chapter of Laozi's *Dao de jing*:

> In the eternal *wu* (absence) we can understand its deep miraculous nature; but in the eternal *you* (presence), we can only see its outer fringe. Actually, these two aspects are the same, but they have different names. Together we call them the Mystery. Where the Mystery is the deepest, is the gate of all that is subtle and wonderful. (*Laozi* s.d., 1)[34]

He explains this by stating that *you* (presence) and *wu* (absence) are both Mystery, and the deepest Mystery is *dao* (as cited in Wang Bo 1991, 42). . . . Therefore, *dao* is identical with *wu* (absence), but also with *you* (presence).

In these three examples, different scholars have used different logical-analytical procedures to explain their opinions. To clarify these differences, let us translate their argumentations into logical inferences.

<u>Hu Shi:</u>

P1. *Dao*   => all existing things
P2. *Wu* (absence) => all existing things

C. *Dao*   = *Wu* (absence)

<u>Yan Lingfeng:</u>

P1. *Dao*   = the mother of all things
P2. *You* (presence) = the mother of all things

C. *Dao*   = *You* (presence)

<u>Zhang Dainian:</u>

P1. *You* (presence) + *Wu* (absence) = Mystery
P2. Mystery   = *Dao*

C. *You* (presence) + *Wu* (absence)   = *Dao*

In fact, we can use this method to prove everything. No matter which view we advocate, no matter on which assumptions or premises our conclusions are based, it is rather easy to find evidence for them in some of the text fragments. Such methods deal with parts of the text and analyze them as isolated meanings. They do not take into consideration the entire context—in other words, they neglect the importance of the contextualization of the meaning.

However, before throwing the baby out with the bathwater, we shall also—once again—take into account that, when properly used,[35] analytical methods can offer us very valuable insights into the realm of Chinese philosophy. With its application of "objective" criteria, the analytical method is especially useful in transcultural philosophy, precisely because it does not consider different evaluations of historically, culturally, or subjectively variable factors. It is, however, strongly recommendable that we use it in combination with other, interpretative methods and always as a tool for clarifying certain quantitatively controllable parts of larger research questions.

4.1.3 Interpreting China through Chinese Interpretation

Chinese hermeneutics has a rich (and very specific) tradition which can be traced back to Wang Bi[36] (226–249) and Guo Xiang[37] (252–312) from the Wei Jin Nanbei Chao period. A most prominent figure who left indelible traces in the history of Chinese interpretative theory was Liu Xie[38] (ca. 455–522), the author of the famous work *Literary Mind and the Carving of Dragons*.[39]

As King Po-Chiu (2016, 76) exposes, Chinese hermeneutics mainly describes various methods of interpreting Chinese thought (mostly through comments and explanatory annotations) rather than problematizing questions regarding why we interpret something in such different ways. According to him, metaphysical discussion is not the subject matter of "Chinese hermeneutics."[40]

Now let us take a closer look upon hermeneutic methods as applied in contemporary China. Very soon, it becomes clear that in this field, we can encounter similar problems as the ones pertaining to the question of the existence of Chinese philosophy:

> If all acts of reading, interpreting, and understanding are seen through the Western hermeneutic lenses, based on the premise that Western hermeneutics is the only legitimate conceptual and philosophical tool, can an accurate image of the Chinese exegetical efforts ever be captured? When Western hermeneutics is taken as the normative and prescriptive manner of reading, cultural particularities are swamped and flattened out

for the spurious cause of analytical unanimity and coherence; and such, in its essentials, is the sin of cultural hegemony, to employ a much-used neologism. (Ng 2013, 374)

On the other hand, some (mostly Western) scholars also express their doubts in the opposite direction, namely doubts regarding the question of whether the Chinese tradition of interpreting the classics is truly comparable with the European hermeneutical method, and hence, whether it is suitable to call it hermeneutics (e.g., Kubin 2005, 312). Here, we have—once again—landed on a marshy ground on which we have to build the entire concept of Chinese philosophy. It is completely clear that Chinese ideational and intellectual tradition did not categorize its thought in accordance with strictly separated disciplines, which means that we cannot find in this tradition systematic ideational branches of epistemology, logic, phenomenology, or, precisely, hermeneutics. However, this does not mean that it does not include a magnificent amount of prosperous and opulent epistemological, logical, phenomenological, and hermeneutic theories. Once again, we cannot but emphasize that the largest difference dividing Chinese and Euro-American thought might be found in their respective classifications.

Gu Ming-dong also points out (2005, 11), although traditional China did not lack conceptual inquiries into reading and writing, its hermeneutic perceptions were scattered in various kinds of discourses and have never been synthesized into a clearly defined system. On the other hand, however, he also argues that the Chinese tradition has formed an implicit system of reading and writing with "fascinating insights that not only predated similar ideas in the West by centuries but also anticipated contemporary ideas of hermeneutic openness and open poetics" (2005, 11). On this basis, he created a modern interpretative instrument based upon the concept of "hermeneutic openness" that proves itself as a very useful tool not only in Chinese, but also in intercultural research. Here, we also have to mention Cheng Chung-ying's innovative theory of "onto-hermeneutics," according to which the Chinese interpretative paradigms are always rooted in a specific understanding of reality. In such a view, understanding is inseparable from being. This paradigm is tightly connected to another special feature of Chinese hermeneutic, namely in its surpassing of the subject-object division and its deep embedment into intersubjective understanding (Wu 2004, 237). Notwithstanding many problems and difficulties with which all scholars dealing with Chinese hermeneutics are necessarily confronted, one can certainly sense a quite optimistic spirit among them: and if there can be socialism with Chinese characteristics, why not a hermeneutics with Chinese characteristics?

Notwithstanding the aforementioned kernels and promising seeds of different interpretative models, most scholars investigating classical Chinese texts still apply interpretative mechanisms derived by Western hermeneutic theories. In the first three decades after the establishment of the People's Republic of China, Chinese intellectuals were in this respect mostly limited to the studies of Hegelian and Marxist theories; from the 1980s on, they have yet again gained access to most of the classical works of modern Euro-American hermeneutics, including Schleiermacher, Dilthey, Heidegger and Gadamer, whose theory of the fusion of horizons soon gained widespread popularity among Chinese theoreticians:

> Overall, however, it has been the influence of Gadamer that has seemed to dominate, even though more informed discussions of a relatively wider range of European hermeneutic philosophical works were already manifest in publications available during the early years of the twenty-first century. (Pfister 2006, 4)

As is well known, his concept of the fusion of horizons was based on an elaborated version of Schleiermacher's notion of the hermeneutic circle, that is, on the idea that one's understanding of a text as a whole is established by reference to the individual parts, and vice versa: the understanding of each individual part is being established by reference to the whole. Neither the whole text nor any individual part can be understood without reference to one another, which can be illustrated by a circular model of comprehension. According to this view, the "fusion of horizons" takes place between the writer and the readers, or the speaker and the listeners in the dialectical process of transferring meanings. In this sense, the concept of horizon refers to the particular situation into which every individual is embedded, whereas the situation is not limited to the vision or perception of what is nearby; hence, the horizon implies an openness of existence and a possibility to overcome one's own prejudices. The fusion of horizons always creates new meanings, for in this dialectical process of mediating and perceiving, it incorporates both horizons and, on the other hand, transcends their individual boundaries. On this basis of free and unlimited horizons, Gu Ming-Dong has drawn his method of traditional Chinese hermeneutic openness, which is rooted in the so-called metaphysical-aesthetic tradition (Gu 2005, 9) of interpretations.[41]

However, while in China, the theories of the Gadamerian discourse (i.e., including Gadamer's predecessors and successors) might represent a precious contribution for a successive establishment of transcultural hermeneutics, this overall enthusiasm could also be gently put on the brakes by raising some questions on the nature of this circle and this horizon.

Of course, the circular character of understanding does not make it impossible to interpret a text; rather, it stresses that the meaning of a text must be found within its context. But the problem is precisely that the very concept of the context has never been sufficiently explained and defined, particularly in view of different layers of reality and different modes of their perception and categorization. In my view, the very term of contextualization and its respective contents can, for instance, at least be divided into external and internal contextualization. The former refers to the cultural, historical, and literary context of the text, and the latter to its inherent conceptual dimensions and their semantic and philosophical implications and developments. Hence, the hermeneutical method is still lacking a binding, inherent consistency.

Recent sinological research has namely still not managed to develop a method of unifying these two kinds of contextualization, and the situation in Chinese-speaking academia on the other hand is not much different in this respect. On the one hand, scholars in China and in Taiwan have developed brilliant theories, which help us understand the historical significance of the time and space of politically, ideologically and culturally conditioned factors in the interpretation of any important classical text. Such theories of external contextualization are mainly written in the area of intellectual history. Contemporary Taiwanese scholar Huang Chun-chieh,[42] for instance, has written several significant works in this field that have clarified many important elements of the historical development of the exegesis of Mencius (see for instance Huang 1997 and 2015). He has also brilliantly shown how and why certain classical works of Chinese tradition have been—for various cultural, political, and ideological reasons—de-contextualized and re-contextualized in the course of their incorporation by Korean and Japanese cultures.

On the other hand we could return here to Cheng Chung-ying, and his aforementioned method of onto-hermeneutics (*benti quanshixue* 本體詮釋學) that was rooted in Gadamerian hermeneutics, but further explored and developed in terms of the Confucian worldview. Cheng believes that the traditional Chinese hermeneutic is ontological; his model is rooted in the presumption, according to which the "understanding of reality and truth is simultaneously the source of meaning and the driving force for seeking understanding" (Cheng 2003b, 290). According to Cheng, no understanding or interpretation can be made without such a reference.

Irrespective of the questionable nature of the notion of truth in the Chinese worldview, the onto-hermeneutics is, in general, doubtless an interesting and innovative approach to the investigation of the traditional Chinese mode of exegesis. However, the problem that has to be discussed in this context is linked to the question of different contextualities underlying all these theoretical approaches. Although Huang and Cheng both write about traditional Chinese hermeneutics, both kinds of hermeneutics (i.e., the one based on the external and the other rooted in the internal contextualization) obviously refer to two very different things.

However, this is by no means the only problem linked to this method. In my view, what is even more questionable, is its premise, which presupposes the existence of a normative intelligible meaning. In Gadamer's own words, the concept of horizon and the fusion of horizons respectively could represent a means to grasp the "own meaning" of a text.

> The concept of "horizon" suggests itself because it expresses the superior breadth of vision that the person who is trying to understand must have....
> We are always affected, in hope and fear, by what is nearest to us, and hence we approach the testimony of the past under its influence. Thus it is constantly necessary to guard against over hastily assimilating the past to our own expectations of meaning. Only then can we listen to tradition in a way that permits it to make its own meaning heard. (Gadamer 1989, 305)

Obviously, this is still a conceptual view of hermeneutic understanding. On the basis of Lacan's insistence on the supposition, according to which this circle is without semantic support, since the meaning is a product of an infinite sliding of the referential surface, Žižek (1976, 75) rejects the hermeneutical circle, which implies the anteriority of the entirety of the semantic horizon in particular statements. In his view, hermeneutics proceeds to the edge of interpretation, but just before reaching it, it covers its eyes for the realization of the fact that there is no original meaning, which could provide a basis for a differential network for the transmission of the reference, because the meaning is always relational.

I do agree that meaning is always relational. Hence, Gadamer's model of the hermeneutical circle, which is based upon a conceptual view of horizons, is indeed problematic. However, instead of mourning over this fact, we should rather search for an un-conceptual foundation of the semantic fusion in the process of interpretation. In my view, Gadamer's paradigm of horizons (which is conceptual in essence) should be replaced through an un-conceptual paradigm, such as *jingjie* 境界 (sphere, atmosphere, aesthetic realm), which has a Buddhist origin and belongs to crucial notions in traditional Chinese metaphysical and literary writings. Hence, in hermeneutical interpretations of Chinese philosophy, we could replace the notion "fusion of horizons" with the term "fusion of *jingjies* or aesthetic realms (境界融合)."

4.1.4 Beyond the Hermeneutic Circle: Fusion of Aesthetic Realms?

This important and typically Chinese aesthetic notion is a hermeneutic means that can help us understand artistic and intellectual creations through the lens of various manifestations of the realm of human life. The *jingjie*—sphere—can only be experienced, but not fully described in concrete language or imagined in purely conceptual thought.

In the beginning, *jingjie* was a term pertaining to geopolitical discourses. Expressing a certain realm limited by boundaries, it was used for mapping out the geopolitical world of ancient China. It evolved into a philosophic-religious discourse of a mental or psychological "territoriality" after it was employed to communicate the Buddhist ideas of spiritual reality and enlightenment in the sense of crossing to the other shore (Han 2014, 86). In other words, the notion of aesthetic realm primarily pertained to the "objective" features of external reality. The internalization of the psychologically transmitted formations of this basic level of *jingjies* is linked to the Buddhist interpretation of its nature. The unification of external and internal elements takes place on the level of transforming these outward formations and images into a specific mental realm (Cheng 1995, 92). According to Christina Han (2014), it further gained many new implications and complex semantic dimensions in the Neo-Confucian discourses of the Song and Ming Dynasties.

In premodern Chinese philosophy, the notion *jingjie* was central to Wang Guowei's[43] (1877–1927) aesthetics. Wang himself defined the concept as follows:

> The "realm" does not only refer to a landscape or scene. The emotions of joy and sorrow, anger, and pleasure also constitute a sort of aesthetic realm in the human heart. (Wang Guowei 2013, 18)[44]

What Wang is referring to in the above quotation is the objectification of psychological state in which the external realm is fused with the inner world. In this way, *jingjie* is a paradigm that appears in order to construct an aesthetic noumenon that manifests something about human life and conveys a certain meaning (Li 2010, 210). In spite of the fact that Wang's theoretical framework was clearly strongly influenced by Western philosophy (especially by Schopenhauer and Nietzsche), it can still be defined as the "revelation of life through the relationship between feeling and scene, and the objectified realm of the artistic subject" (Li Zehou in Samei 2010, xvi). However, this aesthetic realm cannot be reduced to mere integration of feeling and scene, nor to the emotion, sensibility, or motivation of its author or creator. It also implies eliminating the difference between self and the others, and it transcends all utilitarian purposiveness without having to negate the will, desire, and life itself. Therefore, it could also serve as a tool for creating subtle syntheses between traditional Chinese hermeneutic notions, techniques, and approaches on the one hand, and Western philosophies of hermeneutics, on the other hand.[45] As Wang Guowei continues:

> So if a poem captures in words a real scene or a real emotion, it can be said to convey an aesthetic realm. (Wang Guowei 2013, 18)[46]

This is not only true for poetry, painting, or other works of art. Because *jingjie* possesses a noumenal dimension, it can also be discovered in numerous (but certainly not all) good philosophical works. They also contain insights, which convey a philosophical idea not only through conceptual phrases, but rather through that which is engraved between the lines, creating a certain atmosphere, consisting of images, associations, sensations, and emotions, experienced and expressed by their author on the one hand, and perceived and re-experienced by the readers on the other. No wonder that—precisely through the realm of inner experience—philosophy is often linked to literature or poetry. Li Zehou, for instance, has defined it as "science, imbued with poetry" (Li 2016b, 4): as science, it offers us a systematic way of exploring and comprehending reality; as poetry, it walks with us through the opaque jungle of our life, on a long and intimate journey that not only offers us beauty and pleasure, but also forces us to confront fear and melancholy. Philosophy can be a way of life that is rational and artistic at the same time; it not only urges us to search for answers to eternal questions of being, but also to unceasingly raise new ones. It does not remain limited to discovering the world, but also allows for its ongoing creative change. *Jingjie* or the aesthetic realm might be one of the most typical hermeneutic paraphernalia of philosophy that was created in China. Because it seems that precisely here, this affinity and subtle closeness between the philosophical depths of rationality and sensitivity could come to life and find its untroubled home—even when it comes to the ultimate existential concerns:

> *Jingjie*, attained through literary appreciation, is the sudden realization and cognition of ultimate reality that embodies the principle of truth, goodness, and beauty simultaneously. The experience contained in *jingjie* is not only aesthetic, but religious and existentialistic as well. Our close reading of Wang's remarks on *jingjie* has revealed the rich spiritual meaning of this concept: the fusion of subject and object through intuition, the consummation of truth, goodness, and beauty, and a deep existential concern. (Wu 2002, 450)

To a certain extent or in certain aspects, *jingjie* can be compared to Heidegger's understanding of "moods" (or attunements),[47] which, for him, reveal the Being of *Dasein*, for according to him, *Dasein* is always in an attunement; the world is discovered in a mood (Heidegger 1996, 126ff, 313ff). It is a very basis on which we can establish our being-in-the-world. In other words, moods establish *how we find ourselves in the world.* Similar to Heidegger's moods, aesthetic realms or jingjies represent a pre-subjective and pre-objective sense of being-in-the-world. Hence, it is completely clear that *jingjie* is not a conceptual, paradigm, but one that can at the most be grasped through situational, contextual approaches. Hence, like Chinese language and Chinese philosophy, interpretations through aesthetic realms are always linked to contexts, as much as concrete experiences. I will try to illustrate such a holistic contextual interpretation with the help of two essays from Zhuangzi. For this purpose, let us first take a closer look to Zhuangzi's famous essay about the seabird:

> Have you not heard of this? Once upon a time, on the outskirts of the land of Lu, a bird of paradise appeared. The Emperor of the land of Lu received

it with the highest honors and expressed his heartfelt welcome to it. He had it transferred to the highest temple, treated it to the most select wines, and offered it the most enchanting music to please it. He had a good number of cattle and sheep slaughtered and he organized a sumptuous banquet. But the bird remained gloomy and depressed, not taking a bite to eat or a sip to drink. After three days, it died, just like that. This is what happens if one feeds birds with food for humans instead of food for birds. Those who know how birds should receive food suitable for them, would have let the bird fly into deep woods, where it would rest on trees. They would have let it fly merrily above sandy ground and soar above rivers and lakes. They would have let it hunt for its own food and feast on the small fish that it likes. It would have followed its flock, and stopped and rested wherever it pleased. It would have complete freedom of movement. Birds are most bothered by human voices. If symphonies of the greatest human musicians were played somewhere in the wild, birds would immediately fly away, all wild beasts would flee and fish would hide in the deepest waters. However, when humans hear such music, they gather around it and enjoy it. Fish can only live in water, but people die in it. Since man and fish have different properties, what they hate and love differs as well. The ancient wise men did not measure individual features of ability and behaviour with the same criteria. The name is created before the reality. Meaning is effected through appropriateness. To follow these principles brings happiness and satisfaction. (*Zhuangzi* s.d., Zhi le, 5)[48]

That which is not a bird, therefore, cannot simply judge on its own and conclude that what is best for them is best for birds. This is a Daoist critique of the Golden rule, advocated by the Confucians, which finds its most famous expression in the advice "not to impose on others what you would not wish done to yourself" (*Lunyu* s.d., Yan Yuan, 2).[49] We must be aware of the fact that we are parts of different worlds, living in different realities.

But let us return to the basic message of the story. Because I am not a bird, I cannot inherently know the likes and dislikes of birds. This, naturally, is merely an assumption of Zhuangzi's method of perception and communication. It is not, by any stretch, a system of logical systematization. In Zhuangzi's basic work, his friend Hui Shi always represents the basic type of argumentation, which attempts to derive logical, universally valid conclusions from assumptions. And in doing so, naturally, he often makes himself abundantly ridiculous. If humans cannot know birds, since we are not birds, shouldn't it

Methods and Approaches 119

also apply that we cannot know fish, since we are not fish? Or, translated into logical inferences:

P1: Humans can not know birds.
P1: Zhuangzi is human.

C: Zhuangzi cannot know birds.

P1: Humans can not know fishes.
P1: Zhuangzi is human.

C: Zhuangzi cannot know fishes.

However, Zhuangzi is not quite convinced that it is all that simple. Let us listen to an anecdote from the *Autumn Water* section in Zhuangzi's *External Chapters*.

Zhuangzi and Huizi are strolling on a bridge over the Hao river. Zhuangzi
   says: How easily the white fish swims to and fro—this is the joy of fish!
Huizi says: But you are not fish, so where can you know what is the joy of fish??
Zhuangzi then says: But you are not me, so how can you know that I do not
   know what is the joy of fish?
Huizi says: I am not you, therefore I cannot understand you; but you are also
   not fish, and therefore you cannot understand fish. That is all.
Zhuangzi says: Well, then, let's go back to the beginning. You asked me:
   Where can you know what is the joy of fish? So at the time you asked me
   that, you must have known that I knew what is the joy of fish. Well, I knew
   this on this bridge over the Hao river (*Zhuangzi* s.d., Qiu shui, 13).[50]

Hmm. Was Zhuangzi here playing with sophisms? He has obviously been playing with words, for the Chinese interrogative *an* 安 can refer to time, space, or manner. It can thus mean *what, how, when,* or *where*. If it was understood in the latter sense, Zhuangzi provided a proper answer. However, if one takes into account the sociocultural context of traditional China at the time when this work was (or is supposed to have been) created, we will readily think that Zhuangzi truly wanted to say something more meaningful with this anecdote, and to impart a message.

Of course, the following is only my subjective interpretation of the two stories—one under many, many others.[51] But since we have already rejected the idea of an absolute text or an absolute meaning, we also have to question the notion of an absolute interpretation. However, the real reason for my adding more water to this flood is because with these interpretations, I would like to demonstrate how a new meaning and understanding can be acquired through the method of unifying (fusing) the aesthetic realms (*jingjies*) that can be experienced in these two separated anecdotes, without relying on their strictly conceptual connotations.

If we try to connect and understand both stories in this way, namely considering the broader essential context of which they are both a part, we can easily see that they are both dealing with human relations (or relations between living beings in general). In Lao Sze-kwan's view, the "fundamental source" of both stories would probably be linked to the question of the nature of intersubjectivity. The common ground in both debates is namely doubtless connected to this problem. It shows us, to speak with Ram Adhar Mall (2000, 6), that, in our attempt to understand one another, we meet to differ and differ to meet.

The first essay emphasizes differences between different beings. If one desires the well-being of everything that exists, one must—according to Zhuangzi—first get used to the fact that we are all different. Only on the basis of knowing this fact, that is, the fact that we all live in different worlds, can one create close mutual contacts. (This—implicitly and latently proposed—fusion of *jingjies* could apply to contacts and relations between birds and people, as well as those between sinologists and the Chinese, or between authors and readers.)

The creation of such contacts and communication, in turn, proves again that we all live in a single, unified world, as the second essay shows. Zhuangzi's comprehension of the joyfulness of fishes resulted from the entire context in which the fishes were observed. Zhuangzi was joyfully strolling in friendly nature, accompanied by his best friend, and he enjoyed the whole situation, of which the fishes were also a part. Hence, his joyfulness could not be separated from the fishes and vice versa. It was precisely this very unification in joy (a fusion of these joyful *jingjies*), which made his innate, complete, and comprehensive understanding of fishes possible.

The aesthetic realms experienced in both stories can show us very clearly that, ultimately, it is human individual subjectivity, which determines what should be regarded as a genuine relationship. The apparent objectivity and independence of the human rational mind has repeatedly been proven to be a false, illusory chimera, which only leads to self-deception. The ruler of Lu from the first essay will never understand the genuine nature of seabirds. But if he tries to experience the aesthetic realm of their existence, and accepts the fact that this realm is different and separated from the realm which limits, defines, and determines his own existence, he could experience a fusion of both aesthetic realms, a fusion that is rooted in separation and difference. The happy fishes from the second essay show through the very fact of their happiness that these differences and separations are the keys to any genuine, vital and creative unity, because a fusion of aesthetic realms is always conditioned by diversity.

Hence, intersubjective understanding is not conditioned by the criteria of objectivity (with agreed-upon names) but rather by the thing itself, that is, by understanding and experiencing the aesthetic realms in which they are embedded. The dynamics of being limited to the intimate world of an individual, on one side, and muddled, continuous merging of all individual worlds into a single one, on the other, permeates our existence and positions us in what we call "time and space." And finally, the fusion of their individual aesthetic realms is precisely the starting point for constructing a tiny bridge of understanding, connecting Zhuangzi and his reader.

4.2 Problems of Transcultural Comparative Philosophy

In recent decades, the method of comparative philosophy has been the subject of many heated debates. Some scholars believe that in principle any philosophy is comparative, for "comparison in general is a basic function/apparatus of critical thinking, which characterizes philosophy" (Ouyang 2018, 244). It certainly holds true that contrasting, that is, distinguishing between and associating different concepts and categories as well as lines, patterns, and models of reasoning belong to the basic features of any form of reasoning, for thinking as such is based upon contrasting objects and forms. However, comparison is a cognitive method that goes beyond simple contrastive procedures and principally surpasses them. In this sense, the term "comparative philosophy" is neither tautological nor redundant (Li Chengyang 2016, 534). However, recent controversies in academic circles have clearly shown that the concept of comparison as such is a rather problematic one. In addition, they have made clear the fact that the very process of comparing different philosophies as such is necessarily linked to numerous methodological problems, which have hitherto not been comprehensively reflected upon and are thus still far from being solved. These problems are certainly even more complex when dealing with transcultural philosophical comparisons. The following citation is one of the many different formulations of these tricky issues and the possible underlying reasons for them:

> The fact that comparative philosophy deals with thought systems of different cultural provenance necessitates a different methodological approach than in the case of focusing on a single philosophical tradition. Comparative methodology is deeply concerned with revealing possible conceptual and heuristic (in)commensurabilities in order to produce a unifying discourse supervening on them. In other words, we have a unifying methodology built on culturally discrete materials. . . . Second, although comparative philosophy creates space where different philosophical traditions can be encapsulated in one philosophical language, it treats the material it works on as culturally discrete. (Banka 2016, 605)

But unfortunately, the problem goes even further, especially in the realm of comparing Chinese and Euro-American philosophies. This is not only connected to the fact that we have a "unifying methodology built on culturally discrete materials." The core problem is that the methodology in question is a system underlying one of the philosophies under comparison, namely the Western one. There is no third, "objective" methodology. And the same applies to the abovementioned "one philosophical language." Because of this, all transcultural philosophical comparisons are rooted in the "now well-known but still persisting (political) reality of overall Western-centric academics" (Coquereau 2016, 152). This is even more troublesome if we reflect upon the fact that genuine and coherent philosophical comparison cannot be limited to the level of paralleling and describing differences and commonalities of different abstract entities. In this sense, transcultural comparative philosophy is certainly more than just

> the erecting, detecting, smudging, and tearing down of borders, borders between philosophical traditions coming from different parts of the world, different time periods, different disciplinary affiliations, and even within a single period and pedigree, between opposite or at least distinguishable persuasions. Philosophical comparisons, more often than not, separate and

connect at the same time what are very likely or unlikely pairs of, or entire sets of, *comparanda* (that which we set out to compare). (Chakrabarti and Weber 2016, 2)

Any comparative discourse or procedure which aims to provide new knowledge, must therefore also include interpretations, evaluations, and hence judgments. In transcultural comparisons, these evaluations are necessarily linked to the abovementioned problems of Western-centric methodology and its axiological presumptions. Therefore, the relatively common supposition of comparative philosophy as a discourse that establishes fruitful interrelations and dialogues between different traditions is not only idealist, but also superficial and, hence, it "may not turn out to be the magic formula to which all comparison can be reduced" (Chakrabarti and Weber 2016, 2).

4.2.1 From Fusion Philosophy to Philosophy of Sublation

On the basis of thorough reflections and analyses of such axiological and conceptual issues, Arindam Chakrabarti and Ralph Weber propose the idea of "fusion philosophy" (Chakrabarti and Weber 2016, 6) as an innovative method to transform traditional comparative philosophy by surpassing its limitations and fixing its inconsistencies. "Fusion philosophy" means cross-cultural philosophizing rather than doing comparative philosophy. In other words, it means "philosophically comparing" rather than merely "comparing philosophies." This challenging idea is based upon a self-critical account of comparative philosophy that has been long overdue. The argument advanced by Chakrabarti and Weber provides us with a sound and ambitious definition for the future of such a new model of cross-cultural philosophies (Coquereau 2016, 152).

However, the notion of fusion seems to be a rather unlucky terminological choice, for it refers to the process or result of joining two or more things together to form a single entity. It is often even associated with the process of melting, which normally results in a unity in which particular elements of the two or more entities that have been melted (or fused together) become completely unrecognizable and are essentially alienated. The amalgamated unity, which arises through a fusion, is, of course, a qualitatively new substance. Now, if we consider fusion as a metaphor for a certain mode of philosophical reasoning, then we have to admit that new philosophical insights are always based upon new cognitive substances. Yet, genuine philosophizing as a creative process can hardly be based upon an amalgamated unity of distorted elements, for it must be based upon certain discrete philosophical grounds.

Instead, we might consider denoting this new methodological transformation with the notion of synthesis philosophy. Synthesis is also a qualitatively new stage of development, and one in which some elements of the two or more entities from which it arises are preserved, and others discarded. However, precisely in philosophy the term synthesis is often overburdened with the orthodox Hegelian view, in which synthesis is a result of two reciprocally excluding and mutually contradictive entities, while comparisons can include both distinctions and commonalities of the *comparanda*. An additional (and perhaps even more severe) problem arises when we consider the mechanistic nature of such dialectical processes, which seem to develop through and by themselves and to proceed more or less automatically from one stage to the next. Thus, a "synthesis philosophy" would probably mostly be seen as something that fails to provide space for new conceptions created by individual minds.

Although the term "sublation" also forms a part of Hegelian lines of thought and could hence be problematic, it is still much less deflated. It encompasses, on the other hand, all three notions that are of crucial importance for any process of creating something new from interactions between two or more different objects or phenomena. In this philosophical sense, it has the three connotations of arising, eliminating, and preserving. Besides, in contrast to "synthesis," the notion of "sublation" refers to a process rather than a stage. Because of all these reasons, I believe a "sublation philosophy" could better and more precisely denote new forms of cross-cultural philosophizing than the term "fusion philosophy" proposed by Chakrabarti and Weber. But ultimately, this is only a question of nomenclature. In spite of the importance of precise designations, what finally counts is certainly the actuality rather than its name.

However, until now, I have only introduced sublation philosophy as an abstract theoretical concept. If I want to bring it to life, I have to show how it can be applied in intercultural philosophical interactions and the ways in which it can possibly lead to new philosophical insights.

Hence, in the following, I intend to demonstrate and concretely exemplify the application of the method of "sublation philosophy" to reinterpret and hopefully clarify some of the complex philosophical intersections between the philosophies of the two of the most influential modern Western thinkers,

Immanuel Kant and Karl Marx, through the lens of interpretations and theoretical developments proposed by the well-known contemporary Chinese theoretician Li Zehou. In this distinct context, Li's sublation of the interaction between the theoretical systems of the two aforementioned German philosophers might also shed some new light upon the question of the precarious relation between apriorism and empiricism. In my view, this relation belongs to the core parts of both differences and similarities that manifest themselves in any contrastive view upon the dominant developmental streams of Chinese and Euro-American philosophy. And, with a bit of luck, this method will also reveal the reasons for these variances, as well as the fact that they can be tracked down to some important paradigmatic differences underlying their respective referential frameworks.

However, my intention of epitomizing the method of sublation on a discrete example is not limited to the revealing of such system-related variances.[52] It does not remain encapsulated into a framework of traditional comparative philosophy in the sense of "identity construction in the face of those who seem different" (Moeller 2018, 32), nor in the sense of "cultivating attitudes toward and a semantics of inclusion" (Moeller 2018, 32) of the "Other," but rather seeks to achieve a complementary relation between many different elements and aspects of transcultural philosophy in a way that can arouse manifold inspirations for new forms of understanding and philosophically co-creating realities.

Therefore, such an endeavour might be worthwhile; even though much (perhaps too much) light has already been shed upon the basic epistemological problem regarding the relation between apriorism and empiricism, such a cross-cultural perspective may offer us a new dimension of their mutual interaction.

In order to illustrate this theoretical methodology, the last two sections of this chapter will be devoted to an illustration of the proposed comparative method. In the following, we will therefore take a look at Li Zehou's, Kant's and Marx's theories through the lens of sublation philosophy.

4.2.2 Transformation of the Empirical into the Transcendental

Li Zehou is one of the most influential contemporary Chinese philosophers. Most often, his central work has been viewed as a philosophy in which the basic framework of Kant's theory was placed upon a social and materialist foundation, and which simultaneously recovered the original Marxist definition of human beings as "*homo faber.*" Yet, while Li Zehou agrees with Marx's emphasis on the primary importance of objective conditions, productive forces, and the material base, he essentially diverges from orthodox Marxism in his conviction that the objective content of human practice cannot be separated from all those factors that constitute human beings as autonomous subjects, especially their creativity, innovativeness, and inclination to act. Li Zehou has tried to fix this Marxian inconsistency with the help of Kantian philosophy, aiming to provide a link between Marx's idea of a "humanized nature" on the one hand, and Kant's understanding of the subject on the other. Hence, at a first glance, Li's theory appears as a kind of interaction between, or even a synthesis of, Marx and Kant.

As soon as one digs a bit deeper into Li Zehou's theory, however, it quickly becomes clear that its Marxist provenance is more or less limited to the basic historic materialist framework. On the other hand, however, an analysis of the Marxist framework which underpins Li's philosophy also reveals several striking similarities which undoubtedly connect it with traditional Chinese, and especially Confucian, discourses. In his later, mature work, Li himself has often clearly revealed and emphasized these commonalities (see, for instance, Li Zehou 1980, 78–9; 1992, 10; 2010, 8; 2016b, 196, 205ff).

But if we now try to compare Li's philosophy with those of his greatest "Western" inspirations, then it is certainly his relation to Kant—rather than the one to Marx—which first raises our interest. By unfolding and mutually contrasting the elementary groundworks of Kant's and Li's systems, we can find rich and diverse material for stimulating contrastive analyses that can lead to promising and possibly innovative results.

Numerous scholars who tried to grasp and analyse Li Zehou's thought from the angle of comparative philosophy have therefore aimed to posit it into a constructive contrast to Immanuel Kant's theory. Such a scheme appeared as an interesting way to approach their theories from different perspectives and in this way to shed new light on certain general issues regarding the nature of human perception and comprehension of external reality.

Let us try to look upon these two philosophical systems in a way that allows us to overcome certain loops and traps illuminated in all recent debates about the methodological problems arising from traditional comparative intercultural philosophy. If we want to apply the method of sublation philosophy in this process of parallel investigations and bring them into a fruitful mutual interaction, we must, as indicated before, ground our methodological schema in the awareness of manifold basic dissimilarities between different frameworks of reference that have defined the theories of each of these two philosophers. Namely, in spite of the overall cosmopolitan nature of his work, Li Zehou's philosophy is—obviously in contrast to Kant's—still rooted in the specifically Chinese theoretical and methodological approaches, which have been delineated in the first chapter of this book. This means that we have to fully consider the all-inclusive nature of this characteristic which thoroughly underlies and permeates Li Zehou's thought and has far-reaching consequences.

The question of gradual conversion of empirical elements into universal mental forms belongs to the key issues by which Li Zehou has altered and transformed Kant's views on pure and practical reason, on the very nature of perception and cognizance, and also on the autonomous human subject and his or her actions. The process of transforming the empirical into the transcendental can be seen as a kind of synthesis of empiricism and rationalism. This transformation takes place in the process of evolutionary sedimentation, in which the experiences of the entire humankind are being transformed into the transcendental forms incorporated in the cultural-psychological formations of each individual mind (Li Zehou 2016a, 1140).

In this view, all forms of understanding are a priori only from the viewpoint of the individual; from the viewpoint of humankind, they are derived from experience, and are therefore a posteriori (Li 1999a, 175–6), for they were gradually shaped through the practice of the human species over millions of years. In this context, he redefined Kant's a priori formations (i.e., the pre-empirical faculties of the human mind, which help us to perceive and to order elements of our sense impressions) mainly by borrowing and applying to this discourse the dialectical methodology of early Marx. This theory of "psycho-sedimentation" (Li 1999a, 175–6) is based on the Marxian concept of practice and is, on the other hand, also comparable to Piaget's view (1969, 356), according to which forms of logic and mathematics, for instance, come from the abstraction of practice-related activities.

It is often claimed that in this respect Li's theory can be considered as an upgrading or a completion of Kant's philosophy (Ding 2002, 248). Nonetheless, in terms of philosophical reflection, this can hardly be the case, because Kant himself has repeatedly warned against a mingling of the empirical with the rational:

> I here ask only whether the nature of the science does not require the empirical part always to be carefully separated from the rational, placing ahead of a genuine (empirical) physics a metaphysics of nature, and ahead of practical anthropology a metaphysics of morals, which must be carefully cleansed of everything empirical, in order to know how much pure reason could achieve in both cases; and from these sources pure reason itself creates its teachings *a priori*, whether the latter enterprise be carried on by all teachers of morals (whose name is legion) or only by some who feel they have a calling for it. (Kant 2001, 5)

Therefore, Li's aim to synthesize the two approaches (or disciplines) within this process of transformation is rooted in the holistic, "one-world" nature of Chinese philosophical tradition, the existence of which has not been acknowledged by most of the traditional European thinkers, including Kant himself:

> That which mixes those pure principles among empirical ones does not even deserve the name of a "philosophy" (for this distinguishes itself from common rational cognition precisely by the fact that what the latter conceives only as mixed in, it expounds in a separate science), still less of a "moral philosophy," because precisely through this mixture it violates the purity of morals and proceeds contrary to its own end. (Kant 2001, 6)

Irrespective of what one might think of such approaches, it is pretty clear that Li's "transformation of the empirical into the transcendental"[53] is by no means an element that could be directly compatible with, or even assimilated into, Kant's transcendental philosophy. Hence, it seems certainly better and more suitable to categorize Li's ethical system as a theory which rests on completely different paradigms that are not comparable to (and even less compatible with) the ones that determine Kant's referential framework. Instead of speaking about Li's theory as a system, based upon Kantian approaches, one could rather presuppose that for Li Zehou, Kant's philosophy was but a valuable source of inspiration.

Li Zehou has explicated the theoretical grounds of such transcendental notions with the help of his own interpretation of Kant's epistemology:

Kant's "transcendental reason" is a uniquely human form of perception and cognition. Where does it come from? Kant has never answered this question. He merely stated that "transcendental" is prior to experience. With my elaboration on the problem of "how is the humankind possible," I have replied to Kant's question: "How is the faculty of thought itself possible." In this context, I have proposed the notion of experience transforming into the transcendental. The transcendental forms of the individual are shaped through the historical sedimentation of experiences.... Heidegger explained the famous Kantian problem of the unknown common origin of sensitivity and cognition as originating in the transcendental imagination, but I believe it is a result of producing and using tools, i.e., of vital practice. Sensitivity arises from individual sensitive experiences of practice, and cognition from psychological forms shaped by the practices of the humankind. (Li Zehou and Liu Xuyuan 2011, 77)

Although there is thus no supernatural or metaphysical origin of human cognition, it is also not simply established in one-to-one correspondence by an empirical world. The transformation of the empirical into the transcendental is a dynamic, nonlinear, and long-lasting procedure, evolving through and within human beings over millions of years, which takes place in their concrete and tangible world. In addition, this process offers human beings possibilities of consciously restraining their natural inclinations, instincts, and desires and adapting their behaviour in accordance with social norms. It leads to the condensation of reason.[54] In such a framework, there is no room for any isolated forms of pure reason, nor for any independent kinds of practical reason in the Kantian sense. Li's pragmatic reason,[55] on the other hand, is an assortment of both types; it is rational and practical at the same time and therefore, it belongs to both epistemology and ethics.

In this framework, no transcendental form can exist independent of experience. The transcendental arises from the empirical through sedimentation, and reason is therefore nothing mysterious but rather something constructed from the historical practices of humankind. Through their formal qualities, these practices are sedimented into human psychological formations. As already mentioned, in Li's view these processes are not only primarily linked to epistemology, but even more to ethics. The transformation of the empirical into the transcendental helps us understand Li's interpretation of the categorical imperative. Just like the classical Chinese concepts of the coherent cosmic structure[56] or inherent knowledge,[57] it is absolute and universal, but simultaneously, it is a result of an incorporative process, which leads from external norms to internal values.

On such basis, it is easier to investigate the grounds of Li's transformation of the empirical into the transcendental. Because of space limitations, however, we cannot go deeper into these issues. But in order to enhance your understanding of the very groundworks of this transformation, and to provide a solid basis for our later reinterpretation of Li's interactions with Kant, I have first to clarify some terminological questions.

In Kant's philosophy, the terms "a priori," "transcendental," and "transcendent" have different meanings. In his *Critique of the Pure Reason*, he explained a priori knowledge as knowledge that does not rely on any kind of experiences. It means "before experiencing," and refers to necessary truths (or knowledge) that are independent of reason. Kant has also clearly and unambiguously defined the notion of transcendental:

> I call all cognition transcendental that is occupied not so much with objects but rather with our a priori concepts of objects in general. A system of such concepts would be called transcendental philosophy. (Kant 1998, 133)

Here, "transcendental" means the necessary conditions for the possibility of every experience. Some a priori truths also refer to transcendental conditions, for example, time and space, basic categorical judgments, or the law of causality. In his *Critique of Judgement*, Kant associated "transcendental" principles with "those, through which we represent *a priori* the universal condition under which alone things can become objects of our cognition generally" (Kant 1911, 181). Hence, the term transcendental refers to that which enables the human mind to constitute concepts, and thus to experience them as objects. In contrast to everyday knowledge, which is knowledge of objects, transcendental knowledge is knowledge of how human beings experience those objects as objects. Kant believes that our consciousness provides us with structures that make this kind of experience possible. The human mind generates both such structures and its own unity through a synthesis.

The term transcendence, on the other hand, refers to that which has surpassed the limits of physical existence and does not necessarily depend on it. The differentiation between the transcendental and transcendent designates the boundary between theoretical knowledge and mere thought, for beyond all possible experience we cannot have theoretical knowledge but can only think. For Kant, the "transcendent," as opposed to the "transcendental," is that which lies beyond what our cognitive ability can reasonably know. In this context, Li emphasizes the important role of experience in the functioning of transcendental structures.

> I certainly believe Kant has paid close attention to experience. In Kant's theory, the transcendental is different from the transcendent. The transcendental is transcendental precisely because on the one hand it precedes experience, but on the other hand it cannot be separated from it. Therefore he wrote at the very beginning of his Critique of the Pure Reason that all began with experience, but experience could not be equated to knowledge. Kant's transcendental categories tell us precisely this, namely, that there can be no science without experience. (Li Zehou and Yang Guorong 2014, 125)

Li reveals that the realm of transcendence is illusionary but still has a positive influence on people, for it provides them with ideals and enhances their activity (Li Zehou and Liu Yuedi 2017, 8). On the other hand, he points out that, due to Kant's dualistic worldview, his noumenon is also a transcendent notion:

> For him, noumenon and reason are without origin and they are simultaneously higher than humankind. Hence, we can speak here about a two-world view. However, I have established a different concept of the thing-in-itself. For me, it is material substance that exists as a synergetic interaction between the universe and human beings. Such a conceptualization is directly linked to my "one-world view," in which both of them are parts of one world. Since they still belong to this one and the same world, this is not a contradiction. (Li Zehou and Liu Yuedi 2017, 8)

In such a context, it becomes clear that Li understands and applies Kant's notion of transcendentality in a different way. In a one-world paradigm, transcendence in the sense of surpassing one world and existing in another is impossible. Hence, Li concludes that in Chinese philosophy there is no transcendence (*chaoyue* 超越) but instead detachment (*chaotuo* 超脱).

But while the Chinese one-world paradigm cannot include transcendence (*chaoyue* 超越), it certainly includes a kind of transcendentality (*chaoyan* 超驗). Li's conceptualization of transforming the empirical into the transcendental is a processual account of the elementary construction of such transcendentality. In this framework, Li has tried to elaborate on some of Kant's central concepts. In this process, he aimed to replace certain "problematic" definitions of such concepts with others that have—in his view—better expressed their positioning into the schema of a processional, dynamic, and materialistic-historical development.

4.2.3 A Dynamic Sublation of Statics

Li's philosophy is rooted in a referential framework, which reminds us in many aspects of the basic paradigmatic network determining the dominant streams of traditional Chinese philosophies. It is holistic, but structured in accordance with binary categories that function through the principle of correlative complementarity. But its main characteristics, perhaps, can be found in its dynamic, processual, and contextual nature, which also belong to the main specific features of the Confucian framework.

In this theoretical reevaluation of Kantian philosophy, Li placed its central framework upon a social and materialist foundation by simultaneously incorporating into it the original Marxist definition of human beings as *homo faber*, that is, as living beings developed through practice and their ability to make and to use tools in a systemic, continuous way. This processual view, which is—in this dynamic aspect—similar to the basic paradigms of traditional Confucian philosophy, allowed him to create an innovative approach to the question of empiricism and transcendentality. In Li Zehou's system, the concepts of the empirical and the transcendental interact in a dynamic, correlative, and mutually complementary way. They are both parts of a processual philosophy in which movement is always followed by a standstill. In such a worldview, they always appear as two different, but essentially interrelated and interdependent, realms of life.

Kant's transcendental forms, on the other hand, are pure and perfect, like frozen images of a timeless world. Even though the empirical sphere is discrete and multifarious, composed of innumerable different moments and countless particularities, it cannot influence the sacred realm of pure rationality. If it could, its impact would have devastating consequences for the entire system of Being, which can only exist without permanent contact with the manifold and changeable varieties of being. Therefore, Kant's system is completely incompatible with Li Zehou's philosophy.

But Li's own system, on the other hand, can readily borrow and apply concepts and ideas from the one created by Kant (just as he could borrow and apply many Marxian concepts and ideas). This asymmetry is possible due to the simple fact that dynamic systems can incorporate static components, but not vice versa. In this sense, Li's philosophy can truly be seen as a sublation of Kant's transcendental theory and Marx's historical materialism. It elevates the apparent contradiction between the empirical and the transcendental to a new dynamic unity, without becoming Kant's worst nightmare, namely a "jack-of-all-trades" (Kant 2001, 4) by directly and thoughtlessly "mixing" the principles of pure reason among those derived by experience.

And this sublation is something that can allow for and enhance many further insights into the specific features of Chinese philosophy, especially in regard to its relation to other (particularly "Western") philosophical systems. It might also help us to answer the question, which has been often raised in the context of comparative intercultural philosophy, of why there is such an asymmetry between the Chinese knowledge of Western philosophy and vice versa. Most of the relevant Western works are translated into Chinese very soon after they have been published in their original languages. But in the Western cultural areas, the situation is completely different:

> There is and continues to be a profound asymmetry in comparative studies. We enter a Chinese bookstore or a Chinese library, and all of the most recent world scholarship is being made available in accurate and accessible Chinese translations. We enter a European or American bookstore or library, and never mind recent Chinese scholarship, but even the monumental works of the greatest minds of Chinese philosophy and culture are absent. (Ames 2020, 1)

Most of the Western prejudices against Chinese philosophy, such as the ones discussed in the beginning of this book, can be seen as arising from such a truly remarkable ignorance and, simultaneously, as their result. As we have seen, the superficial understanding or, to put it more bluntly, the widespread misunderstanding of ancient Chinese texts, continues to hold sway in Western theories on China. Among others, one reason for this situation has to do with the history of sinology as such. The earliest translations of original Confucianist and Daoist texts were the products of Western missionaries who often interpreted them through the lens of Western concepts and methodologies. Another reason for these prejudices might be found in the fact that there are still almost no translations of later philosophical sources in Western languages. While many classical works from the pre-Qin era have been repeatedly translated, the West still does not know much about philosophy from later periods, in which Chinese philosophers began to create systematic theories. With some rare exceptions, the main works of Han and Wei-Jin theoreticians are yet to be rendered into Western languages. Even the pinnacles of medieval Chinese philosophy, namely the Neo-Confucian discourses from the Song and Ming Dynasties, are practically unknown in the Western academia, and the same holds true for almost the entire opus of premodern Chinese philosophy. Considering all this, it is easier to understand why Western scholars have often criticized Chinese as lacking any systematic theory.

Confucius, for instance, lived at a time in which the ancient Greek pre-Socratic philosophy was being developed. And as is well known, the works of pre-Socratic philosophy are also preserved only in a fragmentary form and do not contain any systematic theory. However, nobody equates Western philosophy with pre-Socratic philosophy. In contrast, the original Confucianism and Daoism from the pre-Qin period are still regarded as the sole representatives of the entire range and history of Chinese philosophical thought.

Now, if we try to find a reason for this epistemological asymmetry, we will soon discover that there are many of them. If we look to the eighteenth and nineteenth centuries, it is obvious that in the process of "importing" modernization to semicolonial China, Western ideas came to the country along with its investment capital and technology. In such a situation, Chinese intellectuals were and remain forced to immerse themselves deeply into the wide oeuvre of traditional and modern Western thought, and to confront its "Otherness."

But even if we try to put aside those aspects of the question delineated in this chapter, which are steadfastly and directly linked to Eurocentric and colonial traditions, there are still many other reasons for this discrepancy. Some of these might not be that tightly connected to strictly political causes, but rather to purely epistemological ones. Sometimes it seems as if this asymmetry or discrepancy is also rooted in an epistemological asymmetry or, in other words, in a discrepancy of mutual understanding. It is, of course, a pretty bold supposition to claim that the Chinese philosophers could understand Western philosophy better than vice versa. However, this supposition does not imply that the "Chinese mind"[58] is smarter or more lucid than the minds that enable people to comprehend reality in other parts of the world. Rather, it points to some elementary dissimilarities between the two respective referential frameworks underlying the "Western" and the traditional Chinese theoretical and philosophical discourses and determining their particular methodologies.

In this sense, the discrepancy appearing in the knowledge and understanding of the "Other" has to do with the aforementioned assertion that dynamic systems are able to integrate the static ones, while the latter cannot assimilate the former. In fact, static phases always appear to be a part of dynamic entities. I will try to illustrate this presumption with the metaphor of human breath, which is a dynamic process consisting of inhaling and exhaling. These two phases are processual; they are determined by motion. However, between them there is always a moment of inert motionless. Without this motionless moment, the entire process of dynamic breath would not be possible, for the dynamics of inhaling and exhaling cannot go uninterrupted and continuous into each other. Hence, static moments are not only contingent, but rather necessary parts of dynamic processes. In other words, without standstill there can be no motion. This is why dynamic systems can integrate the static ones. Because of this reason, it is not only possible, but even natural, for people to understand the notions of unchanging entities from the viewpoint of change. The other way around, however, is much more difficult, because static states never include any kind of motion.

Let us now return to the perspective of different referential frameworks and consider the fact that Kant's philosophical system is embedded in the framework that prevailed in the course of European intellectual history. This framework, and all the particular notions within it, refers to meanings and thought patterns that are based upon the unchanging essence of Being. Here, we must consider the fact that the traditional formal logic which represents the basic laws of reasoning in such a framework would not be possible or valid without the unchanging, eternal semantic kernels by which the meanings of all notions are being defined and determined. Li's system, on the other hand, belongs—in its very essence—to the frameworks that prevailed in the Chinese intellectual tradition. As we have seen, this framework is defined by the everlasting change of all elements constituting reality, including the meanings of all notions. This is also the reason why such frameworks allow for the possibility of the (albeit very gradual) transformation of empirical material into transcendental forms.

The philosophy of sublation is based upon a method which views individual theories or systems of thought under comparison from contrasting angles, simultaneously taking into consideration their respective referential frameworks. In this way, it can facilitate new perspectives through which these theories or systems can be seen. In other words, by enabling us to gain insights into some hitherto unrecognized dimensions of their overall structures, it can offer us new, and perhaps different, understandings of particular concepts embedded in them. The contrasting view described in this chapter allowed us to determine the specific relation between static and dynamic states and their role in constituting the basic paradigms of individual philosophical systems. On this basis, we became able to induct a new view on the relation between empirical and transcendental entities, or matter and form.

In this way, proceeding from contrasting perspectives of different material, the philosophy of sublation can offer us fruitful grounds for gaining access to and developing new paths of reasoning.

Epilogue

Relation as the Core of Understanding

In the previous section, we have already tried to describe the transcultural philosophy of sublation alongside the method of "fusion" as elaborated by Chakrabarti and Weber. But in order to posit it into the context of the respective contemporary discourses, it also has to be placed into a relation with some other newly coined concepts designating the multifarious ways of perceiving and interpreting the world (and the culture, in which the human world is always necessarily embedded). The transcultural philosophy of sublation belongs to methods that have been denoted as "post-comparative philosophy" by Hans-Georg Moeller (2018, 42). This means, on the one side, that it belongs to procedures which are—precisely because of its considerations of the semantic essence which defines different, culturally determined referential frameworks—tightly connected to intercultural philosophical vocabularies (see Ames 2011). More specifically, such vocabularies do "not evolve from within the currently dominating philosophical discourses, but, to the contrary, substantially challenge these discourses by confronting them with an 'alien' semantics" (Moeller 2018, 42). In intercultural reinterpretations of Chinese philosophy, the method of sublation must therefore necessarily include constructions of "new networks of technical terms, metaphors, conceptual ideas, and normative claims" (Moeller 2018, 43) from readings of traditional Chinese texts.

On the other side, this method can only evolve in a historical perspective, that is, in a dialogue with all positive and relevant aspects of what we have learned from the past intercultural comparisons. In this sense, comparative philosophy is, of course, the necessary condition for the post-comparative method, and the latter cannot truly develop by thoroughly negating the former, but rather by engaging in a constructive dialogue with it: "The two dimensions, the comparative and post-comparative, mutually support and influence one another. It is important to see them in conjunction in order to appreciate each of them" (Moeller 2018).

Thirdly, and perhaps most importantly, the transcultural philosophical method of sublation is necessarily founded upon relations, and not only because their paradigmatic bases, that is, different frameworks of reference, are actually relational networks connecting different meanings. Besides, the relational nature of this method manifests itself in its linking particular elements from different systems under investigation into new, mutually transformed entities of information, ideas, knowledge, or even wisdom.

This relational nature of the sublation method fits well into the general nature of characteristic Chinese worldviews. As we have seen, classical Chinese cosmologies are dynamic ontologies of interactive structural networks, in which the universe is made up entirely of mutual relations, and no independent, self-sufficient entity can exist without or beside them (Rošker 2012a, 158). All this is vividly reflected in the basic structure of traditional Chinese society and the corresponding form of ethics, in which the personhood of an individual human being is not constituted by her distinctive personality or his unique character, but rather through their relations with other people (Ames 2016, 141).

In such a framework, human understanding is not conditioned by the normative standards of some objectivity, but rather by the object of recognition itself, including the situational context in which it is embedded. As we have seen, our existence is necessarily permeated by dynamic interactions between our being limited to our individual, subjective, and most intimate world on one side, and the muddled, continuous amalgamations of all our individual worlds into a single one, on the other. Therefore, the philosophy of sublation (along with its dynamic structural underpinning, its consideration of referential frameworks, and its hermeneutics of the *jingjie*-fusion) is by no means the single "most suitable" or even less, the "most proper" method for investigating Chinese philosophy. In the field of transcultural methodologies, it simply represents one of the many possible ways to reconcile universality with particularities.

Creative philosophers will always seek to improve their own methods. Even those who genuinely respect different cultural values, epistemologies, and methodologies will always preserve some of their own preferences, subjective insights, and blind-spots (Bunnin 2003, 352). What really matters are solely their equal opportunities, their evaluation devoid of the seemingly omnipresent relations of economic, political, and cultural power. No matter where they arise, and irrespective of their individual originators, such subjective inclinations should be checked by an equally reliable culture of academic criticism and discussion rather than hushed by demands for strict agreement over methods, theories, and doctrines.

This issue is of special importance for the very understanding of philosophy, which is, in essence, not a tool for finding truth, but rather a means for an endless search for constantly changing truths. The task of philosophy is not to establish an objective and eternally valid truth. Because of the situational and emotional nature of human understanding, these truths necessarily always remain merely partial. As such, philosophy needs to continuously re-open old questions and ask new ones (Rošker 2015, 20). Instead of being a "hardcore science," which implies simple justifications and monotonous confirmations of what already exists, it is and should be a constructive, creative, and unending critique of reality. By unceasingly seeking for new methods and simultaneously by developing, upgrading, and changing the existing methodological procedures, we might gradually obtain an insight into some new, challenging approaches to the understanding of our world. Someday, such approaches might even help us to confront differences by transcending the schemas, defined by deep-seated, ingrown prejudices, against so-called Oriental thought.

Notes

Prologue

1 Given the fact that—due to the necessary unawareness of the problems related to differences in reference frameworks and discursive translations (see sections 1.1.3, 1.2, and 1.3 of the present book)—many early Western translations of Chinese philosophical works were dubious regarding the authentic and accurate transmission of paradigms, categories, and concepts, this might even hold true to a certain extent, although not in Hegel's judicious sense.
2 However, to be honest, we have to admit that they were neither fully (in a clearly distinguishable and unambiguously definable manner) developed in Europe before the enlightenment.
3 玄學 Chinese metaphysic (lit.: The teaching of the Obscure).
4 名學 Chinese semantic logic (lit.: The teaching of the names).
5 窮理格物 (a medieval branch of) Chinese epistemology (lit.: Exhaustive investigation of objects).
6 心性 Moral philosophy of the heart-mind and inner nature.
7 理氣 Ontology, based upon a correlative interaction between dynamic structure/s and vital creativity.

Chapter 1

1 *Zhongguo zhexuede fangfalun wenti* 中國哲學的方法論問題.
2 馮耀明.
3 信念剛落.
4 概念之不可轉移性.
5 Although Kuhn did not speak about referential frameworks, but rather about "paradigms," the meaning of these two terms is, in this context, almost interchangeable.
6 我們都知道，中國人做菜是用圓底鍋的，而西方人則喜歡用平底鍋。對於同樣的材料來說，兩種鍋都可以來煮菜，只是煮出來的菜式有些地方近似，有些地方卻可能極不相同。比如說，兩種鍋都可以用來煎雞蛋，這是二者近似的地方。但二者也有不同的功能，因而有不同的限制，例如平底鍋可以用來煎、炒、炸，卻不能像圓底鍋那樣可用來炆、燉、蒸；反之，圓底鍋又不可以像平底鍋那樣容易在平面上做出各種形狀的菜式。。。。這裏的平底鍋與圓底鍋，正好用來比喻不同的概念架構或理論體系。

7 Eric Nelson (2020, 249) even believes that concept of the "intercultural" is better described as the interaction of lifeworlds instead of cultures.

8 Besides, these terms as such are by no means value free; notions like the Middle-East or the Far-East express the degree of distance from the "Center," which is geographically located in the "West."

9 For a detailed explanation of these notions see section 1.3.1 "One-world view or immanent transcendence?"

10 However, this does by no means diminish the fact that was described as a phenomenon of "delinking" by Amin Samir. This notion is tightly linked to the fact that the privileged pole of the dichotomy can and will never freely give up its advantaged position. Chaibomg Hahm formulates this in the following way: "The most powerful acts of criticism, resistance, and defiance comes from those who have been designated as the 'lesser' of the dichotomies who then embrace and empower that definition, using it as the starting point of their resistance" (Hahm 2000, 103).

11 For example, Caputo 1997, Shohat and Stam 1994.

12 This holds true for general evaluations of many crucial values, the structuring of social relations, aesthetic concepts and political or economic systems. Regarding the central subject of this book, Chinese philosophy, this phenomenon can clearly be observed in the way many Chinese theoreticians are dealing with (and interpreting) the classical sources—namely throughout through the lens of European (or "Western") methodological premises.

13 This "leading historical role" is, of course, limited to the periods of renaissance, the industrial revolution, and the Copernican revolution.

14 Twitchett (1925–2006) was a well known British sinologist. He was a renewed scholar, specialized in Chinese history, and is famous as one of the authors and editors of the *Cambridge History of China*.

15 At the other extreme, the term sinologist is also often used to characterize a rather ridiculous caricature compounded of pedantry and a preoccupation with peripheral and precious subjects of little general significance. However, Denis Twitchett rightly reminds us that the pedantry and the preoccupation with trivia are by no means monopolies of the Sinologist: "A glance through current issues

of journals concerned with Western history or the social sciences on the shelves of any library would lead one to suppose that a vigorous training in one of the disciplines is no more prophylactic against the misemployment of advanced techniques of analysis in the pursuit of unimportant topics" (Twichett 1964, 110).

16 If at all, the term "feudalism" applies in China solely for the Western Zhou period (1046–771 BCE). In Europe, feudalism was determined by the hierarchical relationships between different positions within the nobility, and by the farmers and workers (villeins) who invested their physical labor by which they supported the entire social structure, a part of which were also influential religious leaders. Nobility titles, as well as the position of the villeins, were hereditary, which means that the latter were dependent serfs with respect to their lord. In China, on the other hand, the peasants who cultivated the land of the owners, who belonged to the gentry, were basically free to leave. The system was controlled by the bureaucracy class; the positions within this class were not hereditary. Instead, they were based on a form of "meritocracy," that is, the official examination system. In translating the Western term "feudalism" into their language, the Chinese translators have applied the term "fengjian 封建," which was originally a Confucian and legalist notion describing a decentralized system of government during the Zhou Dynasty, based on four elementary occupations. To increase the confusion, the Chinese version of Marxism has (in order to ensure that China also fitted into the "norm," that is, into the Marxist classification of particular stages of social development) defined the entire traditional and premodern period of Chinese social history as a form of "feudalism."

17 The informers were second grade students of the educational sciences at the Universities of Vienna (50), Ljubljana (50), and Hsinchu (103).

18 Which were, of course, rooted in the different social functions of law in the Chinese and the European societies.

19 張岱年.

20 不同的哲學理論包涵不同的概念, 範疇. 不同的民族的哲學理論, 更是具有不同的概念, 範疇.

21 During the last decade, the term "Ruism" as a new translation for "*ru xue*" also became increasingly common in Western sinology.

22 孔夫子.

23 Numerous sinologists have noted the wider connotational scope of the term *ruxue* 儒學. Roger Ames, for example, has shown how this notion refers to a general classical "scholarly tradition" (see Ames 2015, 5). This, of course, does not mean that Daoist and Buddhist texts were included in the Confucian canon, but only confirms how inextricably intertwined these three major idea

systems were. In most forms of Confucian state orthodoxy, for example, the *Shiji* 史記 and *Hanshu* 漢書, the term *Ru* 儒 basically signifies an expert in the Five Classics. In her book on Confucianism and women, Li-Hsiang Lisa Rosenlee also writes:

> The concept of Ru 儒 . . . denotes the inexact Chinese counterpart of the term Confucianism used by Jesuits in the 18th century. . . . The ambiguity of its semantic origins in ancient, pre-Confucian times obscures the connection between Ru as an intellectual discipline and Confucius, as its most prominent spokesperson. Unlike the term Confucianism—its secularized and simplified representation in the West—the complex term Ru can only be approximated as the teaching of the sages and the worthies wherein the ethical teaching of Confucius—the Supreme sage and the First teacher— forms a part, but an important part nevertheless. (Rosenlee 2006, 4)

24 In considering specific features of traditional Chinese philosophy that are common to all schools of ancient and classical Chinese thought, of primary importance are the concept of transcendence in immanence (or immanent transcendence), binary structured holism which functions by means of binary categories (for example *yin-yang*, *you-wu*, *ti-yong*, *ming-shi*, etc.), as well as the principle of complementarity which represents the method of interactions between both implied antipodes. All these specific features will be treated in more detail in later parts of this book.

25 Except recent developments in comparative (especially Chinese West) philosophy (see for instance Wong 2017), many fruitful contributions to the improvement of such multifarious perspectives and dimensions have been elaborated by the pioneers of intercultural philosophy, for example, Ram Adhar Mall (see Mall 1989; 2000) or Franz Martin Wimmer (see Wimmer 2004).

26 Here, we should by no means commit the sin of mistaking one part of a tradition for the whole. Although Confucianism is a very influential stream of Chinese philosophy, and in spite of the fact that it cannot be clearly separated from Daoism and several other streams of thought, it cannot be identified with Chinese philosophy—just the same as modern European enlightenment philosophy cannot be identified with the entirety of Euro-American philosophical discourses, albeit both of them are representative for the respective traditions and ideational histories.

27 This is probably due to the fact that binary contrasts and patterns are an elementary condition and characteristic of human cognition, as well as of the fact that a dialogue or confrontation between two different ideas is a precondition for the evolution of any thought or understanding.

28 Binary categories (*duili fanchou* 對立範疇) belong to the basic features of traditional Chinese philosophy. Such categories can be seen as dualities that seek to attain a state of actuality through relativity, which is expressed through the relation between two oppositional notions. The mutual interactions between the two poles that form such a category are governed by the principle of correlative complementarity, which belongs to the fundamental paradigms of Chinese reasoning and which, inter alia, led to the formation of patterns of specific Chinese analogous reasoning. Some of the generally best known Chinese binary categories are *yinyang* 陰陽 (sunny and shady), *tiyong* 體用 (essence and function), *mingshi* 名實 (name or concept and actuality), *liqi* 理氣 (structure and phenomena), *benmo* 本末 (roots and branches), etc.

29 In the process of the intensive sinification of Marxism, this feature of the dialectical model, belonging to framework B (which was typical for traditional China), was highly problematized by Maoist theoreticians. Hence, they used to call this form of dialectics "simple" (see Lü Xiaolong 1993, 58) or "primitive" (see Pan Tianhua 1995, 14) dialectics (*pusu bianzheng fa* 樸素辯證法, *yuanshi bianzheng fa* 原始辯證法) and criticized it for its conservative nature, that is, for its lacking the component of progress.

30 Many modern Chinese philosophers have focused upon this difference, aiming to solve the alleged contradiction of simultaneous immanence and transcendence in Chinese philosophy; here, we could mention the controversial Modern Confucian paradigm of "immanent transcendence," which is also linked to Mou Zongsan's concept of "double ontology," or the "One-world" view proposed by Li Zehou.

31 In several philosophical systems belonging to framework A—for instance in Kant's philosophy—it could of course be claimed that ethics is an important part of the human self. But even in such contexts, it is only a part of the noumenal nature of the Self, whereas in framework B it is part and parcel of the self that pertains to a concrete human being in any particular situation of a given human life.

32 李澤厚.

33 一个世界观; According to Li's philosophical system, this view arose from and was developed on the foundation of rationalized shamanism.

34 According to Li Zehou, traditional Chinese culture represents "a culture of pleasure" (*legan wenhua* 樂感文化) as opposed to the Western culture of sin (*zuigan wenhua* 罪感文化) or the Japanese culture of shame (*chigan wenhua* 恥感文化).

35 Some theorists, especially from Taiwan, sometimes prefer to use the term *cunyoulun* 存有論 as a more appropriate translation for ontology.

36 使用理性.
37 新儒學—a stream of thought established at the threshold of the twentieth century. Its main aim is the revival of the Chinese ideational tradition.
38 外在超越性.
39 內在超越性.
40 Here, Lee Ming-Huei is referring to Modern Confucians.
41 當代新儒家常借用 »超越性« 和 »內在性« 這兩個概念來詮釋傳統儒家思想(特別是其天道思想), 強調儒家的天道或基本精神是 »超越而內在«, 以與西方宗教中 »超越而外在« 的基本模式相對比.
42 天道高高在上, 有超越的意義. 天道貫注於人身之時, 又內在於人而為人的性. 這時, 天道又是內在的 (Immanent).
43 如果有 »天命« 的感覺, 首先要有超越感 (Sense of Transcendence), 承認一超越的存在, 然後可說.
44 李明輝.
45 當代新儒家在使用"內在超越"的概念時, 顯然認為, "內在性"與"超越性"這兩個概念在邏輯上並不矛盾, 這就證明他們並非依郝, 安二人所認定的嚴格意義來使用"內在性"一詞. 因此, 郝, 安二人的批評顯然是基於誤解. For the full controversy between Lee, Hall, and Ames, see Lee Ming-huei 2001 and 2002 (especially Chapter 1), as well as Hall and Ames 1987 and 1998 (especially Chapter 9).
46 牟宗三.
47 董仲舒.
48 人心即天心, 人性即神性.
49 體用不二.
50 緊張關係.
51 鄭家棟發現, 牟宗三是由某種"天人相分"即由講述"人不即是天"(承認有某種外在超越對象), 而逐漸轉到"即人即天", 即強調"內在超越", 人的"心性"即"天道"本身上來的. 這樣一來, 人既有此"內在的超越"、心中的上帝, 也就不需要去"畏"那作為對象存在的超越的上帝?
52 所以我說它只是宋明理學在現代的"迴光返照"、"隔世迴響", 構不成一個新的時期, "恐怕難得再有後來者能在這塊基地上開拓出多少真正哲學的新東西來了", "如不改弦更張, 只在原地踏步, 看來已到窮途".
53 陳來.
54 One could certainly presuppose that the human heart-mind is not completely restricted by concrete given sensual experiences, even though it is rooted in the actual limitations of the human physical body. Even according to the strictly materialistic worldview, the human brain has a limitless potential to

construct new, previously inexistent knowledge by shaping new synapses, which arise from innumerable possibilities of new relations between different neurons. Besides, new relational knowledge is also created by every single new idea that is being shaped by the human heart-mind. Since all these relations can occur in countless particular combinations, it could be claimed that human consciousness, that is, the very foundation of the Chinese heart-mind, is epistemologically and axiologically infinite. In this sense it is immanent, but in this immanence there is also the possibility of transcendence. (Hence, following Levine, Husserl, and Whitehead, some scholars also translate the Chinese term *neizai chaouye* 內在超越 as "transcendence in immanence," instead of "immanent transcendence," which seems to be a more appropriate translation.)

55 劉述先.
56 公曰：「敢問君子何貴乎天道也？」孔子對曰：「貴其『不已』。
57 Although this model is by no means dualistic, it is still binarily structured and dynamic. Hence, we could also consider it as a kind of an alterable model in which pairs of entities (no matter whether they belong to objects, qualities, patterns, or realms) can interact according to the correlative principle of complementarity. In such a model, immanence and transcendence are indeed not necessarily in a mutual contradiction—although they are, of course, in mutual opposition. Here, immanence is (similar to Confucianism) demarcated by a forceful ability of assimilation, which enables it to integrate within itself its dual opposition (whereby this opposition cannot be equated with negation), and therefore to unite within itself all their mutual differences. In this continuously changing dynamic correlative holistic model, immanence is hence (similar to Confucianism in relation to Daoism) still dominant; however, in Chinese philosophy, both realms can still be seen as mutually interdependent and complementary.
58 徐復觀.
59 道德本心, 道德自我.
60 The "Chinese" (*Han ren*) were first mentioned as a people with a distinct culture during the early centuries of the Zhou Dynasty (1066–221 BCE). While we cannot speak of state borders in the modern sense, this term indicates that already at that early date there existed a clear boundary between the agrarian culture of the Chinese Dynasties and various nomadic tribes. The emerging Chinese civilization was also linked to a unified cultural domain by the language and script, which the rulers of the Zhou Dynasty took over from the cultures of the Shang (Yin) Dynasty and introduced throughout their territories. The bronze

inscriptions of the Zhou period with their long texts simplified the ideographs, reduced strokes, and standardized the characters. From the mid-Zhou period on, bamboo slips became a widespread writing material. However, the characters still differed from region to region, for the script became standardized only with the unification of the empire in 221 BCE.

61 While the nomadic origin of the Zhou continues to be debated in both the Chinese academic world and in Western sinology, strong support for this thesis can be found in the chapter "Zhou benji" of *Shi ji (Historical Notes,* see next footnote). In their philosophical and religious approaches, the representatives of the second generation generally subscribed to Xu Fuguan's historical researches, especially those found in the chapter "The pre-Qin Period (Xian Qin bian)" in his study *The History of Human Nature Theories in China (Zhongguo renxing lun shi).* For my own part, in the present study I will focus primarily on the interpretations of the Modern Confucian scholars.

62 后稷卒，子不窋立。不窋末年，夏后氏政衰，去稷不務，不窋以失其官而犇戎狄之間。不窋卒，子鞠立。鞠卒，子公劉立。公劉雖在戎狄之間，復修后稷之業，務耕種，行地宜，自漆、沮度渭，取材用，行者有資，居者有畜積，民賴其慶。百姓懷之，多徙而保歸焉。周道之興自此始，故詩人歌樂思其德。公劉卒，子慶節立，國於豳.

63 Of course, this point is still open to further discussion. We can interpret his famous saying "If we cannot comprehend the living, how can we comprehend the spirits? (曰: 未知生, 焉知死) (*Lunyu* s.d., Xian jin: 12)" as a clear statement that the afterlife was a priori inaccessible to human perception or comprehension. On the other hand, this sentence could also be translated as "If you cannot comprehend the living, how can you comprehend the spirits?"

64 至於鬼神祭祀這種風俗, 孔子在知識上不能證明其必有,
但也不能在知識上證明其必無, 而主張將其改造為對祖先的孝敬,
一表現自己的誠敬仁愛之德. 因此,
孔子及由孔子發展下來的祭祀, 實質上不是宗教性的活動,
是使每一個人以自己為中心的自私之念通過祭祀而得到一種澄汰與純化.

65 For example, as in the following two poems: "The Great Heaven is not righteous, and the ruler cannot find peace. And yet, he does not calm his heart, but instead tries furiously to alter Heaven (昊天不平、我王不寧。不懲其心、覆怨其正)" (*Shi jing* s.d., Xia ya, Jie nan shan 9). "Heaven does not feed us and we are doubtful, because we do not know where to go (天不我將。靡所止疑)" (*Shi jing* s.d., Da ya, Sang rou 3).

66 Zhou You Wang 周幽王, 795–771 BCE.

67 See Jaspers 2003, 98.

68 這是一個重要的轉機，它標誌著中國文化開始走入卡爾·雅斯貝斯（Karl Jaspers）所說的軸心時代。值得關注的是，與其他文明不同，中國的軸心時代變化的最顯著特點是沒有走向神學，而是從神學脫離開來.

69 Chen Lai (1996, 4), for instance, explains this counter-tendency by the fact that in China the great religious crisis occurred before the emergence of the "axial period." Because this morally defined religion dating from the early Zhou Dynasty had gradually lost all its moral luster and Heaven itself, the previously "religious" faith was replaced by a faith in the rational structure of the universe, and "Heaven" became "Nature."

70 方東美.

71 這個文化傳統的形成, 主要的是從宗教精神體現出來,
而成為高度的倫理文化. 孔子承受之而予以適當的整理.

72 人類的文化, 都是從宗教開始, 中國也不例外.
但是文化形成一種明確而合理的觀念,
因而與人類行為以提高向上的影響力量,
則需發展到有某程度的自覺性. 宗教可以誘發人的自覺; 但原始宗教,
常常是由對天滅人禍的恐怖情緒而來的原始性地對神秘之力的皈依,
並不能表示何種自覺的意識. 即在高度發展的宗教中, 也因人,
因時代之不同, 而可成為人地自覺的助力; 也可成為人地自覺的阻礙.
從遺留到現在的殷代銅器來看, 中國文化, 到殷代已經有了很長的歷史,
完成了相當高度的發達. 但從甲骨文中, 可以看出殷人的精神生活,
還未脫離原始狀態; 他們的宗教, 還是原始性的宗教. 當時他們的
行為, 似乎是通過卜辭而完全決定於外在的神—祖宗神, 自然神,
及上帝. 周人的貢獻, 便是在傳統的宗教生活中, 注入了自覺的精神;
把文化在器物方面的成就, 提升而為觀念方面的展開,
以啟發中國道德地人文精神的建立.

73 天的人文化.

74 According to Xu Fuguan, the idea of reverence predominated precisely because of the "consciousness of anxiety" (*youhuan yishi*), which he sees as a fundamental psychological feature of ancient Chinese society (Xu Fuguan 2005, 24).

75 Hence, this discourse cannot be considered merely in terms of the explicit formulation of moral discourses, but must be understood as the internalization and awareness of one's Moral Self. The following saying by Confucius makes this explicit: "The Master said, 'I would rather not speak.' Zi Gong replied, 'If you do not speak, what can we, your disciples, narrate?' The Master replied: 'Does Heaven speak? The four seasons pursue their courses, and all things are constantly being produced, but does Heaven say anything?'" (子曰：「予欲無言。」子貢曰：

「子如不言,則小子何述焉?」子曰:「天何言哉?四時行焉,百物生焉,天何言哉?」) (*Lunyu* s.d., Yang huo 19).

76 在孔子之前,...這些道德觀念都表現為外面的知識,
行為,是在客觀世界的關係中比定出來的,
還不能算有意識的開間了一種內在的人文世界.只有經過孔子的創造,
才將這種客觀的人文世界轉變為內在的人文世界.只有經過孔子的創造,
才將這種客觀的人文世界轉變為內在的人文世界,
從而開啟了人類無限融合於向上之機,形成了中國道德精神.

77 See *Lunyu* s.d., Xian wen 35 (下學而上達).

78 孔子的所謂天命或天道或天,用最簡捷的語言表達出來,
實際上是知道德的超經驗性格而言.

79 Confucius expressed this concept as: "My inner virtue was produced by Heaven (天生德於予)" (*Lunyu* s.d., Shu er 23). Also: "I do not blame Heaven. I do not complain against men. My studies lie on the physical level, and my penetration rises to the metaphysical one. But only Heaven knows me!" (不怨天,不尤人。下學而上達。知我者,其天乎!) (*Lunyu* s.d., Xian wen 35).

80 According to the Confucian *Analects*, unity with Heaven could only be reached by a nobleman (*junzi*): "Yao as a sovereign was a true nobleman! He was extraordinarily majestic! Only Heaven is truly grand, and only Yao corresponded to it" (大哉,堯之為君也！巍巍乎！唯天為大,唯堯則之) (*Lunyu* s.d., Tai bo 19).

81 Confucius stressed that humanity was established in each person through the realization of a moral life: "True humanity means being able to practice five virtues everywhere under heaven (能行五者於天下,為仁矣)" (*Lunyu* s.d., Yang huo: 6). Proper moral conduct also manifests itself in overcoming oneself (i.e., one's selfish interests) and in rituality as a symbolic identification with Heaven/Nature and the universe: "To subdue one's self and turn to rituality, is perfect virtue. If you can do this for one day, all under heaven will ascribe perfect virtue to you" (克己復禮為仁。一日克己復禮,天下歸仁焉)" (*Lunyu* s.d., Yan yuan: 1). This clearly indicates the possibility of obtaining unity with one's natural and social environment through experiencing humanity.

82 That Confucius' philosophy was more than a set of simple regulations within a body of moral teaching is evident in the following saying: "At fifteen, I was eager to learn. At thirty, I stood firm on my own legs. At forty, I had no doubts. At fifty, I understood the Heavenly Mandate. At sixty, my ears were open for following the truth. At seventy, I could follow what my heart desired, without violating what was right (子曰：'吾十有五而志于學,三十而立,四十而不惑,

五十而知天命，六十而耳順，七十而從心所欲，不踰矩.)" (*Lunyu* s.d., Wei zheng: 4).

83　天何言哉 (*Lunyu* s.d., Yang huo: 19); 天不言 (*Mengzi* s.d., Wang zhang 5).
84　The Chinese holistic world view has been traditionally expressed by the phrase "Unity of men and nature" (天人合一).
85　For example, distinctions between subject and object, substance and phenomena, creator and creation, etc.
86　The analogical model used in the context of traditional Chinese logic differs from the classical European model in terms of both its methods and functions (see Cui and Zhang 2005, 25–41).
87　故曰，蓋師是而无非，師治而无亂乎？是未明天地之理，萬物之情者也。是猶師天而无地，師陰而无陽，其不可行明矣。
88　在陰陽言，則用在陽而體在陰，然動靜無端，陰陽無始，不可分先後。今只就起處言之，畢竟動前又是靜，用前又是體，感前又是寂，陽前又是陰，而寂前又是感，靜前又是動，將何者為先後？不可只道今日動便為始，而昨日靜更不說也。如鼻息，言呼吸則辭順，不可道吸呼。畢竟呼前又是吸，吸前又是呼。

Chapter 2

1　This structure is a relational order, because no entity within it can exist or be coherently treated or comprehended in isolation from other entities. This reciprocal interconnectedness means that no object can appear in separation from other objects. They are all linked by different dynamic and changeable or modifiable relations, which form a flexible structural network.
2　A detailed analysis and description of the formation, development, and the specific features of this structural order that mostly manifests itself in the concept of structural patterns or structural principles *Li* 理 can be found in my book *Traditional Chinese Philosophy and the Paradigm of Structure* (2012a).
3　Ethical and axiological elements of such structural networks will be treated more in detail in the next section.
4　Graham's translation of a chapter "Mingshi lun 名實論" in the book *Mozi* 墨子.
5　In pinyin: Laozi and Han Feizi.
6　韓非子.
7　短長, 方圓, 堅脆, 輕重, 白黑之謂理.
8　荀子.

9. 形體色理以目異. A later commentator, Yang Jing, points out that in this context the character *li* signifies a structural pattern: 楊倞注: 理, 紋理也 (qf. *Gu Hanyu da cidian* 2000). John Knoblock translates *li* as "design" (*Xunzi*, trans. Knoblock 1994, 129).
10. 取牛肉必新殺者，薄切之，必絕其理.
11. 莊子.
12. 依乎天理.
13. 王乃使玉人理其璞而得寶焉.
14. 三十而有室, 始理男事.
15. Compiled in ca. 100 CE, by Xu Shen 許慎.
16. 理, 治玉也.
17. Regarding the philosophical connotations of such an understanding, we should bear in mind the conservatism which so often appears as a decisive factor in traditional Chinese, especially Confucian, axiology, and the elements of a specifically Chinese aesthetic that attributes greater value to Art that seeks to express itself in accordance with the visible structures of Nature, than to a creativity that gives form to new modes of expression which did not exist before.
18. 凡物者有形者, 易裁也, 易割也. 何以論之, 有形則有短長, 有短長則有大小, 有方圓. 有方圓則有堅脆. 有堅脆則有輕重, 有白黑. 短長, 大小, 方圓, 堅脆, 輕重, 白黑謂之理.理定而物易割也. 故欲成方圓, 而隨於規矩, 則萬事之功形矣. 而萬物莫不有規矩. 聖人盡隨於萬物的規矩, 則事無不事, 功無不功. 凡理者方圓長短堅脆之分也故理定而後物可道.
19. 萬物殊理, 道不私, 故無名.
20. 然一物之中, 天理完具.
21. For an example of the evaluation of society as a system of relations in comparison with the individual, see the results of an intercultural comparative research in Rošker 2012, 40.
22. However, because in the Western world the term "role" is mostly understood as "playing a part or a character that is different from one's true self," which can lead to a misunderstanding of the essence of Confucian ethics, I prefer to denote it with the (although a bit vague) phrase "Confucian relational ethics" or simply with "Confucian ethics of relations."
23. Recently this notion has been introduced and described by several Western sinologists; see for instance Lai 2016, 109.
24. 管子; an important political text written in the Spring and Autumn period (770–476 BCE).
25. 坦氣修通，凡物開靜，形生理 (*Guanzi* s.d., You Guan, 1).
26. 有氣則生，無氣則死 (*Guanzi* s.d., Shu Yuan, 1).

27 陽癉憤盈，土氣震發 ... 自今至于初吉，陽氣俱蒸，土膏其動。
28 As, for instance, distinctions between subject and object, substance and phenomena, creator and creation.
29 In the philosophy of Zhu Xi 朱熹 (1130–1200), who is the most well-known representative of the Neo-Confucian discourses, the binary patterns tended to transform into a semi-dualistic pattern (see Rošker 2016) because they relied too heavily on a mechanistic rationality. Such approaches resulted in a deformation of the holistic tradition in philosophy, in which the binary poles of structure (*li*) and vital creativity (*qi*) were harmonized, thereby preserving the harmonic unity of facts, values, and the sphere of aesthetic experience. Hence, numerous scholars share the opinion that Neo-Confucian philosophers headed by Zhu Xi represented a turnaround in Chinese tradition. This was often expressed through the optics of its alleged "germs of dualism" (see for instance Forke 1934, 173). However, it was still a mixture between both models; and what matters most in the context of the present study is the fact that, even in their function of basic cosmological elements, *li* and *qi* were never seen as idea and matter respectively by any of the traditional Chinese philosophers—including Zhu Xi.
30 張載.
31 氣之聚散於太虛由冰釋於水 (Zhang Zai 1989, 389).
32 Huainanzi, a Han period (206 BCE–8 CE) Daoist-oriented master of Chinese philosophy, said that before the birth of Heaven and Earth, there was only a formless, fluid state called *taizhao*, like a clear transparent void. This void, which is the beginning of Dao, gave birth to the universe. The universe in turn produced *qi*. That part of *qi* which was light and limpid, floated up to form Heaven, whereas the part of qi which was heavy and turbid coagulated to become Earth. Therefore, *qi* can be understood as protomaterial, a vital creative force that gives "form" to everything in the universe (Xu 1999, 967).
33 I have added the italic form in order to highlight the part of Le Gall's translation that is relevant to the present discussion.
34 *Zhong yong* 中庸, mostly translated as *The Doctrine of the Mean* or the *Middle Way*. Ezra Pound has explained it as "the unswerving" or "un-wobbling" pivot.
35 Particularly in Chapters 2, 40, and 42.
36 這是我常講的 "中國辯證法." 不是P∨¬P 而是P≠P±。認為 "過猶不及," 即中庸是也.
37 從上古以來, 中國思想一直強調 "中," "和." "中," "和" 就是 "度" 的實現和對象化 (客觀化).

38 因此, 反對放從慾望, 也反對消滅慾望,
而要求在現實的世俗生活中取得精神的平寧和幸福亦即 '中庸,' 就成為基本要點. 這 . . . 是在有限中得到無限.

Chapter 3

1. This chapter includes contents from my article "Classical Chinese Logic," originally published in 2015 in *Philosophy Compass*.
2. While the first Chinese translations of a number of medieval texts on Aristotelian logic date from the seventeenth century, in China, the question of whether Chinese thought possesses a logic in the Aristotelian sense, and, if not, whether it has its own specific logic, arose mainly after the introduction of Western philosophical and scientific thought in the nineteenth century. This issue then acquired a particular importance after the cultural revolution of the so-called May Fourth movement, in 1919 (see Cheng 1965, 195–6).
3. The reasons for the decline of the latter in early medieval China are multiple and linked mainly to complex historical events and processes that shaped specific social conditions that proved to be unfavorable for the evolution of scientific thought and methodologies.
4. Actually, this is not a specific feature of Chinese logical reasoning, for the logic of disputation (in the sense of arguments and counter-arguments, that is, of thesis and antithesis) was also developed in ancient Greece. However, this form of logical method was not elaborated in later periods because the European tradition focused on the development of formal logic instead. In the history of traditional European logic, even Aristotelian logic implied two main methods: evidences and disputation. Later developments focused on syllogisms, which depended on evidences, while disputation was gradually forgotten (Li Xiankun 2001, 353). A renewed interest in the logic of argumentation by a number of modern logicians (e.g., Chaïm Perelman) only occurred in the latter half of the twentieth century.
5. 惠施.
6. 公孫龍.
7. 白馬非馬.
8. 后期墨家.
9. 墨翟.
10. 墨子.
11. However, Hansen's claim about the concept of truth in Chinese philosophy has been challenged by several scholars (e.g., Lenk 1991; Sun 2007; Cheng 1965, etc.).

Chris Fraser, for instance, exposes that Chad Hansen's hypothesis, according to which both early and later Mohist texts apply only pragmatic, not semantic, terms of evaluation and treat "appropriate word or language usage," not semantic truth. Fraser argues that although the early Moist "three standards" are indeed criteria of a general notion of correct *dao* (way), not specifically of truth, their application may still include questions of truth. He shows in detail that, in contrast to Hansen's opinion, the Mohists can justifiably be said to have a concept of semantic truth (Fraser 2012a, 351).

12 今日適越而昔至也.
13 We will be dealing with this concept in more detail in the chapter on analogies.
14 In different contexts, the notion *gu* can also be translated as "cause" or "reason" (for something to take place).
15 For example, quantifiers like "all" (*jie* 皆) or "some" (*huo* 或), disjunctions like "either . . . or" (*huo . . . huo* 或。。。或) and conditionals like "suppositions" (*jia* 假).
16 抱朴子
17 葛洪
18 「堅白」是無用之說 . . . 邪學。
19 As Xunzi explains, "honor" has two "starting points," honor with respect to moral standing and honor with respect to social status. A person can be morally honorable while having low social status or socially honored while being morally disgraceful (Fraser 2013a, 17).
20 While some scholars (e.g., Sun Zhongyuan) insist that analogism in Chinese logic (especially Mohist logic) was identical to Aristotelian three-part argumentation (or the three-branch method), there is no convincing evidence for this view, and it has never found acceptance in the academic community. Already at the beginning of the twentieth century, Hu Shi (1963) questioned Zhang Binglin's assertion that the later Mohist school had developed a theory of three-part argumentation, arguing that the Mohist theories were based on causality rather than deduction (see Cui and Zhang 2005, 25).
21 This assumption appears in classical Chinese epistemology which, on the basis of the relation between language and reality, tried to standardize (*chang*) linguistic structures "rationally" (i.e., in accordance with the most appropriate structural regulation (*dao*) of language as an expression of all that exists) in order to improve and harmonize political and social relations within society (Hansen 1989, 75). Zhang Dongsun's approach here can also be compared to some recent researches in linguistic logic, which focus on linguistic pragmatism (Li Xiankun 2001, 353–4).
22 This does not mean that ontological discourses are entirely absent in early Chinese philosophical texts. However, classical Chinese philosophers dealt with

	ontological questions within the scope of an implicit ontology, in which this discipline was not clearly distinguished from ethics and epistemology.
23	As mentioned, this kind of dual oppositions is called "binary categories."
24	Here, it may be argued that that Chinese logic is more consistent with modern predicate logic.
25	See for instance the Mohist passage on cows and horses (*Mozi* s.d., Jingxia: 168) in which they have introduced the problem of antinomy. While a herd can consist of cows and horses (A and B), it cannot be regarded as a herd of cows (A), nor as a herd of horses (B). Another example can be drawn from Gonsun Long's famous *White Horse Dispute*: Something which is white colour (A) and horse (B) is neither (only) a white colour (A), nor (just) a horse (B) (see *Gongsun Longzi* s.d., Bai ma fei ma: 1–14).
26	See for instance the Mohist definition of the notion "filling": What does not fill anything is dimensionless (*Mozi* s.d., Jing shuo shang: 66).
27	This chapter includes a reworked version of my article "Structural Relations and Analogies in Classical Chinese Logic," which was originally published in *Philosophy East & West*, Vol. 67, No. 3 (2017), 841–3.
28	Most scholars agree that the Mohist logic is based upon causality rather than deduction (see Cui and Zhang 2005, 25).
29	Here, it is important to remember that the later Mohist School and the School of Names were much more analytical in their methods than either Confucianism or Daoism, because they expressed their philosophical arguments with an analytical language.
30	In the sense of messages that were communicated via language; in this context, the notion of meaning is connected to words or phrases that refer to concepts.
31	告諸往而知來者.
32	不憤不啟，不悱不發，舉一隅不以三隅反，則不復也.
33	仁者，己欲立而立人，己欲達而達人。能近取譬，可謂仁之方也已.
34	This is a latent supposition that was considered, but never explicitly defined by Confucius. The definition was provided later by his follower Mengzi 孟子. The concept of kind, however, is also mentioned in earlier Confucian classics, for example, in the *Book of Ritual* (*Li ji* 禮記).
35	One of the ancient Chinese mythological rulers, a model saint in the system of Confucian ethics.
36	舜，人也；我，亦人也.
37	聖人之于民，亦類也.
38	In the *Analects*, it mostly means social classes, for example: "The master said, 'In teachings there is no distinction between different classes' 子曰：「有教無類。」" (*Lunyu* s.d., Wei Ling Gong: 39).

39 故凡同類者，舉相似也，何獨至於人而疑之？聖人與我同類者。
40 犬馬之與我不同類也.
41 聖人先得我心之所同然耳。
42 至於心, 獨無所同然乎？心之所同然者何也？謂理也，義也。
43 物類之起，必有所始... 施薪若一，火就燥也；平地若一，水就濕也。草木疇生，禽獸群焉，物各從其類也.
44 艸木枝葉必類本.
45 以類行雜，以一行萬.
46 後期墨家.
47 推類之難說. This chapter also includes the first occurrence of a phrase that is still used in modern Chinese to denote the method of analogical inference (*tuilei* 推類).
48 In the *Mozi*, this notion is somehow ambiguous, for it is not always clear whether it refers to two objects belonging to the same kind, or to two kinds that are similar to each other. The Mohists seem to apply it in the former (see for instance *Mozi* s.d., II, Shang xian zhong: 7; III, Shang xian xia 1), but also in the latter meaning (e.g., *Mozi* s.d., I, Qin shi: 6; III, Shang tong shang: 3). The absence of this semantic demarcation line might be rooted in its verbal connotation, which means "to unite" or "to unify two entities into the same one" (see *Mozi* s.d., II, Shang xian zhong: 6; III, Shang tong shang: 4).
49 至同無不同，至異無不異.
50 Fraser (2013) exposes that "there may originally have been further criteria, as only a series of fragments remain of the text or texts that treated these issues."
51 異：木與夜孰長？
52 In this context, the word meaning implies the denotations, reference, or ideas associated with a particular word or phrase.
53 名, 達, 類, 私.
54 名物, 達也. 有實, 必待之名也. 命之馬, 類也. 若實也者, 必以是名也. 命之臧, 私也. 是名也止於實也.
55 正名而期, 質請而喻, 辨異而不過, 推類而不悖.
56 同, 重, 體, 合, 類.同.
57 二名一實，重同也。不外於兼，體同也。俱處於室，合同也。有以同，類同也.
58 異, 二, 不體, 不合, 不類.
59 異：二必異，二也。不連屬，不體也。不同所，不合也。不有同，不類也。
60 以名舉實，以辭抒意.
61 辭也者，兼異實之名以論一意也.

62 推類之難，說在之大小 (*Mozi* s.d., Jing xia 102). The original text might be corrupt here. There is an issue about both the beginning and the ending of this canon regarding the breaks between the canon and the previous, as well as the following explanations (see for instance Graham 1978, 349; note 267). But whatever variation is accepted, the subject is clearly the size of the classes. In this regard, I have followed the analysis and interpretation of Ian Johnston (2010, 466), which is well-grounded and persuasive.
63 謂四足獸, 與牛馬與, 物盡異, 大小也. 此然是必然, 則具.
64 大同而與小同異，此之謂小同異；萬物畢同畢異，此之謂大同異 (*Zhuangzi* s.d., Tian xia 7).
65 Or, at the semantic level, to their intension and extension respectively.
66 牛與馬惟異, 以牛有齒, 馬有尾, 說牛之非馬也, 不可. 是俱有, 不遍有, 遍無有. 曰'牛與馬不類, 用牛有角, 馬無角, 是類不同也'. 若舉牛有角, 馬無角, 以是為類之不同也, 是狂舉也. 猶牛有齒, 馬有尾.
67 辟, 侔, 援, 推.
68 For example: let us suppose that R is a transitive relation; if there is a relation R (a, b) and at the same time there is a relation R (a, c), then it must be valid for all relations R that R (a, b) and R (b, c) both necessarily include R (a, c).
69 驪馬, 馬也; 乘驪馬, 乘馬也。獲, 人也; 愛獲, 愛人也.
70 雖盜人人也, 愛盜, 非愛人也.
71 This claim was clearly related to the ideological stance of the later Mohists, who—in contrast to their staunchest opponents, the Confucians—advocated universal love but were not opposed to capital punishment. They thus had to reconcile this contradiction.
72 雖盜人人也, 愛盜非愛人也.
73 奚以明之？惡多盜, 非惡多人也；欲無盜, 非欲無人也。世相與共是之。若若是, 則雖盜人人也, 愛盜非愛人也.
74 世相與共是之.
75 狗, 犬也, 而殺狗非殺犬也.
76 而萬物之理, 各以其類相動也.
77 Specific Chinese models for investigating questions related to knowledge and comprehension were thus premised by the idea of a structurally ordered external reality. Because the order of the universe is organic, it follows the flowing current of dynamic and vivid structural principles, which guides all beings and manifests itself in the notion of *li* 理. Human consciousness is likewise structured in congruence with this open and all-pervasive organic system. Therefore, the elementary principles and axioms of our cognition are not arbitrary or

coincidental, but are always tracking down the paths of this dynamic structure. The congruence, compatibility and correspondence of both structures is the fundamental precondition enabling us to perceive the object from the world around us. Zhu Xi, for instance, has described this epistemological condition in the following way: "The structural patterns of things can be explored by following their intrinsic nature and by adapting ourselves to it. In this way, we will find the structure that connects our inwardness with the external world. 自家知得物之理如此，則因其理之自然而應之，便見合內外之理" (Zhu Xi s.d., Daxue, 295).

78 For a detailed explanation of this relation and its development see Rošker 2012, 51–2.

79 交正分之謂理。順理而不失之謂道.

80 Homer Dubs, who interprets *lei* 類 as classification and *li* 理 as principles, translates this passage as a conditional sentence: "If the classification is not violated, although it is old, the principle remains the same" (Dubs 1966, 74). Analogously we could translate it as "If the kinds are not in mutual contradiction, then the (underlying) structure remains the same all the time." The passage contains a discussion about ordering society that evolves around the question of whether the old principles are still suitable for governing the present world; in the context of this interpretation, it could mean that the basic structure of this order is the same no matter the specific situations and conditions that change through time.

81 類不悖，雖久同理.

82 三物必具，然後足以生。夫辭以故生，以理長，以類行也者。立辭而不明於其所生，妄也。

83 狗, 犬也.

84 E.g. 驪馬，馬也; 獲, 人也; etc.

85 世相與共是之 (*Mozi* s.d., XI, Xiao qu: 5).

86 殺盜人非殺人也.

87 「殺盜非殺人也」，此惑於用名以亂名者也。

88 The transfer of information or their "value" from the system of formal signs into the system of natural language as such is namely already rather problematic, for the former is a system of defined values, while the latter also contains moral and ideological implications. As a striking indicator of axiological (or semantic) differences that can appear in a quite simple "translation" of a certain sentence from the formal into the natural language, let's take a look at the following example: "$\neg p \longrightarrow q \longleftrightarrow \neg p \longrightarrow q$." If we express the variable p with the phrase "to be against us," and the variable q with the phrase "to be with us," we can

"translate" the left part of the above (logically valid) formula into the natural language with the phrase "whoever is not with us is against us" and the right part with "whoever is not against us is with us." Although in the system of formal signs both sides of the equivalence have the same validity and although the equivalence as such is formally true, the moral implications (and along with them the messages provided by the contents) that manifest themselves in their translation into the natural language are not only not equivalent, but even in contradiction to one another.

89 獲之親，人也；獲事其親，非事人也。

90 We can see this from several similar examples in the *Mohist Canon* that are not necessarily connected to ethical issues, for instance: "Black horses are horses; riding a black horse is riding a horse," (驪馬，馬也；乘驪馬，乘馬也, *Mozi* s.d., Xiao qu, 4), while it also holds true that "A boat is wood, but entering into a boat is not entering wood" (船，木也；入船，非入木也, *Mozi* s.d., Xiao qu, 5). Black horses are a subset of the kind of all horses, and boats are a subset of all wood. But in respect to our dealing with them, one of them still remains a subset, while the other becomes an object, belonging to a different kind.

Chapter 4

1 境界融合.
2 東林書院.
3 顧憲成.
4 高攀龍.
5 王夫之.
6 顧炎武.
7 黃宗羲.
8 戴震.
9 馮友蘭.
10 子學時代.
11 經學時代.
12 金岳霖.
13 張申府.
14 綜合創新論.
15 在金岳霖與馮友蘭那裡, 對中國傳統哲學的繼承是 浸透在他們的哲學研究中的, 而到了張岱年, 終於將 這種對傳統哲學的繼承轉化為一種自覺的方法論. 可以說, 較之金, 馮二人, 張岱年不僅更注意對中國傳統哲學特徵的 整體把握, 也更注重繼承傳統的方法論原則... 張岱年對中國傳統哲學的繼承, 就其廣度而言, 遠遠超出了 金岳霖, 也超過了馮友蘭, 顯示他對傳統哲學繼承的'綜合性'.

16. *Zhide zhijue yu Zhongguo zhexue* 智的直覺與中國.
17. 勞思光.
18. 所謂『基源問題研究法』, 是以邏輯意義的理論還原為始點, 而以史學考證工作為助力, 以統攝個別哲學活動於一定設準之下為歸宿。... 我們著手整理哲學理論的時候, 我們首先有一個基本了解, 就是一切個人或學派的思想理論, 根本上必是對某一問題的答覆或解答。我們如果找到了這個問題, 我們即可以掌握這一部份理論的總脈絡。反過來說, 這個理論的一切內容實際上皆是以這個問題為根源。
19. 杜保瑞.
20. 功夫理論.
21. 李賢忠.
22. 王博.
23. 老子.
24. 胡適.
25. 道 生 一, 一 生 二, 二 生 三, 三 生 萬 物.
26. 天下萬物生於有, 有生於無.
27. 嚴靈峰.
28. 道生一, 一生二, 二生三, 三生萬物.
29. 這就是說明'道'為'萬物之母'.
30. 天下萬物生於有.
31. 有, 名萬物之母.
32. 可見, '有' 也 是 萬 物 之 母. 是 則, ... 老 子 以 '道' 為 有, 與 '有' 同體, 無可置疑.
33. 張岱年.
34. 故常無欲以觀其妙; 常有欲以觀其徼。此兩者, 同出而異名, 同謂之玄。玄之又玄, 眾妙之門。
35. In my oppinion, a "proper application" of the analytic method in philosophical research is possible when it answers at least the following three conditions: 1. Proper or suitable context; 2. Proper or suitable research question; 3. Coherence with the respective referential framework.
36. 王弼.
37. 郭象.
38. 劉勰.
39. 文心雕龍.

40 Because of this richness, many important contemporary works were published in the recent years (see for instance Tu 2000 and 2005). However, many other scholars, on the other hand, directly compare traditional Chinese and modern European hermeneutic theories (Ng 2005, 297–310).

41 Although I have predominantly limited this section to the new insights of Chinese (including overseas Chinese) scholars, Western sinologists have also proposed some new directions in interpreting China or developing a modern Chinese hermeneutics. "David Hall and Roger Ames pinpoint what they call 'analogical or correlative thinking' as the First order strategy of coming to grips with reality and the human condition in classical Chinese culture. Tu Weiming sees Confucianism as a moral universe in which the self, with its immanent qualities of fundamental goodness, is the locus of ultimate transformation, in the sense of soteriological transcendence. In pondering the 'trouble with Confucianism' in the context of modernity, Wm. Theodore de Bary posits the critical, prophetic role of the *chüntzu* (the noble man) as the fulcrum of a politico-social community in which this figure must play the ambiguous roles of a conscientious critic of the dynastic state, a loyal servant of the ruler, and a caring representative of the people whose voice could only speak through him. Thomas Metzger suggests looking at Neo-Confucianism as a shared cultural 'grammar' that involves a 'sense of predicament,' the result of the nagging awareness that there is a chasm between the idealized goal of life—transforming state and society by the heroic moral self—and the dismal realities of the given world—the source of the anxiety of moral failure" (Chow, Ng and Henderson 1999, 1).

42 黃俊傑.

43 Besides being the first scholar to introduce to China the works of Nietzsche, Schopenhauer, and Kant, Wang Guowei initiated the comparative study of Western and Chinese aesthetics. Similar to Li Zehou's thoughts, the idea of "human life" was the basic foundation of all aesthetic studies also for Wang Guowei. On this basis, he created an aesthetics of life in the sense of modern humanitarianism and purposelessness by elaborating Zhuangzi's category of "the use through the useless *(Wu yong zhi yong* 無用之用*)*" in aesthetic activities (*Zhuangzi* s.d., Nei pian. Renjian shi: 9).

44 境非獨謂景物也。喜怒哀樂，亦人心中之一境界。

45 Wang Guowei used the term *jingjie* or aesthetic realm interchangeable with the concept of *yijing* 意境 or artistic conception (Cheng 1995, 93). This notion is a kind of imaginary domain, which is—similar to the aesthetic realm—also based upon a fusion of emotion and scene or situation (*qingjing jiaorong* 情景交融,

see ibid., 95). However, what the artistic conception implies is more centred upon the mindful awareness of the here and now, which is conveyed by artistic creation. In his writings about the artistic conception Li Zehou (see for instance Li 2010) hence always highlights that it is—precisely because of this fusion or the unity it implies—completely useless and redundant to seek comprehension through any kind of conceptual medium between feeling and object.

46　故能寫真景物，真感情著，謂之有境界。

47　*Stimmung*. The term has often been translated into English as "mood"; however, in my opinion, attunement is a more appropriate translation.

48　且女獨不聞邪？昔者海鳥止於魯郊，魯侯御而觴之於廟，奏九韶以為樂，具太牢以為善。鳥乃眩視憂悲，不敢食一臠，不敢飲一杯，三日而死。此以己養養鳥也，非以鳥養養鳥也。夫以鳥養養鳥者，宜栖之深林，遊之壇陸，浮之江湖，食之鰍鯈，隨行列而止，委蛇而處。彼唯人言之惡聞，奚以夫譊譊為乎！咸池、九韶之樂，張之洞庭之野，鳥聞之而飛，獸聞之而走，魚聞之而下入，人卒聞之，相與還而觀之。魚處水而生，人處水而死，故必相與異，其好惡故異也。故先聖不一其能，不同其事。名止於實，義設於適，是之謂條達而福持。

49　己所不欲，勿施於人.

50　莊子與惠子遊於濠梁之上。莊子曰：「儵魚出遊從容，是魚樂也。」惠子曰：「子非魚，安知魚之樂？」莊子曰：「子非我，安知我不知魚之樂？」惠子曰：「我非子，固不知子矣；子固非魚也，子之不知魚之樂全矣。」莊子曰：「請循其本。子曰『汝安知魚樂』云者，既已知吾知之而問我，我知之濠上也。

51　Throughout history, there have been thousands of different interpetations of this charming story. The most recent ones can be enjoyed in the collection *Zhuangzi and the Happy Fish* (2015), edited by Robert T. Ames and Takahiro Nakajima. The editors wrote in the description of the anthology that they have brought together

> essays from the broadest possible compass of scholarship, offering interpretations that range from formal logic to alternative epistemologies to transcendental mysticism. Many were commissioned by the editors and appear for the first time. Some of them have been available in other languages—Chinese, Japanese, German, Spanish—and were translated especially for this anthology. And several older essays were chosen for the quality and variety of their arguments, formulated over years of engagement by their authors. All, however, demonstrate that the Zhuangzi as a text and as a philosophy is never one thing; indeed, it has always been and continues to be, many different things to many different people.

52 As already mentioned, these discrepancies are merely the results of different frameworks of reference, which have been elaborated in detail in previous chapters. But these frameworks, again, are no more than (albeit important) conceptual tools that enable us to see and understand different semantic constitutions and hence, different philosophical perspectives of a concrete subject matter under comparison. Therefore, the awareness of these discrepancies merely represents a necessary condition for the application of the sublation method.
53 *Jingyan bian xianyan* 經驗變先驗.
54 理性凝聚.
55 實用理性.
56 天理.
57 良知.
58 This is, of course, an ironic statement. Even though serious academic works have been written on this very topic (see for instance Moore 1967; Allinson 1989; De Mente 2009, etc), I am naturally well aware of the fact that the human mind has no geographical provenience, nor a gender or a cultural determination.

Glossary

Chinese word	English meaning
An 安	Classical interrogative, meaning *What? How? When?* or *Where?*
Bai ma fei ma 白馬非馬	A white horse is not a horse
Bao Puzi 抱朴子	*The Master Who Preserves Simplicity*
Ben 本	Root, origin
Benti quanshixue 本體詮釋學	Onto-hermeneutics
Benti 本體	Noumenon
Bentilun 本體論	Ontology
Bianfa 變法	Reform, change of law
Bianxue 變學	Theories of argumentation
Bianzhe 變者	Dialecticians, debaters
Bu ran 不然	Not so (in logic)
Buzhu 不窋	A ruler of the early Zhou Dynasty, son of the mythological founder Hou Ji
Chang 常	Standardization (in logic)
Chen Lai 陳來	Contemporary Chinese philosopher
Cheng Zhongying (Cheng Chung-ying 成中英)	Contemporary overseas Chinese philosopher
Chong tong 重同	Synonyms (in Mohist logic)
Chongbai Moluo 崇拜摩罗	Contemporary Chinese scholar
Ci 詞	Proposition (in logic)
Ci 辭	Words or phrases
Daode jing 道德經	*The Classic of the Way and its Virtue*
Dai Zhen 戴震	Premodern Chinese philosopher
Dao 道	Dao, the Way, the ultimate (or original) principle
Daode benxin 道德本心	Moral Self (literally: the original moral heart-mind)
Daode ziwo 道德自我	Moral Self
Deng Xi 鄧析	Pre-Qin philosopher, Nominalist (School of Names)
Dong Zhongshu 董仲舒	Han dynasty scholar
Donglin shuyuan 東林書院	Donglin academy
Du Baorui (Duh Bao-Ruei) 杜保瑞	Contemporary Taiwanese scholar
Du 度	Proper measure
Duan 端	Dimensionless tip of a solid object
Falü 法律	Law, legislation
Fang Dongmei 方東美	Modern Confucian philosopher (second generation)
Fei 非	Wrong/false
Feng Yaoming 馮耀明	Contemporary Chinese scholar
Feng Youlan 馮友蘭	Modern Chinese philosopher

Chinese word	English meaning
Fengjian 封建	The Chinese term denoting the social system during the Zhou Dynasty, based on four basic occupations. The term also served as the Chinese translation of the European notion of feudalism.
Gainiande buke zhuanyixing 概念之不可轉移性	The non-transferability of concepts
Gao Panlong 高攀龍	Medieval philosopher
Ge Hong 葛洪	Early medieval philosopher
Gongfu lilun 功夫理論	Theory of skills
Gongsun Long 公孫龍	Pre-Qin logician, nominalist
Gou 狗	Cur
Gu Xiancheng 顧憲成	Medieval philosopher
Gu Yanwu 顧炎武	Premodern Chinese philosopher
Gu 故	Evidence (in logic) or reason
Guanxi 關係	Relationships
Guanxizhuyi 關係主義	Relationalism
Guo Xiang 郭象	Wei-Jin period philosopher
Guoyu 國語	*State records*
Han Feizi 韓非子	Ancient Chinese Legalist philosopher
Hanshu 漢書	The official dynastic history of the Former Han dynasty
Hou ji 后稷	Mythological founding ancestor of the Zhou Dynasty
Houqi Mojia 後期墨家	Later Mohists
Hu Shi 胡適	Modern Chinese philosopher
Huang Junjie (Huang Chun-chieh) 黃俊傑	Contemporary Taiwanese scholar
Huang Zongxi 黃宗羲	Premodern Chinese philosopher
Hui Shi 惠施	Pre-Qin logician, nominalist
Huo . . . huo 或。。。或	Either . . . or (in logic)
Huo 或	Some (in logic)
Jia 假	Supposition (in logic)
Jianbai 堅白	Hart and white (logical category)
Jie 皆	All (in logic)
Jin Yuelin 金岳霖	Modern Chinese philosopher
Jing xue shidai 經學時代	Period of the Classics
Jingjie ronghe 境界融合	The fusion of (aesthetic) realms
Jingjie zhexue 境界哲學	Philosophy of aesthetic realms
Jingjie 境界	(aesthetic) realm
Jingyan bian xianyan 經驗變先驗	Transformation of empirical into the transcendental
Jinzhang guanxi 緊張關係	Tensely relation
Jiyuan 基源	Fundamental source
Ju yun 居運	Residence and migration
Kaozheng 考證	Traditional Chinese textual criticism
Ke 可	Acceptable (in logic the link between consecutive statements)
Kong fuzi 孔夫子	Confucius

Chinese word	English meaning
Lao Siguang 勞思光 (Lao Sze-kwang)	Contemporary Chinese philosopher
Laozi 老子	Pre-Qin Daoist philosopher
Lee Ming-huei 李明輝	Contemporary Taiwanese philosopher
Lei 類	Kind (in logic)
Leitong 類同	Sameness/similarity of kind
Leiyi 類異	Differences of kind
Li Gong 李塨	Pre-modern philosopher
Li ji 禮記	*Book of Rites*
Li Xianzhong (Lee Hsien-Chung) 李賢忠	Contemporary Taiwanese scholar
Li xue 理學	School of the structural principle
Li yi fen shu 理一分殊	One structural principle (consists of) many structural patterns
Li Zehou 李澤厚	Contemporary Chinese philosopher
Li 理	Structure, pattern, structural order, structural principle
Li 里	Mile, the fonetic part of the character li (structure)
Liang shu 量數	Amount and number
Liangzhi 良知	Inborn knowledge
Liu Shu-hsien 劉述先	Modern Confucian philosopher (Third generation)
Liu Xie 劉勰	The pioneer of Chinese aesthetics, hermeneutics, and literary theory
Lu Xun 魯迅	Chinese writer
Lü 律	Law, regulation, discipline, control
Lunli 倫理	Ethics (lit.: the structure of human relations)
Mengzi 孟子	Mencius, Mengzi
Ming jia 名家	School of names, Nomenalists
Ming xue 名學	Theories of names
Ming 名	Names or concepts
Mingbian 名變	Names and disputation
Mingshi 名實	Name and actuality (binary category)
Mo Di 墨翟	Pre-Qin philosopher
Mo 侔	Type of Chinese analogy (deduction from a parallel series of words or phrases)
Mou Zongsan 牟宗三	Modern Confucian philosopher (second generation)
Mozi 墨子	*Master Mo*
Neizai chaoyuexing 內在超越性	Immanent transcendence
Pei Wenzhong 裴文中	Chinese paleontologist, archaeologist, and anthropologist
Pi 辟	Type of Chinese analogy (explanation by examples)
Qi 氣	Vital potential, vital creativeness
Qin 秦	Chinese Dynasty (221–206 BCE)
Qingjing jiaorong 情景交融	Fusion of emotion and sccene or situation
Quan 犬	Dog
Ran 然	So (in logic)
Ren dao 人道	Way of men

Chinese word	English meaning
Ren xing 人性	Humanness (often translated as human nature)
Ren 仁	Humaneness
Ru 儒	Scholar, Confucian
Ruxue 儒學	The teachings of the scholars, Confucianism
Shi 實	Realities
Shi 是	Right/true
Shiji 史記	*The Records of the Historian*
Shiyong lixing 使用理性	Pragmatic rationality
Shuowen jiezi 說文解字	*Explanation of Texts and Interpretation of Characters*
Sixiang danwei 思想單位	Thought unit
Suoyu 所與	The Given
Ti 體	Body, stem
Tian 天	Heaven, nature
Tian dao 天道	The way of heaven (nature)
Tian ming 天命	Decree of Heaven
Tian zi 天子	Son of Heaven
Tiande renwenhua 天的人文化	The humanization of heaven
Tianren heyi 天人合一	The unity of human beings and nature (or heaven)
Tiyong bu er 體用不二	Inseparabilty of substance and function
Tiyong 體用	Essence and function (binary category)
Tong 同	Sameness/similarity, identity
Tongbian 通變	Continuity through change
Tu qi 土氣	The earthly qi (the vital potential of the earth)
Tui 推	Type of Chinese analogy (agreements with certain views through the negation of contrary claims)
Waizai chaoyuexing 外在超越性	External transcendence
Wang Bi 王弼	Wei-Jin period philosopher
Wang Bo 王博	Contemporary Chinese philosopher
Wang Fuzhi 王夫之	Premodern philosopher
Wang Guowei 王國維	Premodern Chinese scholar
Wenxin diaolong 文心雕龍	*Literary Mind and the Carving of Dragons*
Wu 無	Absence
Wu hou 無厚	Dimensionessless
Wu lun 五倫	Five cardinal relations in the Confucian role-ethics
Wu yong zhi yong 無用之用	The use through the uselessness
Xi zhai 習齋	School og practical knowledge
Xiaoshuo 小說	Chinese novel
Xin 心	Heart-mind
Xin ruxue 新儒學	Modern Confucianism
Xin xue 心學	School of heart-mind
Xing mao 形貌	Shape and visual appearance
Xingti 性體	Innate moral substance
Xinnian ganluo 信念剛落	Frameworks of presumptions
Xu Fuguan 徐復觀	Modern Confucian philosopher (second generation)
Xuan Zang 玄奘	Buddhist monk

Chinese word	English meaning
Xunzi 荀子	Ancient Chinese Confucian philosopher
Yan Linfeng 嚴靈峰	Modern Chinese philosopher
Yan Yuan 顏元	Premodern philosopher
Yang Guorong 楊國榮	Contemporary Chinese scholar
Yang qi 陽氣	The dynamic and active qi
Yang Zebo 楊澤波	Contemporary Chinese scholar
Yi jing 易經	*The Book of Changes*
Yi 意	Meaning (in logic)
Yi 異	Difference, distinction
Yi 義	Righteousness, justice
Yige shijie guan 一個世界觀	One-world view
Yijing 意境	Artistic conception
Yinming xue 因明學	Indian Buddhist logic Hetuvidya
Yinyang 陰陽	Yin and yang, sunny and shady (binary category)
You 有	Presence
Yu 玉	Jade
Yuan 援	Type of Chinese analogy (potentially similar views)
Zhang Dainian 張岱年	Modern Chinese philosopher
Zhang Shenfu 張申府	Modern Chinese philosopher
Zhang Zai 張載	Chinese philosopher (1020–77)
Zheng Jiadong 鄭家棟	Contemporary Chinese scholar
Zhengming lun 正名論	Theory of proper names
Zhi 指	Reference
Zhi tong 至同	Sameness
Zhi yi 至異	Difference
Zhide zhijue yu Zhongguo zhexue 智的直覺與中國哲學	*Intellectual Intuition and Chinese Philosophy*
Zhong yong 中庸	The principle of equilibrity (of binary categories)
Zhongguo tong 中國通	A colloquial expression, denoting a foreign expert on Chinese history and culture
Zhongguo zhexuede fangfalunwenti 中國哲學的方法論問題	*The Methodological Problems of the Chinese Philosophy*
Zhou You Wang 周幽王	Ruler You of the Zhou Dynasty
Zhuangzi 莊子	Ancient Chinese Daoist philosopher
Zi xue shidai 子學時代	Period of the masters
Zi 子	Son, child, philosophers in the pre-Qin period
Zi 自	Self, myself
Zijuexing 自覺性	Self-awareness
Zilü 自律	Autonomy, self-governance, self-discipline
Zonghe chuanxin lun 綜合創新論	Creative synthesis

Sources and Literature

Al-Azm, Sadiq Jalal. 1980. "Orientalism and Orientalism in Reverse." In *Europe Solidaire Sans Frontiéres*. http://www.europe-solidaire.org/spip.php?article20360.

Allinson, Robert E., ed. 1989. *Understanding the Chinese Mind – The Philosophical Roots*. Oxford, New York: Oxford University Press.

Ames, Roger T. 2011. *Confucian Role Ethics: A Vocabulary*. Honolulu: University of Hawaii Press.

Ames, Roger T. 2015. "Classical Daoism in an Age of Globalization." *Taiwan Journal of East Asian Studies* 12(no. 2, Issue 24): 105–48.

Ames, Roger T. 2016. "Theorizing 'Person' in Confucian Ethics: A Good Place to Start." *Sungkyun Journal of East Asian Studies* 16(2): 141–62.

Ames, Roger T. 2020. "Translating China." Project. http://en.yiduobufen.com/.

Ames, Roger T. and Takahiro Nakajima. 2015. *Zhuangzi and the Happy Fish*. Honolulu: University of Hawai'i Press.

Banka, Rafal. 2016. "Psychological Argumentation in Confucian Ethics as a Methodological Issue in Cross-Cultural Philosophy." *Dao: A Journal of Comparative Philosophy* 2016(15): 591–606.

Bauer, Wolfgang. 2000. *Geschichte der Chinesichen Philosophie*. München: C.H. Beck.

Benesch, Walter. 1997. "The Place of Chinese Logics in Comparative Logics: Chinese Logics Revisited." In *Asian Thought and Culture, Vol 28: New Essays in Chinese Philosophy*, edited by Cheng Hsueh-li, 3–58. New York: Peter Lang.

Bresciani, Umberto. 2001. *Reinventing Confucianism – The New Confucian Movement*. Taipei: Taipei Ricci Institute for Chinese Studies.

Bunnin, Nicholas. 2003. "Contemporary Chinese Philosophy and Philosophical Analysis." *Journal of Chinese Philosophy* 30(3–4): 341–56.

Caputo, John D. 1997. *Deconstruction in a Nutshell: A Conversation with Jacques Derrida*. New York: Fordham University Press.

Carleo, Robert A. and Paul D'Ambrosio. 2015. "Confucianism in Contemporary Contexts: Li Zehou and 21st Century Philosophy." Paper presented at the international conference Li Zehou and Confucian Philosophy. October 2015. Honolulu: University of Hawaii at Manoa, the East West Center.

Chakrabarti, Arindam and Ralph Weber. 2016. "Introduction." In *Comparative Philosophy without Borders*, edited by Arindam Chakrabarti and Ralph Weber, 1–33. London: Bloomsbury Academic.

Chen, Lai 陈来. 1996. *Gudai zongjiao yu lunli – ru jia sixiangde genyuan* 古代宗教与伦理——儒家思想的根源 [*Ancient Religions and Ethics – The Foundation of Confucian Thought*]. Beijing: Sanlian shudian.

Cheng, Chung-Ying. 1965. "Inquiries into Classical Chinese Logic." *Philosophy East and West* 15(3–4): 195–216.

Cheng, Chung-Ying. 1987. "Logic and Language in Chinese Philosophy." *Journal of Chinese Philosophy* 1987(14): 285–307.

Cheng, Chung-Ying. 2003a. "Qi (Ch'i). Vital Force." In *Encyclopedia of Chinese Philosophy*, edited by Antonio S. Cua, 615–17. New York and London: Routledge.

Cheng, Chung-Ying. 2003b. "Inquiring Into the Primary Model: *Yi Jing* and the Onto-Hermeneutical Tradition." *Journal of Chinese Philosophy* 30(3–4): 289–312.

Cheng, Fuwang 成复旺, ed. 1995. *Zhongguo meixue fanchou cidian* 中國美學範疇詞典 [*A Dictionary of Chinese Aesthetic categories*]. Beijing: Zhongguo Renmin daxue chuban she.

Chmelewski, Janusz. 1965. "Notes on Early Chinese Logic." *Rocznik orientalistycny* 28(2): 87–111.

Chomsky, Noam. 1968. *Language and Mind*. New York: Cambridge University Press.

Chow, Kai-wing, On Cho Ng, and John B. Henderson, eds. 1999. *Imagining Boundaries: Changing Confucian Doctrines, Texts, and Hermeneutics*. New York: SUNY.

Coquereau, Elise. 2016. "From Comparative Philosophy to Fusion Philosophy." *Journal of World Philosophies* 1: 152–4. doi: 10.2979/jourworlphil.1.1.13.

Creller, Aaron. 2014. *Making Space for Knowing: A Capacious Alternative to Propositional Knowledge*. Ph.D Dissertation. Honolulu: University of Hawai'i at Manoa.

Cua, Antonio S. 1971. "Reflections on the Structure of Confucian Ethics." *Philosophy East and West* 21(2): 125–40.

Cui, Qingtian 崔清田 and Wen Gongyi 溫公頤, eds. 2001. 中國邏輯史教程. Tianjin: Nankai daxue chuban she.

Cui, Qingtian and Xiaoguang Zhang. 2005. "Chinese Logical Analogism." *Asian and African Studies* 9/3: 14–24.

Dai, Yuanfang, ed. 2020. *Transcultural Feminist Philosophy: Rethinking Difference and Solidarity Through Chinese—American Encounters*. Lanham: Lexington Books.

D'Ambrosio, Paul, Robert Carleo, and Andrew Lambert. 2016. "On Li Zehou's Philosophy: An Introduction by Three Translators." *Philosophy East and West* 66(4): 1057–67.

Defoort, Carine. 2001. "Is There such a Thing as Chinese Philosophy? Arguments of an Implicit Debate." *Philosophy East and West* 51(3): 393–413.

De Mente, Boye Lafayette. 2009. *The Chinese Mind: Understanding Traditional Chinese Beliefs and Their Influence on Contemporary Culture*. North Claredon: Tuttle Publishing.

De Reu, Wim. 2006. "Right Words Seem Wrong: Neglected Paradoxes in Early Chinese Philosophical Texts." *Philosophy East and West* 65(2): 281–300.

Derrida, Jaques. 2004. "Uniterrupted Dialogue: Between two Infinities, a Poem." *Research in Phenomenology* 2004(34): 3–19.

Ding, Zijiang John. 2002. "Li Zehou: Chinese Aesthetics from a Post-Marxist and Confucian Perspective." In *Contemporary Chinese Philosophy*, edited by Chung-ying Cheng and Nicholas Bunnin, 246–57. Oxford: Blackwell Publishers.

Dirlik, Arif 1994. "The Postcolonial Aura: Third World Criticism in the Age of Global Capitalism." *Critical Inquiry* 20(2): 328–56.

Dubs, Homer H. 1966. *The Works of Hsüntze*. Taibei: Ch'eng wen Publishing.

Duh, Bao-Ruei (Du Baorui) 杜保瑞. 2013. *Zhongguo zhexue fangfa lun* 中國哲學的方法論 [*The Methodology of Chinese Philosophy*]. Taibei: Taiwan shangwu yinshuguan.

Elstein, David. 2015. "Contemporary Confucianism." In *The Routledge Companion to Virtue Ethics*, edited by Lorraine Besser-Jones and Michael Slote, 237–51. New York and London: Routledge, Taylor & Francis Group.

Fang, Dongmei 方東美. 2004. *Xin rujia zhexue shiba jiang* 新儒家哲學十八講 [*Eighteen Lectures in New Confucian Philosophy*]. Taibei: Liming wenhua chuban she.

Fang, Keli 方克立 and Jinquan Li 李錦全, eds. 1995. *Xiandai xin ruxue xue'an* 現代新儒家學案. [*Studies in Modern New Confucianism*]. 3 Vols. Beijing: Zhongguo shehui kexue chuban she.

Feng, Yaoming (Fung Yiu-ming) 馮耀明. 1989. *Zhongguo zhexuede fangfa lun wenti* 中國哲學的方法論問題 [*The Methodological Problems of Chinese Philosophy*]. Taibei: Yunchen wenhua shiye.

Forke, Alfred. 1934. *Geschichte der mittelalterlichen Chinesischen Philosophie* II. Hamburg: R.Oldenbourg.

Fraser, Chris. 2007. "Language and Ontology in Early Chinese Thought." *Philosophy East and West* 57(4): 420–56.

Fraser, Chris. 2012. "Introduction: Language and Logic in Later Moism." *Journal of Chinese Philosophy* 39(3): 327–32.

Fraser, Chris. 2013a. "*Mohist Canons*." *The Stanford Encyclopedia of Philosophy*, edited by Edward N. Zalta. http://plato.stanford.edu/archives/fall2013/entries/mohist-canons/.

Fraser, Chris. 2013b. "Distinctions, Judgment, and Reasoning in Classical Chinese Thought." *History and Philosophy of Logic* 34(1): 1–24.

Fredericks, James. 1988. "The Kyoto School: Modern Buddhist Philosophy and the Search for a Transcultural Theology." *Horizons* 15(2): 299–315.

Fung, Yiu-Ming. 2012. "A Logical Perspective on the Parallelism in Later Moism." *Journal of Chinese Philosophy* 39(3): 333–50.

Gadamer, Hans-Georg. 1989. *Truth and Method*. 2nd ed. Translated by J. Weinsheimer and D. G. Marshall. New York: Crossroad.

Ge, Hong 葛洪. s.d. *Bao Puzi* 抱朴子 [*The Master Who Preserves Simplicity*]. *Chinese Text Project* website, accessed September 29, 2020. https://ctext.org/baopuzi.

Geaney, Jane. 2002. *Epistemology of the Senses in Early Chines Thought*. Honolulu: University of Hawai'i Press.

Gongsun, Longzi 公孫龍子. s.d. *Bai ma lun* 白馬論 [*White Horse Discourse*]. *Chinese Text Project* website, accessed December 29, 2016. http://ctext.org/gongsunlongzi.

Graham, Agnus Charles. 1970. "Chuang Tzu's Essay on Seeing Things as Equal." *Journal of the History of Religions* 9(2–3): 137–59.

Graham, Agnus Charles. 1978. *Later Mohist Logic, Ethics and Science*. Hong Kong, London: Chinese University Press.

Graham, Agnus Charles. 1989. *Disputers of the Tao – Philosophical Argument in Ancient China*. Chicago: Open Court Publishing.

Gu Hanyu da cidian 古漢語大辭典 [*A Large Dictionary of Classical Chinese*]. 2000. Edited by Xu Fu. Shanghai: Shanghai cishu chuban she.

Guanzi 館子 [*Master Guan*]. s.d. *Chinese Text Project* website, accessed December 29, 2015. http://ctext.org/guanzi.

Guoyu 國語 [*State Records*]. s.d. *Chinese Text Project* website, accessed December 29, 2015. http://ctext.org/guo-yu.

Gu, Ming Dong. 2005. *Chinese Theories of reading and Writing: A Route to Hermeneutics and Open Poetics*. New York: SUNY.

Gu, Ming Dong. 2013. *Sinologism: An Alternative to Orientalism and Postcolonialism*. New York: Routledge.

Hahm, Chaibong. 2000. "How the East was Won: Orientalism and the New Confucian Discourse in East Asia." *Development and Society* 29(1): 97–109.

Hall, David L. and Roger T. Ames. 1987. *Thinking through Confucius*. Albany, New York: State University of New York Press.

Hall, David L. and Roger T. Ames. 1998. *Thinking from the Han: Self, Truth, and Transcendence in Chinese and Western Culture*. Albany: State University of New York Press.

Han, Christina. 2014. "Envisioning the Territoy of the Sage: The Neo-Confucian Discourse of *Jingjie*." *Journal of Confucian Philosophy and Culture* 2014(22): 85–109.

Han Feizi 韓非子. s.d. *Chinese Text Project* website, accessed July 25, 2013. http://ctext.org/hanfeizi.

Hansen, Chad. 1983. *Language and Logic in Ancient China*. Ann Arbour: University of Michigan.

Hansen, Chad. 1985. "Chinese Language, Chinese Philosophy, and 'Truth.'" *The Journal of Asian Studies* 44/3: 491–519.

Hansen, Chad. 1989. "Language in the Heart-Mind." In *Understanding the Chinese Mind: The Philosophical Roots*, edited by Robert E. Allinson, 75–124. Oxford, New York: Oxford University Press.

Harbsmeier, Christoph. 1988. "Language and Logic." In *Science and Civilization in China*, edited by Joseph Needham. Cambridge: Cambridge University Press.

Harbsmeier, Christoph. 1989. "Marginalia Sino-logica." In *Understanding the Chinese Mind: The Philosophical Roots*, edited by Robert E. Allinson, 125–66. Oxford, New York: Oxford University Press.

Hegel, Georg Wilhelm Friedrich. 1969. *Vorlesungen über die Geschichte der Philosophie*. Frankfurt/Main: Suhrkamp.

Heidegger, Martin. 1996. *Being and Time – A Translation of Sein und Zeit*. Translated by Joan Stammbaugh. Albany: SUNY.

Heubel, Fabian. 2011. "Kant and Transcultural Critique: Toward a Contemporary Philosophy of Self-Cultivation." *Journal of Chinese Philosophy* 38 (4): 584–601.

Heubel, Fabian 何乏筆. 2014. "Hunza xiandaihua, kua wenhua zhuanxiang yu Hanyu sixiang de pipanxing chong gou (yu Zhu Li'an dui yi hua) 混雜現代化、跨文化轉向與漢語思想的批判性重構（與朱利安「對一話」" [Hybrid Modernization, Transcultural Shift and a Critical Reconstruction of Sinophone Thought]. In *Sixiang yu fangfa: quainqiuhua shidai Zhong Xi duihuade keneng*, edited by Fang Weigui, 86–135. Beijing: Beijing daxue chuban she.

Holyoak, Keith. 2008. "Relations in Semantic Memory." In *Memory and Mind: A Festschrift for Gordon H. Bower*, edited by M. A. Gluck, J. R. Anderson, and S. K. Kosslyn, 144–59. New York: Erlbaum.

Hu, Shi 胡適. 1963. 先秦名學史 (The History of pre-Qin Logic). Shanghai: Xuelin chuban she.

Hu, Weixi 胡偉希. 2002. *Zhishi, luoji yu jiazhi – Zhongguo xin shizai lun sichaode xingqi* 知識，邏輯與價值 — 中國新實在論思潮 的興起 [Knowledge, Logic and Values – the Rise of New Chinese Realism]. Beijing: Qinghua daxue chuban she.

Huang, Chun-chieh. 1997. "Characteristics of Chinese Hermeneutics Exhibited in the History of Mencius in Exegesis." *Zhongguo wenzhe yanjiu jikan* 1997(7): 281–302.

Huang, Chun-chieh. 2015. *East Asian Confucianisms Texts in Contexts*. Goettingen and Taipei: V&R unipress, National Taiwan University Press.

Jaspers, Karl. 2003. *Way to Wisdom*. New Haven: Yale University Press.

Jiang, Xinyan. 2002. "Zhang Dongsun: Pluralist Epistemology and Chinese Philosophy." In *Contemporary Chinese Philosophy*, edited by Cheng Chung-Ying and Nicholas Bunnin, 57–81. Oxford: Blackwell Publishers.

Jin, Yuelin 金岳霖. 1978. *Lun Dao* 論道 [On Dao]. Beijing: Shangwu yinshu guan.

Johnston, Ian. 2010. *The Mozi: A Complete Translation*. Translated and annotated by Ian Johnston. Hong Kong: Chinese University Publishing.

Kant, Immanuel. 1911. *Critique of Aesthetic Judgment*. Translated by James Creed Meredith. Oxford: The Clarendon Press.

Kant, Immanuel. 1998. *Critique of Pure Reason*. Translated by Paul Guyer and Allen W. Wood. Cambridge: Cambridge University Press.

Kant, Immanuel. 2001. *Groundwork for the Metaphysics of Morals*. Edited and translated by Allen W. Wood. New Haven and London: Yale University Press.

King, Po-Chiu. 2016. *Thome H. Fang, Tang Junyi, and Huayan Thought: A Confucian Appropriation of Buddhist Ideas in Response to Scientism in Twentieth-Century China*. Leiden: Brill.

Knowlton, Barbara J. and Keith J. Holyoak 2009. "Prefrontal Substrate of Human Relational Reasoning." In *The Cognitive Neurosciences*, edited by M. S. Gazzaniga, 1005–17. Cambridge, MA and London: MIT Press.

Kubin, Wolfgang. 2005. "Chinese 'Hermeneutics' – a Chimera? Preliminary Remarks on Differences of Understanding." In *Interpretation and Intellectual Change*, edited by Tu Ching-I, 311–20. New Brunswick and London: Transaction Publishers.

Kuhn, Thomas S. 1996. *The Structure of Scientific Revolutions*. Chicago: University of Chicago Press.

Kuijper, Hans. 2000. "Is Sinology a Science?" *China Report* 36(3): 331–54.

Kurtz, Joachim. 2011. *The Discovery of Chinese Logic*. Leiden, Boston: Brill.

Lai, Karyn. 2016. "Close Personal Relationships and the Situated Self: The Confucian Analects and Feminist Philosophy." In *The Bloomsbury Research Handbook of Chinese Philosophy and Gender*, edited by Ann A. Pang-White, 111–26. London, Oxford, New York, New Delhi, Sydney: Bloomsbury Academic.

Lao, Siguang (Lao, Sze-Kwang) 勞思光. 1980. *Zhongguo zhexue shi.* 中國哲學史 [*The History of Chinese Philosophy*]. Hong Kong: Chinese University Press.

Laozi 老子. s.d. *Dao de jing* 道德經 [*The Classic of the Way and Its Virtue*]. *Chinese Text Project* website, accessed on January 12, 2017. http://ctext.org/dao-de-jing.

Lary, Diana. 2006. "Edward Said: Orientalism and Occidentalism." *Journal of the Canadian Historical Association / Revue de la Société historique du Canada* 17(2): 3–15.

Le Gall, Stanislas P. 2006. *Le philosophe tchou hi, sa doctrine, son influence*. Ville de Saguenay: Chicoutimi.

Lee, Ming-Huei (Li, Minghui) 李明輝. 2001. *Dangdai ruxuede ziwo zhuanhua* 當代儒學的自我轉化 [*The Self-Transformation of Contemporary Confucianism*]. Beijing: Zhongguo shehui kexue chuban she.

Lee, Ming-Huei (Li, Minghui) 李明輝. 2002. "Zai lun Rujia sixiang zhongde 'neizai chaoyuexing' wenti 再論儒家思想中的「內在超越性」問題 [A Revisited View of the Problem of 'Immanent Transcendence' in Confucian Thought]." In *Zhongguo sichao yu wailai wenhua* [*Chinese Thought Currents and Foreign*

Cultures], edited by Liu Shu-hsien, 223–40. Taibei: Zhongyang yanjiu yuan, Zhongguo wenzhe yanjiusuo.

Lee, Ming-Huei. 2013. *Konfuzianischer Humanismus – Transkulturelle Kontexte*. Bielefeld: Transcript Verlag.

Lenk, Hans. 1991. "Logik, cheng ming und Interpretationskonstrukte. Bemerkungen zum interpretationistischen Internalismus der konfuzianistischen Erkenntnistheorie." *Zeitschrift für philosophische Forschung* 45(3): 391–401.

Li, Chenyang. 2016. "Comparative Philosophy and Cultural Patterns." *Dao: A Journal of Comparative Philosophy* 15(4): 533–46.

Li ji 禮記 [*The Book of Rites*]. s.d. *Chinese Text Project* website, accessed June 22, 2016. http://ctext.org/liji.

Li, Xiankun 李先焜. 2001. "Jindai luoji kexuede fazhan (xia) - Xifang xiandai luoji tantao 近代邏輯科學的發展. 下. 西方現代邏輯探討 [The development of the logical science in the pre-modern period. Part 2. Discoveries of modern Western logic]." In *Zhongguo luojishi jiaocheng*, edited by Wen Gongyi and Qingtian Cui, 350-87. Tianjin: Nankai daxue chuban she.

Li, Zehou 李泽厚. 1980. "Kongzi zai pingjia 孔子再評價 [A Reevaluation of Confucius]." *Zhongguo shehui kexue* 2: 77–96.

Li, Zehou 李泽厚. 1985. *Zhongguo gudai sixiang shilun* 中國古代思想史論 [*A History of Classical Chinese Thought*]. Beijing: Renmin chuban she.

Li, Zehou 李泽厚. 1992. "Ruxue zuowei Zhongguo wenhua zhuliude yiyi 儒學作為中國文化主流的意義 [The significance of Confucianism as the mainstream of Chinese culture]." *Kongzi yanjiu* 1992(1): 9–10.

Li, Zehou. 1999a. "Subjectivity and 'Subjectality': A Response." *Philosophy East and West* 49(2): 174–83.

Li, Zehou 李泽厚. 1999b. *Jimao wushuo* 己卯五说 [*Five Essays from 1999*]. Beijing: Zhongguo dianying chuban she.

Li, Zehou 李泽厚. 2002. *Lishi benti lun* 历史本体论 [*Historical Ontology*]. Beijing: Sanlian shudian.

Li, Zehou. 2010. *The Chinese Aesthetic Tradition*. Translated by Maija Bell Samei. Honolulu: University of Hawai'i Press.

Li, Zehou 李泽厚. 2015. *You wu dao li, shi li gui ren* 由巫到礼，释礼归仁 [*From Shamanism to Rituality, Explaining Rituality as a Return to the Humanness*]. Beijing: Sanlian shudian.

Li, Zehou. 2016a. "A Response to Michael Sandel and Other Matters." Translated by Paul D'Ambrosio and Robert A. Carleo. *Philosophy East and West* 66(4): 1068-147.

Li, Zehou 李泽厚. 2016b. "Li Zehou duitan lu 李泽厚对谈录 [Recordings of Li Zehou's Conversations]." *Dai yue ting yu zhu jilu*, accessed May 19, 2016. http://www.doc88.com/p-7030124841.html.

Li, Zehou and Jane Cauvel. 2006. *Four Essays on Aesthetics: Toward a Global View.* Lanham: Lexington Books.

Li, Zehou 李澤厚 and Xuyuan Liu 劉緒源. 2011. "Li Zehou tan xueshu sixiang san jieduan 李澤厚談學术思想三階段 [Li Zehou Discusses the Three Phases of His Academic Thought]." *Shanghai wenxue* 2011(1): 72–7.

Li, Zehou 李澤厚 and Liu Yuedi 劉悅笛. 2017. "Li Zehou, Liu Yuedi 2017 nian zhexue duitan lu (xia): Ziyou yizhi, yinguo lü yu jueding lun 李澤厚、劉悅笛 2017 年哲學對談錄（下）自由意志、因果律與決定論 [The philosophical debate between Li Zehou and Liu Yuedi from 2017, Part II: Free will, the law of causality and determinism]." In *Ziyou ruan zhide boke*, 1–10. Accessed June 26, 2018. http://blog.sina.com.cn/s/blog_5fab50bf0102x7dq.html.

Li, Zehou 李澤厚 and Yang Guorong 楊國榮. 2014. "Lunli wenti ji qita—guocheng fenxide shijiao 倫理問題及其他—過程分析的視角 [About Ethics and Other Issues—from the Perspective of Processual Analysis]." *Shehui kexue* 2014(9): 117–28.

Liu, Fenrong, Jeremy Seligman, and Johan van Benthem. 2011. "The History of Logic in China: An Introduction." *Studies in Logic* 4(3): 1–2.

Liu, Fenrong and Wujing Yang. 2010. "A Brief History of Chinese Logic." *Journal of Indian Council of Philosophical Research* 27: 101–23.

Liu, Junda 劉軍大. 1996. "Shilun Zhongguo zhexue fangfalunde jiben tezheng. 试论中国哲学方法论的基本特征 [A Debate on the Characteristics of the methodology of Chinese Philosophy]." *Wuling xuekan* 1996(4): 14–28.

Liu, Shu-hsien. 1972. "The Confucian Approach to the Problem of Transcendence and Immanence." *Philosophy East and West* 22(1): 45–52.

Liu, Shu-hsien. 2003. "Mou Zongsan (Mou Tsung-san)." In *Encyclopedia of Chinese Philosophy*, edited by Antonio S. Cua, 480–5. New York: Routledge.

Lunyu 論語 [*The Analects*]. s.d. *Chinese Text Project* website, accessed March 1, 2017. http://ctext.org/analects.

Luo, Jiachang 羅嘉昌, and Zheng Jiadong 鄭家棟. 1994. "Zhubiande hua 主編的話 [Chief Editor's Words]." *Chang yu you - Zhongwai zhexuede bijiao yu rongtong* 場與有 - 中外哲學的比較與融通 [*Field and Being - The Comparison and Fusion of Chinese and Non-Chinese Philosophies*] Vol. 1, 1–3. Beijing: Donfang chuban she.

Lü, Buwei 呂不韋. s.d. *Lü shi Chunqiu* 呂氏春秋. *Chinese Text Project* website, accessed February 7, 2016. http://ctext.org/lv-shi-chun-qiu.

Lü, Xiaolong 呂孝龍. 1993. "Yinyang bian yi shengsheng bu xi–lun 'Yi jing' zhong pusu bianzhengfa sixiangde meixue jiazhi 陰陽變易生生不息——論「易經」中樸素辯證法思想 的美學價值 [The Change of Yinyang and the Continuity of Life – On the Aesthetic Value of the Simple Dialectical Thought in the 'Book of Changes']." *Yunnan shifan daxue xuebao Zhexue shehui kexue ban* 1993(3): 58–65.

Mall, Ram Adhar et al. 1989. *Die drei Geburtsorte der Philosophie. China, Indien, Europa*. Bonn: Bouvier.

Mall, Ram Adhar. 2000. *Intercultural Philosophy*. New York: Rowman & Littlefield Publishers, Inc.

Mengzi 孟子 [*Mencius*]. s.d. *Chinese Text Project* website, accessed July 7, 2015. http://ctext.org/mengzi.

Mittal, Ayesha. 2015. "Eurocentric Criticism: The Problem with 'Orientalism' and Post-Colonial Theory." *Ayesha Mittal Writes: Pop Culture, History and Politics through a Feminist and Racial Lens* website, accessed February 6, 2017. https://amittalwrites.wordpress.com/2015/04/13/eurocentric-criticism-the-problem-with-orientalism-and-post-colonial-theory/.

Mo bian zhu xu 墨辯注敘. s.d. *Chinese Text Project* website, accessed February 7, 2016. http://ctext.org/mo-bian-zhu-xu.

Moeller, Hans-Georg. 2018. "On Comparative and Post-Comparative Philosophy." In *Appreciating the Chinese Difference: Engaging Roger T. Ames on Methods, Issues, and Roles*, edited by Jim Behuniak, 31–45. Albany: State University of New York Press.

Moore, Charles A. 1967. *The Chinese Mind: Essentials of Chinese Philosophy and Culture*. Honolulu: University of Hawai'I Press.

Mou, Bo. 1999. "The Structure of the Chinese Language and Ontological Insights: A Collective-Noun Hypothesis." *Philosophy East and West* 4(1): 45–62.

Mou, Zongsan 牟宗三. 1971. *Zhide zhijue yu Zhongguo zhexue* 智的直覺與中國哲學. Taipei: Taiwan shangwu yinshu guan.

Mou, Zongsan 牟宗三. 1975: *Xianxiang yu wu zishen* 現象與物自身. Taibei: Xuesheng shuju.

Mou, Zongsan 牟宗三. 1990. *Zhongguo zhexuede tezhi* 中國哲學的特質 [*Specific Features of Chinese Philosophy*]. Taibei: Taiwan xuesheng shuju.

Mozi 墨子. s.d. *Chinese Text Project* website, accessed July 7, 2015. http://ctext.org/mozi.

Nelson, Eric. 2020. "Intercultural Philosophy and Intercultural Hermeneutics: A Response to Defoort, Wenning, and Marchal." *Philosophy East & West* 70(1): 247–59.

Ng, On-Cho. 2005. "Affinity and Aporia: A Confucian Engagement with Gadamer's Hermeneutics." In *Interpretation and Intellectual Change*, edited by Ching-I Tu, 297–310. New Brunswick and London: Transaction Publishers.

Ng, On-Cho. 2013. "Chinese Philosophy, Hermeneutics, and Onto-Hermeneutics." *Journal of Chinese Philosophy* 30(3, 4): 373–85.

Nielsen, Greg. 1995. "Bakhtin and Habermas: Toward a Transcultural Ethics." *Theory and Society* 24 (6): 803–35.

Ongun, Ömer. 2016. "From Interculturalism to Transculturality: The Puzzling Form of Cultures Today." *Intercultural learning* website, accessed July 7, 2020. http://ectp.eu/efillife/?p=1816.

Ouyang, Min. 2012. "There Is no Need for Zhongguo Zhexue to be Philosophy." *Asian Philosophy* 22(3): 199–223.

Ouyang, Xiao. 2018. "Rethinking Comparative Philosophical Methodology: In Response to Weber's Criticism." *Philosophy East and West* 68 (1): 242–56.

Pan, Tianhua 潘天華. 1995. "'Sunzi binfa' biyuju tese 「孫子兵法」比喻句特色 [The Characteristics of the Metaphor Sentences in 'The Art of War']." *Xiuci xuexi* 1995(1): 14–15.

Paul, Gregor. 2008. *Einführung in die Interkulturelle Philosophie*. Darmstadt: WBG.

Perelman, Chaïm. 1984. "The New Rhetoric and the Rhetoricians: Remembrances and Comments." *Quarterly Journal of Speech* 70(1): 188–96.

Pfister, Laureen. 2006. "Hermeneutics: Philosophical Understanding And Basic Orientations." *Journal of Chinese Philosophy* 33(1): 3–23.

Piaget, Jean. 1969. *The Mechanisms of Perception*. London: Routledge.

Pound, Ezra, trans. 1951. *Confucius: The Great Digest; The Unwobbling Pivot*. New York: New Directions.

Roetz, Heiner. 2008. "Confucianism between Tradition and Modernity, Religion, and Secularization: Questions to Tu Weiming." *Dao – Journal for Comparative Philosophy* 2008/7: 367–80.

Rosemont, Henry Jr. and Roger T. Ames, trans., eds. 2009. *The Chinese Classic of Family Reverence: A Philosophical Translation of the Xiaojing*. Honolulu: University of Hawai'i Press.

Rosemont, Henry Jr., and Roger T. Ames. 2016. *Confucian Role Ethics: A Moral Vision for the 21st Century?* Taibei: National Taiwan University Press.

Rosenlee, Li-Hsiang Lisa. 2006. *Confucianism and Women: A Philosophical Interpretation*. New York: State University of New York Press.

Rošker, Jana S. 2012. "Cultural Conditionality of Comprehension: The Perception of Autonomy in China." In *Reinventing Identities: The Poetics of Language Use in Contemporary China*, edited by Tian Hailong 田海龍, Cao Qing 曹清, et al., 26–42. Tianjin: Nankai daxue chuban she.

Rošker, Jana S. 2012a. *Traditional Chinese Philosophy and the Paradigm of Structure*. Newcastle upon Tyne: Cambridge Scholars Publishing.

Rošker, Jana S. 2012b. "Structure and Creativeness: a Reinterpretation of the Neo-Confucian binary category Li and Qi." In *Origin(s) of Design in Nature: A Fresh, Interdisciplinary Look at How Design Emerges in Complex Systems, Especially Life (Cellular Origin, Life in Extreme Habitats and Astrobiology)*, vol. 23, edited by Liz Swan, Richard Gordon, and Joseph Seckbach, 273–85. Dordrecht [et al.]: Springer.

Rošker, Jana S. 2015. "Intercultural methodology in researching Chinese philosophy." *Zhexue yu wenhua yuekan* 42(3): 55–76.

Rošker, Jana S. 2016. *The Rebirth of The Moral Self: The Second Generation Of The Modern Confucians and Their Modernization Discourses*. Hong Kong, Honolulu: Chinese University Press and University of Hawai'i Press.

Rošker, Jana S. 2017. "Structural Relations and Analogies in Classical Chinese Logic." *Philosophy East & West* 67(3): 841–63.

Rüssen, Jörn. 2004. "How to Overcome Eurocentrism? Approaches to a Culture of Recognition by History in the 21st Century." *Taiwan Journal of East Asian Studies* June 2004: 59–74.

Said, Edward W. 1978. *Orientalism*. New York: Pantheon Books.

Samei, Maija Bell. 2010. Translator's introduction to *The Chinese Aesthetic Tradition* by Li Zehou, ix–xix. Honolulu: University of Hawai'i Press.

Shen, Youding 沈有鼎. 1980. *Mo jingde luoji xue* 墨經的邏輯學. Beijing: Zhongguo shehui kexue chuban she.

Shi ji 史記 [*Book of History*]. s.d. *Chinese Text Project* website, accessed July 7, 2016. http://ctext.org/shiji.

Shi jiing 詩經 [*Book of Poetry*]. s.d. *Chinese Text Project* website, accessed July 7, 2016. http://ctext.org/book-of-poetry.

Shohat, Ella and Robert Stam. 1994. *Unthinking Eurocentrism: Multiculturalism and the Media*. London and New York: Routledge.

Shun, Kwong-loi. 2009. "Studying Confucian and Comparative Ethics: Methodological Reflections." *Journal of Chinese Philosophy* 36(3): 455–78.

Shuowen jiezi 說文解字 [*Explanation of Texts and Interpretation of Characters*]. s.d. *Chinese Text Project* website, accessed July 7, 2016. http://ctext.org/shuo-wen-jie-zi.

Siegel, Harvey. 1999. "Multiculturalism and the Possibility of Transcultural Educational and Philosophical Ideals." *Philosophy* 74 (3): 387–409.

Silius, Vytis. 2020. "Diversifying Academic Philosophy." *Asian Studies* 8(2): 257–80.

Sprintzen, David. 2009. *Critique of Western Philosophy and Social Theory*. New York: Palgrave Macmillan.

Stenberg, Josh. 2014. "Two Questions about Categories in the Relationship of Chinese Literature to World Literature." *Canadian Review of Comparative Literature / Revue Canadienne de Littérature Comparée* 41(3): 287–303.

Sun, Zhongyuan and Saihua Song. 2007. "Meta-research in Chinese Logic." *Frontiers in Philosophy of China* 2(1): 50–69.

Tian, Chenshan. 2002. "Tongbian in the Chinese Reading of Dialectical Materialism." *Philosophy East and West* 52(1): 126–44.

Tu, Ching-I, ed. 2000. *Classics and Interpretations: The Hermeneutic Traditions in Chinese Culture*. New Brunswick and London: Transaction Publishers.

Tu, Ching-I, ed. 2005. *Interpretation and Intellectual Change*. New Brunswick and London: Transaction Publishers.
Twitchett, Denis. 1964. "A Lone Cheer for Sinology." *The Journal of Asian Studies* 24(1): 109–12.
Valera, Eduardo Pérez J. 1972a. "Toward a Transcultural Philosophy (I)." *Monumenta Nipponica* 27(1): 39–64.
Valera, Eduardo Pérez J. 1972b. "Toward a Transcultural Philosophy (II)." *Monumenta Nipponica* 27(2): 175–89.
Vukovich, Daniel. 2010. "China in Theory: the Orientalist Production of Knowledge in the Global Economy." *Cultural Critique* 2010(76): 148–72.
Wang, Bo 王博. 1991: "Laozi zhexue zhong 'Dao', You', 'Wu' de guanxi tantao 老子哲学中 '道', '有', '无' 的关系试探." *Zhexue yanjiu* 1991(8): 38–44.
Wang, Guowei 王国维. 2013. *Renjian cihua* 人间词话 [*Poetic Remarks in the Human World*]. Beijing: Fenghuang chuban she.
Wang, Jing. 1996. "Li Zehou and the Marxist Reconstruction of Confucianism." In *High Culture Fever: Politics, Aesthetics, and Ideology in Deng's China*, 93–117. Berkeley: University of California Press.
Wang, Kexi. 2005. "The Ancient Chinese and Informal Logic in Ancient China." *Asian and African Studies* 9(2): 55–67.
Wang, Shuren. 2009. "The Roots of Chinese Philosophy and Culture — An Introduction to 'Xiang' and 'Xiang Thinking'." *Frontiers of Philosophy in China* 4(1): 1–12.
Welsch, Wolfgang. 1999. "Transculturality-The Puzzling Form of Cultures Today." In *Spaces of Culture: City, Nation, World*, edited by Mike Feather stone and Scott Lash, 194–213. London: Sage.
West, Cornel. 1993. "Lecture: Beyond Eurocentrism and Multiculturalism." *Modern Philology* 90(Supplement): 144–51.
Willaschek, Marcus. 1992. *Praktische Vernunft: Handlungstheorie und Moralbegründung bei Kant*. Stuttgart: Verlag J.B. Metzler.
Wimmer, Franz Martin. 2004. *Interkulturelle Philosophie*. Vienna: UTB.
Wixted, John Timothy. 1989. "Reverse Orientalism." *Sino-Japanese Studies* 2(1): 17–27.
Wong, David. 2017. "Comparative Philosophy: Chinese and Western." *The Stanford Encyclopedia of Philosophy*, Spring 2017 Edition, edited by Edward N. Zalta. https://plato.stanford.edu/archives/spr2017/entries/comparphil-chiwes/.
Wu, Jiang. 2002. "What Is Jingjie? Defining Confucian Spirituality in the Modern Chinese Intellectual Context." *Monumenta Serica* 2002(50): 441–62.
Wu, Kuan-min. 2004. "Distinctive Features of Chinese Hermeneutics. A Review of *Classics and interpretation*: *The hermeneutic Traditions in Chinese Culture*, edited by Ching-I Tu." *Taiwan Journal of East Asian Studies* 2004(2): 233–47.

Xu, Fuguan 徐復觀. 1987. "中國人性論史-先秦篇 [The Theory of Human Nature- The pre-Qin Chapter]." In *Xiandai xin ruxue xue'an* 現代新儒家學案, 647–62, edited by Fang Keli 方克立, Li Jinquan 李錦全. Beijing: Zhongguo shehui kexue chuban she.

Xu, Fuguan 徐復觀. 1995. "Zhou chu zongjiao zhong renwen jingshende yuedong 周初宗教中人文精神的躍動." In *Xiandai xin ruxue xue'an* 現代新儒家學案, edited by Fang Keli 方克立, Li Jinquan 李錦全, Vol.3, 647–60. Beijing: Zhongguo shehui kexue chuban she.

Xu, Fuguan 徐復觀. 2005. *Zhongguo renxing lun shi* 中國人性論史 [*The History of Humanness*]. Beijing: Huadong shifan daxue chuban she.

Xu, Jian. 1999. "Body, Discourse, and the Cultural Politics of Contemporary Chinese Qigong." *The Journal of Asian Studies* 58(4): 961–91.

Xunzi 荀子 [*Master Xun*]. s.d. *Chinese Text Project* website, accessed July 25, 2010. http://ctext.org/xunzi.

Xunzi 荀子 [*Master Xun*]. 1994. *A Translation and Study of the Complete Works*, translated by John Knoblock. Stanford: Stanford University Press.

Yang, Guorong. 2008. "Being and Value: From the Perspective of Chinese-Western Comparative Philosophy." *Philosophy East and West* 58(2): 267–282.

Yang, Zebo 杨泽波. 2007. "Mou Zongsan chaoyue cunyou lun boyi – cong xian Qin tianlunde fazhan guiji kan Mou Zongsan chaoyue cunyou lunde quexian 牟宗三超越存有论驳议—— 从先秦天论的发展轨迹看牟宗三超越存有论的缺陷." In *Zhongguo lunwen xiazai zhongxin*. Accesed on July 15, 2012. http://202.194.14.19/CN/Y2004/V0/I5/109.

Zhang, Dainian 張岱年. 2003. *Zhongguo zhexueshi fangfalun fafan* 中國哲學史方法論發凡 [*An Outline of the Methodology of the History of Chinese Philosophy*]. Beijing: Zhonghua shuju.

Zhang, Dongsun 張東蓀. 1964. *Zhishi yu wenhua* 知識與文化. Beijing: Zhongguo guangbo dianshi chuban she.

Zhang, Zai 張載. 1989. "Zheng meng 正蒙 [Correction of Ignorance]." In *Xingli da quan 4: Kongzi wenhua da quan*, edited by Hu Guang. Jinan: Shandong youyi shushe.

Zhang, Zhiwei. 2006. "'Chinese Philosophy' or 'Chinese Thought'?" *Contemporary Chinese Thought* 37(2): 38–54.

Zhao, Chang 趙昌, ed. 2007. "Zhongguo zhexue yanjiu ying yunxu yunyong luoji fenxi fangfa – Feng Youlan dui luoji fenxi fangfade shouyin yu chuangxin 中國哲學研究應允許運用邏輯分析方法 – 馮友蘭對邏輯分析方法的授引與創新 [The Research in Chinese Philosophy Should Allow the Application of the Analytical Method – Feng Youlan's Adoption of the Method of Logical Analysis and its Creative and Innovative Application]." *Guangmin ribao*, August 15, 2007. Accessed April 13, 2017. http://theory.people.com.cn/BIG5/49157/49164/6117876.html.

Zhou, Dunyi 周敦頤. s.d. *Zhou Dunyi ji* 周敦頤集 [*Zhou Dunyi's Collection*]. *Chinese Philosophical E-text Archive Song* (宋) *through Qing* (清) *Texts* website, accessed March 3, 2017. http://sangle.web.wesleyan.edu/etext/song-qing/song-qing.html.

Zhou yi 周易 [*The Book of Changes*]. s.d. *Chinese Text Project* website, accessed September 3, 2016. http://ctext.org/book-of-changes.

Zhu, Xi 朱熹. 1996. *Zhu Xi ji* 朱熹集. Edited by Jun Bo and Guo Qi. Chengdu: Sichuan jiaoyu chuban she.

Zhuangzi 莊子. s.d. *Chinese Text Project* website, accessed March 12, 2016. http://ctext.org/zhuangzi.

Žižek, Slavoj. 1976. Hermenevtika in psihoanaliza. *Anthropos* 3/6: 69–98.

Index

absence 108–9
aesthetics, aesthetic realm 101–2, 107, 115–17, 120–1
Ames, Roger 40–2, 62–3, 82
Analects (*Lunyu*) 76, 86–7
analysis (analytical method) 12, 81–2, 103–6
ancestors 46–7, 49
a-priori 34, 39, 125
autonomy 27–8
axiology, axiological 11–12, 14, 16, 25, 33–4, 62, 79, 83, 90, 95, 98, 123

binary categories 5, 32–3, 35, 53–6, 69, 132
Book of Changes (*Yi jing*; *Zhou Yi*) 33, 59–60, 68–9, 74–5, 86, 96
Book of History (*Shiji*) 46
Book of Rites (*Li ji*) 60, 96

capitalism, capitalist 16–17
categories 4–5, 12, 23–35, 53–6, 69–70, 90–1, 101–4, 121, 132
Chen Lai 43–4, 48
Cheng Chung-Ying 74, 82, 111, 113
Chinese analogy 68, 87, 96
Chinese philosophy 1–7, 11–13, 20, 30, 35–45, 52–68, 74, 80, 101–7, 110–11, 115–17, 131–4, 137–8
Chinese thought 1–6, 29, 44, 68–71, 74, 79, 81, 101–6, 110
cognitive, cognition 9–10, 37, 58, 78, 80, 83–4, 87–92, 97, 117, 121, 124, 128–31
comparative (philosophy) 18, 27, 29, 31, 101–2, 105, 121–6, 133, 137
complementarity, complementary 32–7, 54–6, 66–71, 81, 125, 132
comprehension 2, 5–6, 10–12, 28, 58, 79, 102, 112, 120, 126
concepts 2, 9–12, 23–4, 27–32, 51, 56, 59, 68–70, 73–7, 81–5, 101–2, 130, 132–3

Confucianism 29, 39–43, 49–52, 77–8, 134
Confucius 3, 29, 46–52, 86–8
context, contextuality 107, 113–14
continuity through change 33, 69
cosmic order 36, 57–8, 97
creativeness 64, 66
culture (Chinese culture) 13, 18–22, 45–6, 49, 61–3

dao (the Way) 40, 44, 51, 61, 97, 104, 107–9
Dao de jing 69, 108–9
Daoism 74, 78, 118, 134
decree of Heaven 41, 49, *see also* heavenly mandate
Defoort, Carine 2, 6
Derrida, Jacques 3–4
dialectics 69–70
discursive translations 27–9
dynamic relations 57–64

empirical, empiricism 125, 127–36
epistemology 5, 7, 11, 14, 19, 39, 58, 78, 85, 105, 128–9
essence and function (binary category) 42, 53
Euro-American (Western) 1–26, 29–32, 35–7, 40–8, 54–63, 66–70, 80–3, 90, 101–7, 110–12, 116, 122–6, 133–5

family 46–7, 63
Feng Yaoming (Fung Yiu-ming) 9–10, 107
fusion (philosophy, philosophy of fusion) 26, 101–2, 112–17, 120–1, 123–5

god 36, 42–3, 45–53
Gongsun Long 75, 104
Graham, Agnus 59, 68, 80

Hall, David   40-1, 82
Hansen, Chad   7, 76, 82
Harbsmeier, Christoph   59-60, 82
heaven, nature, *tian*   34, 36, 38-52, 64, 104
heavenly mandate   48-51
Hegel, Georg Friedrich Wilhelm   3-4, 33, 48, 69
Heidegger, Martin   105, 112, 117
hermeneutics, hermeneutical method   101-3, 110-17
humaneness   34-5, 40, 43, 87
humanism   7, 30, 44, 49-50
humanness   34, 39-40, 42, 44
Hu Shi   103, 108-9

identity   75, 81, 91, 104, 125
immanence, immanent   15, 33-4, 40-1, 68
immanent transcendence   5, 35-6, 39-45, 48, 51-3, 57
inference   78-9, 83-95, 98, 108-9, 119
intuition   34, 117

Jin Yuelin   104-5
jingjie   102, 107, 115-17, 120, 138, *see also* aesthetic realm

Kant, Immanuel   30, 53, 105-6, 125-33, 135
kinship   62-3
Kuijper, Hans   21-2, 27

language   2-3, 6, 9-11, 16, 21-9, 61, 73-4, 79-85, 96-8, 115, 117
Lao Siguang (Lao Sze-kwang)   106, 120
Laozi   69-70, 108-9
law, legislation   28, 54, 68, 81, 99
Le Gall, Stanislas P.   67-8
li and *qi*   5, 53, 64-8, 70
Li Zehou   36-9, 41, 43-5, 63, 70-1, 105-6, 116, 125-32
logic   32-3, 53-6, 59, 73-99, 102-9, 119
    Chinese   59, 73-99, 103, 107
    formal   32, 55-6, 78, 80, 84, 90, 99, 135
    semantic   32, 97, 99
lunli (ethics)   62-3

Marx, Karl   125-7, 132-3
Mencius, Mengzi   40, 86-8, 96, 113
metaphysics   5, 14-15, 35, 42-5, 128
methods, methodology   4-7, 9-14, 21-32, 53-4, 69, 74-9, 84, 89-90, 93-6, 101-39
modern Confucianism   29, 39, 43, 103
Mohist, Mohists   75-8, 81, 85-7, 89-99, 103
Mou Zongsan   39-43, 105
Mozi, Mo Di   74-5, 77, 86, 89-99

name and actuality   53, 91, 95, 124
neo-Confucianism   42-3, 59, 70
network   37, 57-8, 62-3, 97-9, 132, 138
noumenon   33, 36-9, 42, 116, 131

one-world view   5, 36-45, 57, 131
ontology   35-9, 63, 80, 82, 105
orientalism (reversed orientalism)   14-21

perception   7, 9, 11-13, 46-7, 55-8, 118, 126-7
phenomenology   5, 107, 111
presence   108-9
proper measure   68-71

reality   1, 5-7, 9, 11, 16-17, 23, 30-4, 42, 48, 55-8, 64, 69, 73, 76, 78, 82, 85, 99, 111, 113-18, 126, 134, 135, 139
referential framework (framework of reference)   9-56, 70, 83, 97-9, 101-2, 125-9, 132, 135-6
relationalism   62-3
relationships   28, 33, 37, 43, 62-3, 68
religion, religious   35, 39-52, 63, 117
righteousness   49, 51
Roetz, Heiner   7, 52
role ethics   62-3

School of names, Nomenalists   75-6, 78, 81, 85, 92, 103
School of structure, School of the structural principle   43, 104
semantics   62, 82, 137
similarity, sameness   73, 83, 88-93, 96, 98
sinology   15, 20-7, 46, 62, 83, 133
spirituality   35, 45, 53
structure, structuralism   57-62, 66-71, 78 85, 95, 97-9

sublation   33, 123–5, 127, 132–8
    method of   125, 127, 137–8
    philosophy of sublation, sublation
        philosophy   123–5, 127, 135–8
substance   33, 37, 41–2, 51–2, 55, 80

textual criticism   26–7
theory of proper names   76, 91
transcendence, transcendent   3, 15,
    33–45, 48–53, 71
transcendental   125–36
transcultural   4, 7, 11–14, 29, 102, 105,
    110, 113, 121–5, 137–8
    methodology   138
    philosophy   4, 13, 110, 122,
        125, 137–8
transformation   48–50, 124–30

unity of human beings and
    nature   34, 36, 42

values   12, 17, 38, 51, 95, 106, 130
vital potential   64–6

Wang Bo   107–9
Wang Guowei   116
Way of Heaven   36, 40, 43, 45, 51
Western philosophy   1, 4–5, 30–1, 36, 41,
    80, 116, 133–4
white horse   75

Xu Fuguan   45–52
Xunzi   60, 76, 86, 88–92, 97, 99

Yang Guorong   38, 131

Zhang Dainian   104–5, 109
Zhang Dongsun   80–1, 105
Zhu Xi   55, 70
Zhuangzi   54–5, 60–1, 117–21
Žižek, Slavoj   114

www.ingramcontent.com/pod-product-compliance
Lightning Source LLC
Chambersburg PA
CBHW061834300426
44115CB00013B/2381